CHINA IN TRANSITION

HUMAN CAPITAL AND ECONOMIC TRANSFORMATION OF CHINA

CHINA IN TRANSITION

Additional books and e-books in this series can be found on Nova's website under the Series tab.

CHINA IN TRANSITION

HUMAN CAPITAL AND ECONOMIC TRANSFORMATION OF CHINA

YANQING JIANG

AND

YINGJIE LI

nova science publishers
New York

NOTICE TO THE READER

Library of Congress Cataloging-in-Publication Data

ISBN: 978-1-53619-272-8

Published by Nova Science Publishers, Inc. † New York

CONTENTS

Preface		**vii**
Acknowledgments		**ix**
Chapter 1	Economic Transformation	**1**
Chapter 2	China in Transformation	**11**
Chapter 3	Human Capital	**27**
Chapter 4	Human Capital in China	**41**
Chapter 5	Labor-Force Human Capital	**83**
Chapter 6	Technology Diffusion	**97**
Chapter 7	Structural Change	**113**
Chapter 8	Development Strategies	**133**
Chapter 9	Structure and Inequality	**155**
Chapter 10	The Role of Human Capital	**173**
Chapter 11	A Theoretical Model	**185**
References		**221**

About the Authors **229**

Index **231**

PREFACE

Market-oriented reforms initiated four decades ago have constantly fueled a high speed of development in China. The country's industrial structure has experienced rapid evolution. In the meantime, especially in the general context of globalization, the country has also opened to foreign trade and foreign direct investment, transforming itself from a virtually completely closed economy into a major trading nation and the largest developing-country destination for foreign direct investment in the world. Human capital is thought to be one of the key factors that shape the transformation of the Chinese economy. With different human capital Intensities, uneven development is one major issue in the process of China's industrial transformation under new trends of globalization. Substantial disparities across different Chinese regions, e.g., the gaps in regional industrial development and those in incomes and living standards have been one prominent feature of China, and are (needless to say) closely related to different speeds of human capital accumulation. This book therefore aims to explore the potential and actual mechanisms through which human capital accumulation and human capital intensity may affect industrial development and development disparities in China. The book is able to provide the readers with new facts and new findings that shed light on their understanding of important issues related to human capital and economic transformation of China.

ACKNOWLEDGMENTS

The authors acknowledge the funding support of the research project No. 41004263 of Shanghai International Studies University.

Chapter 1

ECONOMIC TRANSFORMATION

Economic transformation is a macroeconomic issue that deserves close and widespread attention. In this chapter, we will discuss some essential points about economic transformation, including its definition, classification, related theories as well as their implications. After that we will be able to move on to focus on the processes of transformations in modern China.

1.1. ECONOMIC TRANSFORMATION

Economic transformation loosely indicates the general process of changing from a state of economic operation system to another. In the process, there are usually four key factors: the target of transformation, the initial transformation conditions, the transformation process modes and the ultimate states of the transformation. The initial transformation condition is the beginning of economic transformations. In order to realize the target of transformation, an economic goal should choose its paths to change from the initial condition. Actually, the process of moving from an initial condition into an ultimate condition is very important. Different economic environments and measures may lead to different results, and then will have a profound influence on the target of transformation.

Before we discuss the definition of economic transformation, we should know something about the word transformation. This is the common concept in almost all research fields. It is a basic concept, which is firstly used in mathematics, medical science, linguistics and other research fields. With the development, this concept is gradually used in sociology and economics theories.

When it comes to the definition of economic transformation, it means that the economic structures and systems in a nation or an area are experiencing a fundamental change. It can be the shift of the mode of economic growth. It can be the promotion of economic structure. It can be the change of pillar industries. It is the process of national economic revolution from quantitative change to qualitative change.

This is not a special phenomenon in socialist economy and society. No matter in which kind of a country, the economic structure and system cannot be perfect. Every country in the world is faced with a variety of economic problems. The economic transformation gives countries a potential for self-improvement. As a result, economic transformation has become a word that is used frequently in reports on the work of the government.

1.2. A Classification of Economic Transformations

As for economic transformations, there are many kinds of standards for classification. The two commonly used classifications methods are as follows:

1. According to the state of transformation: system transformation and structure transformation

System transformation is the process that transfers from a highly centralized redistributive economy to a market economy system. This kind of transformation is aimed to realize the system shift and innovation in a short period. This is a fundamental change in a national economic system, even in the political system.

Structure transformation is the process that transfers from a traditional society to a modern society. This kind of transformation is aimed at the change in modes of economic growth. It will last for a long time and will profoundly influence the course of rural and urban development. In terms of the economic structure, it includes industrial structure, technical structure, market structure, talents structure, labor force structure and so on. It is a matter about how to allocate and utilize resource effectively and efficiently, and eventually, keep the balance of supply and demand in all kinds of markets.

However, some scholars divide the state of economic transformation into four categories: economic system transformation, development strategy transformation, mode of economic growth transformation and structure transformation. The more detailed classification provides the basis for the research of specific economic transformation problems.

2. According to the speed of transformation: radical transformation and gradual transformation

Radical transformation is a fast and comprehensive reform. The government wants to operate the reform as much as it can. It took place in Russia and some Eastern Europe countries, which was called the "Shock Therapy." In this kind of transformation, the government will push forward a lot of policies to transfer the society, regardless of the economic fluctuation and social instability.

Gradual transformation is much more moderate. This kind of transformation means a self-perfection of economic system. It often refers to a part or a stage of reform. Compared with the radical transformation, it will not cause an obvious economic fluctuation and social instability. In China, the gradual transformation is described as the process to cross the river by feeling the stones, and now, this is the most common pattern of transformations.

To sum up, the former pays more attention to the output of transformations while the latter attaches importance to the process itself.

1.3. The Theories About Economic Transformation

From the 1970s, many socialist countries were experiencing the radical transformations, which caused heated discussion in academic circles. A variety of transformation theories came out at that time. Scholars put forward theoretical hypothesis, potential explanations and policy suggestions. In this part, we will discuss some classical theories and explain the existence of economic transformations.

1.3.1. Transformation Theory Based on Imperfect Information

This theory was put forward by an American economist named Joseph Stiglitz. He explained economic transformation based on information economics rather than traditional economics. In his explaining model, the market is not perfect. It is very likely to suffer from the problem of incomplete information so that the society does not realize the Pareto optimality. When it comes to the mode of transformations, Joseph Stiglitz holds the view that the structure transformation should be push forward corresponding with the process of stable economic growth. In order to achieve them, the government should play an important role in the operation and supervision of all industries, especially the banking industry. Besides, the government ought to promote education to improve the quality of domestic human capital. Meanwhile, creating a social environment with complete information is quiet urgent in some countries in transformation in that these countries that lack complete information are likely to have weak ability to correct marker failure. In a word, Joseph Stiglitz's theory stresses the importance of information and the government's role in economic transformations.

1.3.2. Transformation Theory Based on Institutional Change

Douglass C North, an American economist, is the representative scholar in the research of the Institution Change Theory. In this theory, the change of theories means the renovation of the system frameworks. To understand the theory, we can view the institution as a kind of public good. It is produced by the individuals or organizations. This is not the key point of this question. Because of the production of the institutions, according to the knowledge from Microeconomics, we can get a supply curve of institutions. We all know that the resource that human being can make use of is limited. Besides, the individuals or organizations are not completely rational. So the supply of institution has its own limit. With the continuous changes of internal and external environment, people will come up with new demand for this kind of public good and then institution change will take place.

1.3.3. Transformation Theory Based on the Industry Life Cycle

The Industry Life Cycle Theory holds the view that every industry will experience four periods including formation, growth, maturity and decline. In the formation period, the number of related enterprises increases dramatically which forms the rudiment of the industry. In order to support the formation of the industry, the demand for professional human capital increases. The growth period is the time for expansion and the industry needs different kinds of production factors. After that, the industry develops into its maturity period. In this period, the production process becomes standard and the technology gets mature. Both market demand and market supply is stable. In the end, the industry will enter a recession in which market demand decreases while the importance of industrial structure begins to decline. At the same time, new demand will appear and a new industry life cycle starts.

1.4. Major Challenges for Economic Transformation

In the early days, China's economic development mode is quite extensive. The characteristics of industries are high input, high pollution and high consumption. However, cost and price are quite low and consequently the profit is low. This kind of economic development mode has a negative effect on demand-supply structure, urban-rural development and income distribution. In the end, it led to economic structural contradiction.

The first challenge is imbalance of demand structure. Demand can be divided into domestic demand and external demand. Domestic demand includes consumption and investment while external demand is exportation. Consumption is usually the main driving force for economic growth. Investment is another driving force to enlarge domestic demand. Based on the expenditure accounting approach, GDP is the sum of consumption, investment, government purchases and net exports. As a result, economists hold the view that consumption, investment and exportation are the main driving forces for economic growth. As to the traditional mode of economic growth, GDP depends much on foreign trade in China. In 2004, the index of dependence on foreign trade was up to 70%, which reflected that the economic structure was not reasonable at that time. That is to say, the market in China was oversupplied while domestic demand was insufficient.

Table 1.4.1. The proportions of three industries in China from 1976 to 2018 (Unit: %)

Year	Proportion of Three Industries (%)		
	Primary Industry	Secondary Industry	Tertiary Industry
1976	32.8	45.4	21.7
1977	29.4	47.1	23.4
1978	28.1	48.2	23.7
1979	31.2	47.4	21.4
1980	30.1	48.5	21.4
1981	31.8	46.4	21.8
1982	33.3	45.0	21.7
1983	33.0	44.6	22.4
1984	32.0	43.3	24.7
1985	28.4	43.1	28.5
1986	27.1	44.0	28.9
1987	26.8	43.9	29.3
1988	25.7	44.1	30.2
1989	25.0	43.0	32.0
1990	27.1	41.6	31.3
1991	24.5	42.1	33.4
1992	21.8	43.9	34.3
1993	19.9	47.4	32.7
1994	20.2	47.9	31.9
1995	20.5	48.8	30.7
1996	20.4	49.5	30.1
1997	19.1	50.0	30.9
1998	18.4	48.7	32.9
1999	16.5	45.8	37.7
2000	15.1	45.9	39.0
2001	14.4	45.1	40.5
2002	13.7	44.8	41.5
2003	12.8	46.0	41.2
2004	13.4	46.2	40.4
2005	12.2	47.7	40.1
2006	11.3	48.7	40.0
2007	11.1	48.5	40.4
2008	11.3	48.6	40.1
2009	10.3	46.3	43.4
2010	10.1	46.8	43.1
2011	9.2	46.5	44.3
2012	9.1	45.4	45.5
2013	8.9	44.2	46.9
2014	8.7	43.3	48.0
2015	8.4	41.1	50.5
2016	8.1	40.1	51.8
2017	7.6	40.5	51.9
2018	7.2	40.7	52.2

Source: China Statistical Yearbook from 1975 to 2018.

Table 1.4.2. DPI of urban and rural resident in China from 1976 to 2018 (Unit: CNY)

Year	DPI of Residents in China	
	Urban	Rural
1978	133.57	343.4
1979	160.17	405
1980	191.33	477.6
1981	223.44	500.4
1982	270.11	535.3
1983	309.77	564.6
1984	355.33	652.1
1985	397.6	739.1
1986	423.76	900.9
1987	462.55	1002.1
1988	544.94	1180.2
1989	601.51	1373.93
1990	686.3	1510.2
1991	708.6	1700.6
1992	784	2026.6
1993	921.6	2577.4
1994	1221	3496.2
1995	1577.7	4283
1996	1926.1	4838.9
1997	2090.1	5160.3
1998	2162	5425.1
1999	2210.3	5854.02
2000	2253.4	6280
2001	2366.4	6859.6
2002	2475.6	7702.8
2003	2622.2	8472.2
2004	2936.4	9421.6
2005	3254.9	10493
2006	3587	11759.5
2007	4140.4	13785.8
2008	4760.62	15780.76
2009	5153.17	17174.65
2010	5919.01	19109.44
2011	6977.29	21809.78
2012	7916.58	24564.72
2013	8895.91	26955.1
2014	9892	29381
2015	10772	31790.31
2016	12363.4	33616.2
2017	13432.4	36396.2
2018	14617	39250.8
2019	16020.67	42358.8

Source: CSMAR Database.

The second challenge is imbalance of the industry structure. Industry structure means the distribution of factors among industries. The classification of three industries was first established by Fishcher (1935), a New Zealand economist. In the book *The Confliction between Security and Progress*, this kind of classification method of industries was put forward. He divided the world's development history into three periods. The first period is before the Industry Revolution when human beings were mainly engaged in agriculture and animal husbandry. The second period is the time of the Industry Revolution when manufacturing industry got rapidly promoted. The third period is the time about the development and rise of the service industry. The industries emerging in the three periods correspond to three industries respectively. When it comes to China, from 1980, the proportion of primary industry in GDP kept dropping. Currently, the second industry is the main driving force of China's economic growth, and also has great significance for economic transformation and upgrading. However, because of uneven human capital and some other reasons, the transformation in the second industry is always on the way. At the same time, the third industry is getting promoted rapidly during the recent years. The proportion of the third industry in 2018 has been raised up to 52.2%.

In a word, how to balance the industry structure has become a huge problem in economic transformation.

The third challenge is the typical dual economic structure. In this kind of economy, the urban economy dominated by modern manufacturing industry and the rural economy dominated by small-scale peasant economy coexist. In China, infrastructures in cities are well-developed while those in rural town are not perfectly developed. This phenomenon shows the imbalance of urban and rural development. If this problem is not well handled, there is a risk to drop into the "Middle-income Trap."

The fourth challenge is the imbalance of income distribution. The distribution of national income generally refers to the distribution process in all sectors of the national economy, production units, non-production units and residents. In China, income distribution means three parts that include primary distribution, second distribution and final distribution. From 1978, citizens' living standard has basically changed from poverty to overall well-off. However, at the same time, the problem of uneven distribution of national income is increasingly prominent.

Chapter 2

CHINA IN TRANSFORMATION

Since the founding of the People's Republic of China, China has experienced two significant economic transformations. In this chapter, we will discuss the transformations happened in China based on the background we talked about in Chapter One.

2.1. THE TRANSFORMATION HISTORY IN CHINA

China, which is the biggest developing country in the world, has experienced many reforms initiated four decades ago. After these reforms, we have witnessed the amazing developments in China. During the past 40 years, the Chinese government has insisted the market-oriented principle, and at the same time, China's industrial structure has experienced great revolutions. Meanwhile, China put forward the policy of openness and is willing to participate in international trade in global markets. Developing in this way, China has become the second biggest economy and the biggest trading country in the world. However, when it comes to advanced technology and human capital, people will come up with America, Europe or other developed nations or areas while China is often regarded as a global super factory. Actually you will say that it is the phenomena of specializing and exchanging in world trade according to the classic trade theory. However, when a country gradually opens to the global markets on trade, foreign direct investment, the global capital market and so on, the government will reconsider the developing pattern and make some changes. It is related to transformation. That is to say, human capital is thought to be the key factor to shape the development and transformation of the Chinese economy.

From 1949, the target of transformation is to develop the national economy and establish a set of economic systems with Chinese characteristics. So the government launched the development strategy of the Five-year Plan to concentrate on the construction of heavy industry. Meanwhile, the government paid much attention to the ownership transformation. In a word, this transformation is about the shift of the economic system from a new democratic economy to a planned economy.

The second transformation began at the time of reform and opening up. In this transformation, importance was much attached to breaking the shackles of the planned economic system. With national ideological emancipation, the government began to push forward rural and urban reform. Township development is the important content of rural reformation and modernization in China. It is a driving power to speed up the progress of Chinese characteristic urbanization. Because of this transformation, the socialist market economy system has been preliminarily established. There is no doubt that the reform is the important reason for China's economic miracle.

In order to know more about economic transformation, we need to learn about the development history after the founding of new China.

The period of new democratic economic system in China was from 1949 to 1952. During this period, new China was just founded. After the war for many years, the political system, military strength and economic foundation of the whole nation were quite weak. And there was a very strong uncertainty in the future. In order to establish the socialist system as soon as possible, at this time, China stressed the importance of the planned economy, which was in urgent need. At the same time, the government knew the disadvantages of a planned economy and hoped to stimulate the economy with the help of market means. Therefore, in the period of new democratic economic system, the state emphasized the establishment of the planned economy, and at the same time, it did not give up the market as a means to promote economic development.

The period of planned economy in China was from 1953 to 1977. In order to establish the socialist system as soon as possible, the Chinese government made great efforts to carry out the first five year plan, land system transformation and three major industries transformations to realize the transformation and upgrading of the economic system. From 1953 to 1957, in order to quickly establish the socialist system, the central government adopted a highly centralized planned economic system. At this time, the Chinese government almost completely abandoned the market mechanism as a means to promote the operation of the economy by means of government orders and plans, and vigorously developed the public economy and state-owned enterprises. However, a high degree of centralization also produced a lot of problems, which were mainly reflected in the waste of resources, low labor productivity, low enthusiasm of labors for production. In order to solve the problems brought by the highly centralized planned economy, the central government decided to decentralize part of the power. Therefore, from 1958 to 1960, the Chinese government decentralized part of its power according to the actual situation, from complete central management to the coexistence of central and local mandatory plans. Since 1960, China was faced with serious natural disasters and complex international situation. In order to get rid of the predicament, China still adjusted to a highly centralized planned economy from 1961 to 1964, commanding the operation of the country through unified instructions. From 1965 to the beginning of reform and opening up, due to the needs of economic development, the government adjusted its policies and chose to decentralize part of its power. But generally speaking, in this stage, China realized the transformation and upgrading from the new democratic economic system to the planned economic system, which laid an economic foundation for the social nature of China's socialism.

Since 1978, China entered a new period of reform and opening up, as well as a period of economic transformation. The planned economy which had last for quite a long time has led to the rigidity of the economic system, the lack of vitality of the whole society, and the lack of impetus for economic development. From 1978 to 1984, China entered the period of transformation and upgrading from planned economy to a market economy. During this period, China began to emphasize the role of the market in the allocation of resources and put forward the mode of economic development with the planned economy as the main factor and market regulation as the supplement. This is the first time that the importance of the market regulation mechanism has been emphasized since the founding of new China. However, at this period, as the whole nation had just been in the situation of transformation, the principle of taking planned economy as the main part and market regulation as the supplement still emphasizes the importance of the planned economy. It holds that the public ownership economy is the most important part in the development of market economy, and the market mechanism is only the supplement and regulation of the planned economy.

With the deepening of reform and opening up, people's thinking became more and more open, and the academic field had begun to re-examine the role and value of market economy based on western economics. Therefore, since 1985, the Chinese government began to put forward the concept of the planned market economy, which had made obvious progress with the principle of "the planned economy as the main factor and market regulation as the supplement" emphasized in the previous stage. During this period, the government did not emphasize the idea that the planned economy was superior to the market economy, but believed that both the market economy and the planned economy were effective means in economic development, both of which could promote the development of a nation's economy. But at this time, because many people held the view that the market economy and the social nature of capitalism were inseparable, the transformation and upgrading of this period had been greatly resisted from all walks of life.

In 1987, the Chinese government put forward the economic development mode of "the state regulates the market and the market guides the enterprises." During this period, the difference between socialism and capitalism was completely distinguished, which was only a social nature. At this period, more and more people recognized that the planned economy and the market economy are both means to promote social and economic development, and cannot be used to determine the social nature of a country. They also emphasized the role of the market in the allocation of resources and overcome the disadvantages of "the planned market economy." Therefore, this period was the most intense period of China's social and economic transformation and upgrading.

Since 1988, the whole society was in a period of rapid transformation and development. People began to question the direction of marketization since the reform and opening up, and the debate about whether the reform is capitalist or socialist gradually emerged. Therefore, at this period, the whole society returned to the period of planned economy as the main and market regulation as the supplement. The social and economic transformation was in the situation of the ice age again.

Since 1992, China's reform entered a key historical stage. In this period, on the basis of the conception of "socialist market economy," the viewpoint that the market plays a fundamental role in the allocation of resources is put forward and based on which, the theory of the socialist market economy was basically established. Since then, China's market economic system reform entered a new stage. With the need of economic transformation and upgrading, the industrial structure of the whole society undergone dramatic changed, and the efficiency of resource allocation was rapidly improved. Therefore, we generally think that the period from 1992 to 1997 was the period of putting forward the socialist market economic system.

Since 1998, the concept of the socialist market economy was gradually recognized. In this period, the central government had focused on the reform of state-owned enterprises, financial industry and macro-control in different fields, and achieved good results. Therefore, from 1998 to 2002 is considered to be the establish period of socialist market economic system.

The period from 2003 to 2012 is considered as the stage of perfecting the socialist system. In the process of continuous reform and transformation, we attached more importance to the comprehensive development of economy, society and human capital. However, during this period, all sectors of society once again questioned the direction of economic system reform, which made the role of the market challenged again.

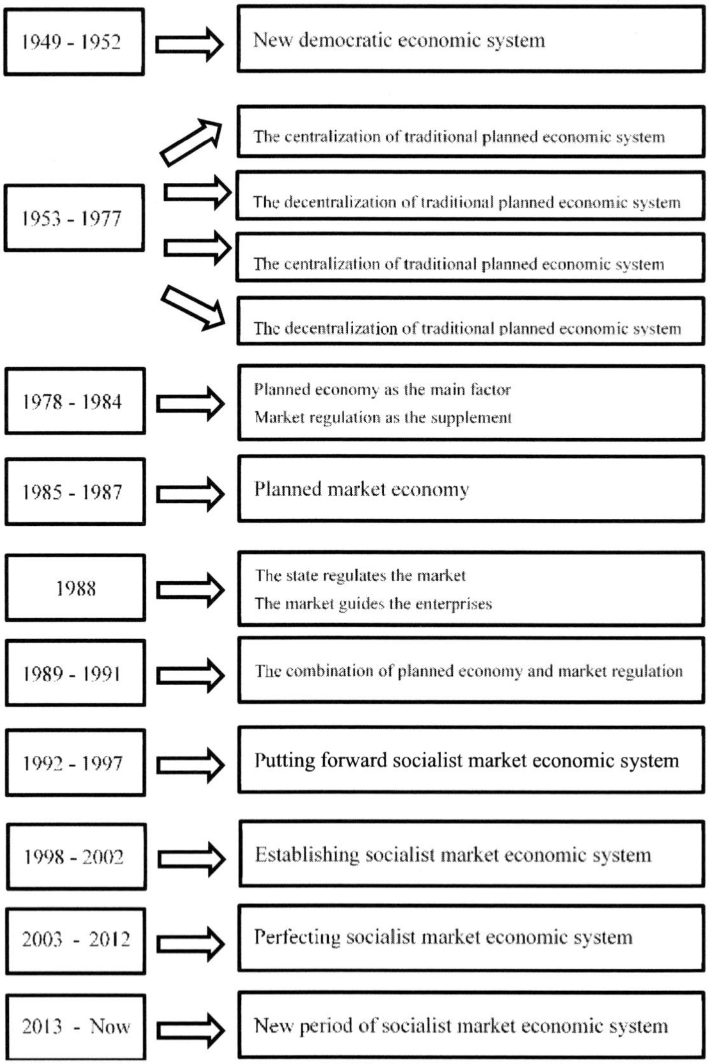

Since 2013, the central government has once again emphasized the role of the market in the allocation of resources, and regarded it as a decisive role rather than a fundamental role, and stressed the role of the government in economic development. At the same time, the government also began to pay attention to the supply side reform, emphasizing the role of human capital in scientific and technological progress, industrial transformation and upgrading, and sustainable economic development. This also marks that the economic system has entered a new stage, and also shows China's determination in the transformation and upgrading of the socialist market economy.

To sum up, this transformation is the shift from a planned economy to a socialist market economy.

2.2. Three Kinds of Transformations in Modern China

If you have the chance to give an interview in China and ask someone whether you have heard the word "transformation," there is no doubt that almost all the people will say "yes." This is the most commonly used word in government reports and social media recently. Now, in China, it is actually a critical time for both economic and social transformation. So, let's begin to explore modern China in transformation.

2.2.1. Transformation of the Development Pattern

Firstly, we need to understand the difference and relationship between quality and quantity. Please image that you are a tailor and you work for 8 hours a day. If you pay more attention to quantity, what you can do is loosen some requirements of the shirt or you can just replace the less efficient machines with more productive machines to shorten the average time on each shirt. If you want to produce good-quality suits, you need to spare more time on each one. In this example, we find that quality and quantity can be judged by the average time of each shirt made, which is more about efficiency. It is a problem to trade off quality for quantity.

Consistent to the two concepts above, from a microscopic point of view, we pay more attention to the relation between economic growth speed and economic benefit. Economic growth speed is something about quantity while economic benefit reveals quality.

Here we begin to explore the meaning of economic growth. The theory of economic growth has developed for many years. In these theories, the most typical one is posed by Edward Fulton Denison, who is a famous economist in America. In his theory, he thought economic growth is decided by two factors. The first factor is the input of resource, including the input of land, capital, labor and other resource. The second factor is total factor productivity, including economy of scales, techniques and so on. Commonly, when the economic benefit is fixed, the economic growth speeds up with the increasing input of resource. Moreover, if the input of resource is fixed, the economic growth speeds up with total factor productivity, vice versa. As a result, the three definitions are related with the equation as follows:

$$Q = \text{Input of resource} \times \text{Economic benefit}$$

Note that Q is the total economic output which means economic growth.

In this equation, we can find that both input of resource and economic benefit have positive effect on the economic growth. That is to say, on the way to develop a country, the government could stimulate the input of resource or improve the quality of development. This is what we call benefit-oriented speed.

It is commonly acknowledged that the reasons for a country to steadily develop are resource and quality and we often consequently consider that these two factors are independent variables. Instead, more people, in practice, hold the view that economic growth inversely affects economic benefit. For example, many retail investors think that the price of a stock will be greatly influenced by the state's economic situation and policies. Meanwhile, many enterprises will also determine their operational strategies based on the economic growth in the past few years. This is the developing pattern named speed-based benefit which is partly caused by economic inertial.

These two economic development patterns are considered as two ways to promote economic development. Nowadays in China, economic growths are often achieved through speed-based benefit. As Yu Bin, the member of the Party Leadership and Director of the General Office of the Development Research Center of the State Council, once said, "As long as the speed of economic growth is more than 10%, almost all the industries and enterprises will make profits, and at the same time, the quality and efficiency of economic development will be significantly improved. Conversely, once the speed of economic growth is less than 8%, many industries and enterprises will get lost, and the quality and efficiency of economic operation will dramatically decline." It significantly reveals that chasing speed-based benefit is the most representative economic development pattern since the market-oriented reform began 40 years ago.

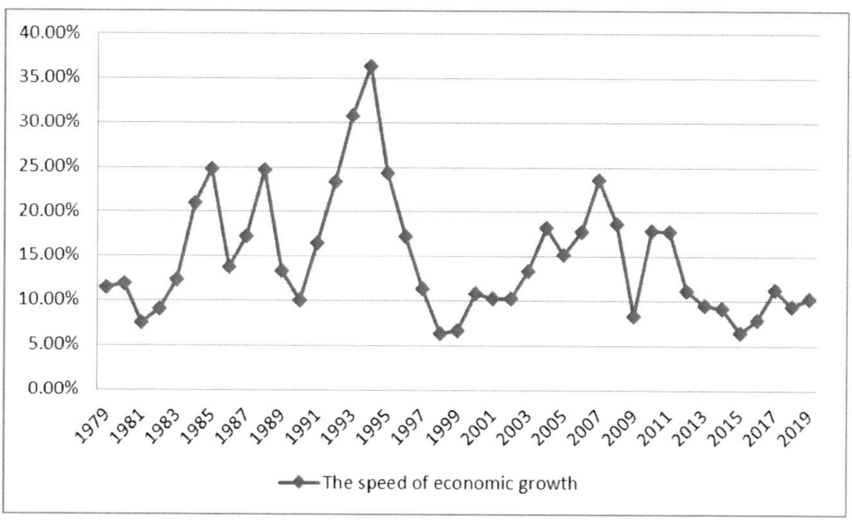

Source: CSMAR Database.

Figure 2.2.1. The speed of economic growth in China from 1979 to 2019.

Table 2.2.1. DPI of urban and rural resident in China from 1978 to 2018

Year	Macroscopic economic growth in China		
	GDP	GNP	GDP Per Capita
Unit	Billion Yuan	Billion Yuan	Yuan
1978	3678.7	3678.7	385
1979	4100.5	4100.5	423
1980	4587.6	4587.6	468
1981	4933.7	4935.8	497
1982	5380.5	5373.4	533
1983	6043.8	6020.9	588
1984	7314.2	7278.5	702
1985	9123.6	9098.9	866
1986	10375.4	10376.2	973
1987	12166.6	12174.6	1123
1988	15174.4	15180.4	1378
1989	17188.4	17179.7	1536
1990	18923.3	18872.9	1663
1991	22050.3	22005.6	1912
1992	27208.2	27194.5	2334
1993	35599.2	35673.2	3027
1994	48548.2	48637.5	4081
1995	60356.6	61339.9	5091
1996	70779.6	71813.6	5898
1997	78802.9	79715	6481
1998	83817.6	85195.5	6860
1999	89366.5	90564.4	7229
2000	99066.1	100280.1	7942
2001	109276.2	110863.1	8717
2002	120480.4	121717.4	9506
2003	136576.3	137422	10666
2004	161415.4	161840.2	12487
2005	185998.9	187318.9	14368
2006	219028.5	219438.5	16738
2007	270704	270092.3	20494
2008	321229.5	319244.6	24100
2009	347934.9	348517.7	26180
2010	410354.1	412119.3	30808
2011	483392.8	487940.2	36302
2012	537329	538580	39874
2013	588141.2	592963.2	43684
2014	642097.6	641280.6	47005
2015	683390.5	685992.9	50028
2016	737074	740060.8	53680
2017	820099.5	820754.3	59201
2018	896915.6	900309.5	64644
2019	988528.9	990865.1	70891.78

Source: CSMAR Database.

At present, after continuous reforms for 40 years, much of the cultivated land has been exploited and capital investment is no longer boosting in a dramatic speed. Meanwhile, the price of labor force continues rising. That is to say, realizing more than 10% speed of economy growth is impossible merely depending on the momentum of economy growth, and based on which, the speed of economy growth has a tendency to decrease with the markets becoming more mature. In 2018, the speed has decreased to 6.6%, which is almost a half of that in 2008. As a result, merely depending on chasing speed-based benefit is not suitable for the economic situation right now. If we insist on promoting economy growth with the inertial of growth, a significant economic contraction is likely to happen, which cannot be accepted right now. Hence, we should consider to relying on input of resources and economy quality to promote economic growth.

After further analysis, we can define resource input and economy quality as a mixed variety in that they have something related. It is known to all that regarding a hypothesis of a rational person, an individual firm will allocate resource properly to maximize the profit. Through this process, adjusting the input of resource is to realize the economies of scale. When an individual firm is in the state of economies of scale, the changes on resource input will firstly affect the efficiency of productivity, and then eventually promote the output. As for a country, this transmission mechanism is the same.

Clearly we could draw a conclusion that nowadays in China, the quality of products and service in many fields, such as agricultural industry, manufacturing industry and service industry, should be improved to promote gradual and steady developments. In order to push forward this transformation, supply-side reform has been carried out for several years. This idea is to produce goods with much added value and find the potential measures to meet diversified demands. Of course, the added value of product is made from human capital. Therefore, human capital is a key factor for economic development and transformation.

2.2.2. Transformation of the Redistribution Pattern

During the period of Economic Reform and Opening up, every industry in China is pursuing the high speed development. The proportion of Chinese GDP in the world's GDP becomes higher, which is from 0.4% (1978) to 15.7% (2018). Looking back on the history of Chinese development, China relies on the inter-industry redistribution of factors to promote economic advancement.

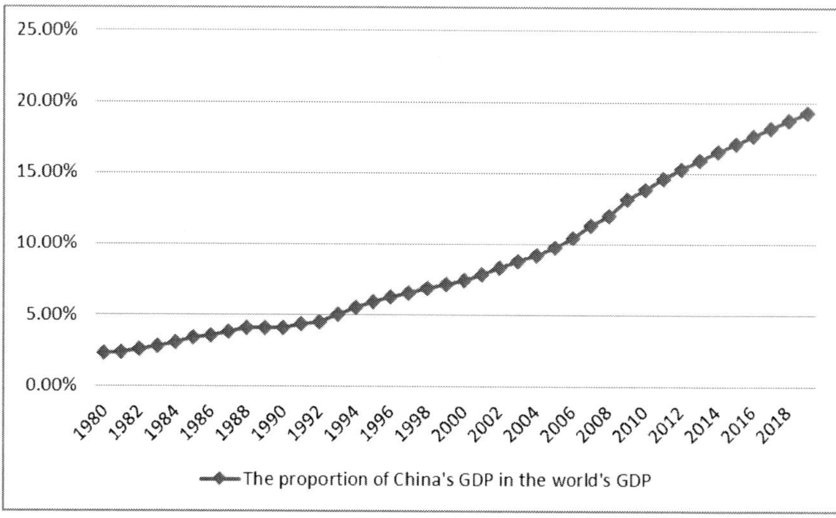

Source: CSMAR Database.

Figure 2.2.2. The Proportion of China's GDP in the World's GDP.

So what is the inter-industry redistribution of factors?

In order to increase the total factor productivity, this is the way to encourage factors to flow from low efficiency sectors to high efficiency sectors by means of reforms and other relative measures. For example, nowadays, almost all parts of the world are experiencing the process of urbanization and China is also included. As a part of the reform, China continuously put forward positive fiscal and monetary policies to stimulate economics. And now China is also in the important stage of urbanization. During this phase, farmers move from rural countryside to cities, becoming a significant engine for development of cities. Simultaneously, this measure solves the problem of the labor whose marginal productivity is nearly zero. Labor resource transfers from agriculture industry to manufacturing industry and tertiary industry with the development of urbanization. Because of the development of science and faster speed of the agricultural modernization, agriculture industry can be properly developed with limited labor force. The inter-industry transfer of labor force can deal with the shortage of city labor force. At the same time, this kind of transformation provided a great amount of effective labor force and market and then promoted the social labor productivity.

However, in the recent few years, the inter-industry transformation has revealed certain sorts of problems. First of all, owing to the law of decreasing marginal returns, the flow of factors has become much steadier than before. If we insist to follow the traditional measure to transfer the factor from agriculture industry to other industry, the transfer efficiency of factors is not satisfactory. Secondly, there is no doubt that a society is in need of all kinds of industries to meet various demands, especially the agriculture industry. Consequently, the government must keep some resource in some so-called relatively low efficiency sectors for social welfare. Meanwhile, the factors used in different industries have their own uniqueness. With the development of technology and science, the transformation of primary factors is useless for some high-tech sectors. Let us look back on the example of urbanization. It really brought many driving forces on the development of economic growth. But there are many problems recently. In China, there is an employment problem that the jobs provided by cities cannot correspond to the increasing number of farmers transferred from rural areas. So nowadays, government has attached great importance on the employment of transferred farmers. Besides, China has the most restrict household registration system in the world and the corresponding land system is not complete. The large scale flow of migrant workers has led to the division of urban and rural labor market, which means the number of agricultural workers decreases dramatically. The people who stay in rural area tend to be the elderly. This situation has become a challenge for the development of agriculture industry.

Moreover, when migrant workers move to towns for the jobs, their social role suddenly changed. Facing a new world and a swiftly changed society, they will gradually change their life style and demand in order to suit the transformation. Before, the labor force without vocational training cannot meet the need of industry development. Therefore, merely depending on the transfer of inter-industry is not reliable. On the contrary, intra-industry transfer has become a promising measure to promote the using efficiency of resource. That is to say, by merger and reorganization, some low efficiency and less competitive corporations will withdraw from the market. In a word, the economic quality can be improved by the promotion of technology and innovation.

2.2.3. Transformation of the Open Fields

The service industry along with the manufacturing industry, gradually open to the world. This kind of change is in need of the corresponding policies. It means that government has paid increasing attention to the development and globalization on service industry. It has become a common sense that when an economy develops to a specific scale, service industry is prone to become an important trigger for social development. With a nation becoming more prosperous, the competitiveness in the market will become much fiercer and a company will refine the specializing. The market consequently has middle service demand. Driven by the profit and market mechanism, the service industry came out. As a result, the existence of service industry is driven by the principle of society development.

Currently, China has played the role of the world factory for a long time in the global market, taking advantage of low labor cost and natural endowments. China takes the job of processing and assembly owing to the comparative advantage in the manufacturing industry. The opening of manufacturing industry is the first step for China to stimulate economy. The manufacturing industry gradually gets involved into the global market by the relative measures such as producing standard improvement, reform of company management, increasing investment in import and export business. Besides, government offers many privileges to export-oriented enterprises. From 2010, China has surpassed the United States, and become the world's largest manufacturer and manufacturing market. We can say that manufacturing industry in China has integrated into the world economy completely. There is no doubt that the opening of manufacturing industry does promote the economic growth. However, we can find that in global competitions, China is in the lowest point in the "Smile Curve," which is not a good signal for China right now. In order to become more competitive, China should transfer the open field, paying more attention to the opening process of service industry. However, because of the varieties of service and the difference between intra-service, service industry has its own characters. Meanwhile, much service is related to a country's absolute power such as banking service, transporting service and so on. As a result, realizing the opening of service industry is not only an urgent need but also a flexible issue.

Nowadays, Chinese government is pushing forward relative policies to encourage the opening of service industries. First of all, government is aiming at reducing the restrictions on market access in service industry and creating a world-class business environment. These measures are as follows:

1) Reduce the amount of capital required for foreign investors
2) Eliminate the requirement on the number of businesses already established by foreign investors
3) Allow foreign-funded service enterprises to provide specific service within the territory of China
4) Ensure foreign enterprises to enjoy national treatment in China

These measures can be used in many fields including investment, culture, entertainment, travelling, auction and so on. Besides, based on the open trade system, government is also aimed at improving the opening quality of cross-culture service trade, promoting economic transformations. Among these actions, the key lies in the international flow of human capital. As for the banking sectors, China has paid attention on five points, including:

1) Eliminate total assets requirements for foreign banks that invest domestically
2) Allow foreign institutions to invest foreign insurance companies in China
3) Relax restrictions on China shareholders in Sino-foreign joint venture banks
4) Allow foreign banks to conduct Chinese capital business
5) Reduce market access standards for foreign banks and insurance institutions

Because of these policies above, China is experiencing the transformation from the manufacturing industry to the service industry.

Chapter 3

HUMAN CAPITAL

With the development of the economy and sciences, the global market has become mature and it is necessary to find a new factor endowment to stimulate an economic transformation, realizing an economic development miracle. Maybe we can find the answer on the existence of human capital. As a result, in this chapter, we will discuss the essence of human capital, including its definition, types, theory and its investment.

3.1. HUMAN CAPITAL

Human capital, which is also called as non-physical capital, is opposite to physical capital in economic analysis. According to the relevant theories of Western Economics, human capital is the capital from labor force, including knowledge, vocational skills, experience, pioneering spirit and so on. The characteristic of human capital is closely connected with personal freedom. That is to say, the ownership of human capital is not transferred with the transfer of product ownership. Different from other kind of factors, human capital has much more potential for appreciation. With the development of industrialization and knowledge economy, human capital has become a key factor endowment in the world. As an active factor, human capital is related to innovation, which is useful for effective allocation of resources and transformation for national economy. As a result, the investment of human capital is a long-term investment and has much more contribution to economic growth.

An individual's innate and acquired abilities are different. Thirdly, the difference of acquired ability is greater. What human capital studies is often acquired ability, which is acquired through family education, academic or non-academic education, vocational training, work experience, labor market flow, and the development of the times. Human capital, like material capital, involves costs and benefits, so it can be used to analyze individual or public decisions. For example, the cost of education refers to the expenses directly paid by students in the process of education and the opportunity cost paid during the study period. The income of education is mainly the salary obtained in the future. Similar to physical capital, human capital also happens. The obsolescence or loss of skills is a reflection of human capital depreciation. This depreciation can be offset by retraining. Therefore, human capital is all kinds of abilities condensed in human body.

3.2. The Types of Human Capital

From the macroscopic level, people often classify human capital according to the length of education. Generally, the individual, whose educational length is relatively long, has higher level of human capital. On the contrary, the individual, whose educational length is relatively short, has lower level of human capital. So we can divide human capital into two types: vocational human capital and average human capital. These two levels of human capitals are related to economic growth. High efficiency economic growth is in need of higher level of human capital.

For more detailed classification, human capital can be divided into three types: basic human capital, skilled human capital, highly qualified human capital. Basic human capital means the labor force only has compulsory education. Skilled human capital has finished secondary education including high school education, vocational high school education and technical secondary school education. Highly qualified human capital has college degree or above. These three types of human capital play different role in industrial revolution and economic growth.

In order to promote the development of enterprises, according to the differences in factor distribution in enterprises, Yinan Wang (2015) divided human capital into three types including basic labor force, management human capital and technical human capital. Basic labor force means employees with basic knowledge and skills. Management human capital means managers and technical human capital means engineers with innovation and creativity. In a word, human capital is often classified according to the quality of labor force.

3.3. Accumulation of Human Capital

Because human capital involves the problem of cost and benefit, this kind of activity that has cost to obtain certain ability is investment activity. Human capital investment and accumulation are designed in the whole life cycle. Academic education investment occurs in the compulsory education stage and higher education stage stipulated by the state. The investment in training will take place throughout the working period, while the investment in health will run through one's whole life. The carrier of human capital is human, without human, the value of human capital cannot be reflected. As a kind of capital similar to material capital, labor force will suffer loss and depreciation. If it is not reinvested, it will gradually lose its value. Therefore, scholars generally believe that health investment is to make up for the depreciation of human capital. Education investment can make the educated rest with new ideas, new theories, new ideas and new methods. The knowledge is conducive to workers to deal with more complex labor and occupy a favorable position in the division of labor. Of course, human capital investment does not end with the end of education. After the investment in education, we can invest in training and train the labor force into experts who can adapt to special work. This kind of investment is continuous with education investment, which makes it easier and more effective for the investee to apply the specific vocational skills acquired from training investment to work, so as to improve production efficiency and ultimately promote the progress of production and society.

Therefore, all walks of life attach great importance to the way of human capital accumulation and investment. There are many ways to accumulate human capital. In this section, we will introduce the formation mechanism of human capital from six aspects.

3.3.1. Education Structure

Educational investment is the most basic and important way to form human capital. Adam Smith believes that before receiving specific education and training. All people's abilities and intelligence are basically the same. The difference of individual abilities is the product of the difference on acquired development and practice. Generally speaking, the relationship between education investment and human capital formation can be expressed as the relationship between education level and human capital quality. To a certain extent, the popularization and quality of basic education and secondary education in a country or region determine the human capital stock level and development potential of the country or region. We can find that the scale and quality of general higher education determine the quantity and quality of high-quality human capital, and the relevant education received in school can also determine the direction and level of labor forces. In other words, basic education improves the potential and efficiency of on-the-job education. At the same time, continuing education and in-service education can be the compensation for the depreciation of human capital and ensure the maintenance and improvement of human capital quality in the long term. Therefore, constructing a reasonable education structure is the most important thing to improve the efficiency of human capital formation.

3.3.2. Learning by Doing

In the process of work, the labor force should think, sum up experience and carry out certain innovative behaviors, which are the actions of "learning by doing." For the R&D positioning of enterprises, firstly, they can choose to become the creators of new products and services, and then they can also choose to become innovative imitators or low-cost producers of successful products in the market. The first kind of R&D positioning needs to rely on a small number of professional inventors. The second chapter requires professionals engaged in production activities to think about how to improve working methods or carry out innovative imitation in their daily work. This is a concept of "learning by doing." That is to say, through daily production and management and experience summary, the quality of labor force is constantly improved. Therefore, for entrepreneurs, professional and technical personnel or general workers, "learning by doing" is an important channel for the formation of human capital.

3.3.3. Technical Progress

Technological progress requires workers to improve their relevant skills and technical level by themselves. This kind of requirement makes the labor forces increase their investment in human capital. On the one hand, with the requirements of skills and technology asked in the production process becoming higher, workers can only actively or passively receive more education and on-the-job training to meet the needs of the labor market. On the other hand, due to the objective needs of technological progress, workers gradually begin to work with higher technical content, which makes them get rid of simple manual labor, and promotes workers to continuously improve their skills and technical level through "learning by doing." At the same time, under the background of technological progress, the labor force with high skills can obtain higher wages and better employment opportunities than those with low skills. The wage difference makes the labor force flow within and between industries.

To sum up, the labor market demand formed by technological progress will lead to the formation of human capital.

3.3.4. Employment Migration

From the perspective of regional differences, there will be differences in the wage level of each region. If the wage level in a certain region is relatively high, labor from other regions will flow into this region, which is a kind of employment migration. Generally speaking, employment migration is not only conducive to the realization of the maximum value of human capital and the continuous appreciation of human capital, but also can make people pay more attention to human capital investment. When human capital flows between regions, it generally needs some skills training and the transfer only on-the-job training can also promote the quality of human capital. In addition, the reasonable flow of human capital between regions can optimize the allocation of human capital and improve the efficiency of economic development. At the same time, the cross regional flow of human capital can realize the introduction and diffusion of technology, and ultimately achieve a win-win situation.

3.3.5. The Cultural Environment

The cultural tradition of the society has a great influence on the investment decision of human capital. Traditional cultural concepts can even determine whether labor force invests in human capital, and determine the degree and direction of human capital investment. For example, the traditional view in ancient China made many people think that technical work is inferior to others while this kind of medium skilled human capital is the most urgent need in China's economic development right now. In contrast, although the rate of return on timely human capital investment is relatively low, most Chinese parents first consider encouraging their children to receive higher education. In this case, the traditional concept of social culture plays a decisive role in the formation of different types of human capital.

3.3.6. The Socioeconomic Environment

The elements of a country's economy will have a positive or negative impact on the formation of human capital. These elements include the level of economic development, economic structure, economic system, market demand, and division of labor, labor market and the rate of return on human capital investment determined by the above factors. The specific effects of these economic factors are as follows: Firstly, from the perspective of a country's economic development level, the higher the country's economic development level, the higher its per capita national income, and then there will be more workers to carry out more education investment and eventually promote the improvement of the quality of human capital. Secondly, from the perspective of a country's economic structure, national economic growth and economic structure adjustment are both conditions and results of human capital structure adjustment. The adjustment of economic structure causes the change of human capital demand, which leads to the adjustment of human capital investment structure. The adjustment of human capital investment structure will have an impact on the existing economic structure. Therefore, economic structure has certain influence on the formation and change of different types of human capital. Thirdly, if a country adopts the market economy system, it means that the competition in the market is relatively sufficient. If enterprises want to establish and maintain their comparative advantages, they must increase the investment in human capital and improve the efficiency of human resource management system. Fourthly, the huge market demand will put forward higher requirements for the production efficiency of enterprises, and workers must improve their skills to meet the requirements of the market. Fifthly, due to the division of labor, there are differences in the work content of workers, which will lead to the formation of different types and quality levels of human capital. Sixthly, as far as the labor market is concerned, if the development of labor market in a country or region is not perfect, it may lead to the unreasonable allocation structure of human capital, and the labor force with higher human capital cannot get the treatment it deserves, which will inhibit the formation of high-quality human capital. On the contrary, if a country's labor market development is relatively perfect, the labor market competition is very full. At this time, due to the existence of the survival of the fittest mechanism, most workers will further improve their human capital level by accepting in-service education and re-education. Therefore, a mature labor market plays a positive role in promoting the formation and promotion of human capital. Seventhly, from the perspective of the rate of return on human capital investment, this index is closely related to the income and cost of human capital investment. If the rate of return on human capital investment of workers in an industry is high, most enterprises and workers in enterprises will invest time, energy and money in improving the level of human capital. On the contrary, if the rate of return on human capital investment of workers in a certain industry is low, most enterprises and workers in enterprises may not invest time, energy and money to improve the level of human capital. Therefore, the appropriate rate of return on human capital investment can promote the speed and quality of human capital formation.

3.4. The Theories About Human Capital

Western human capital theory, unveiled in traditional western economics, can be traced back to the middle of the 17th century. After that, many economists gradually enriched the knowledge of human capital, and eventually, forming a modern theoretical system of human capital. In this part, we will discuss a series of related theories on human capital.

3.4.1. Ideas of Human Capital from William Petty

William Petty, who is a pioneer, firstly underlined that human beings is a great estate which can create value and wealth in his book A Treatise of Taxes and Contribution. As William Petty said, "Labor is the father of wealth while land is the mother of wealth." He held the view that economic growth results from the improvement of labor productivity and the increase in the number of productive workers. He is the first economist who made the quantitative research on human capital. He created a method of estimating people's economic value by discounting the expected income. At the same time, he pointed that the economic value of each human capital varies in that abilities to make money of each human capital vary. William Petty created a precedent for human capital accounting. It is obvious that the views of William Petty on human capital are the beginning of human capital theory.

3.4.2. Ideas of Human Capital from Adam Smith

The concept of human capital originates from Adam Smith's statement on capital division. As a representative of the capitalist class, Adam Smith believes that the differences in abilities that people display in adulthood mainly depend on the acquired practical experience, education and training rather than the innate factors. He regards the ability formed through the acquired practical experience, education and training as human capital and belongs to the category of fixed assets. As a result, human capital means that it is an ability which is obtained through learning and practice is finally transformed into capital fixed on people, and then it can be reversely be used for production practice, personal income improvement, and finally become a part of personal wealth. At the same time, it can increase the level of total social income and become a part of social wealth. Adam Smith highlighted the concept of human capital and its investment, which made a great contribution on human capital theories.

3.4.3. The Human Capital Theory of Theodore Schultz

Theodore Schultz is the founder of the modern human capital theory. He did many researches on definition, investment of human capital and tried to find the relationship between human capital and economic growth. He is the first one to form a basic framework of human capital. In this theory, Theodore Schultz confirmed the definition of human capital which had been excluded from mainstream economic analyses. Theodore Schultz corrected the misunderstandings that exchanges of human capital are not equal to population trade. On the one hand, every individual can choose to advance him or herself and then tries to make a fortune. As a result, human capital can be regarded as a factor which can be exchanged in the market. On the other hand, Theodore Schultz rejected the idea that human capital is homogenous and human capital with heterogeneity is a key factor endowment. Besides, Theodore Schultz underlined the influence of human capital on economic growth. He held the view that not only the quantity but also the quality will affect economic growth. In order to develop economy, an important measure is to accumulate human capita. As for the investment of human capital, Theodore Schultz pointed that everything which is used for improvement of people's productive ability is the investment of human capital, including medical health cost, education cost, training cost, practice cost and other expenditure.

These ideas are a part of modern human capital theories which explain the questions about economic growth and income distribution. To sum up, all these theories reflect the following points:

A. Human capital is the most important factor and human capital theory is an important part of economics.
B. Human capital overweighs physical capital in economic growth. The investment of human capital is directly proportional to national economic investment and the growth rate of human capital is faster than that of physical capital.
C. The core problem of human capital is to improve the quality of population and education investment is the main measure of

human capital investment. The reproduction of human capital should not be merely regarded as a kind of consumption, but also as an investment. The economic benefit of this investment is far greater than that of material investment. Education is the most basic means to improve human capital, so human investment can be regarded as education investment. Obviously, human capital, which is one of the three elements of productivity, can be further decomposed into human capital with different levels of technical knowledge. The output of human capital with high technical knowledge is significantly higher than that of human capital with low technical knowledge.

3.5. The Importance of Human Capital

With the development of economy and social, the importance of human capital has been recognized and public eyes gradually rest on it. And now, the contribution made by human capital is greater than that made by physical capital. Human capital plays an important role in promoting technological progress, improving economic structure, formulating correct development strategy and promoting economic growth.

Firstly, human capital plays an important role in technology advancement. Economists usually divide human capital into skilled human capital and unskilled human capital according to education level, and divide technology advancement into technological innovation activities and technological imitation activities (including technological catch-up activities and technological diffusion activities). Benhabib & Spiegel (1994) constructed the technology diffusion model and found that the increase of the total level of human capital will contribute to the advancement of technology. Vcandenbussche (2006), based on the endogenous economic growth model and empirical analysis, found that the development of technology pioneer industry mainly got benefit from the growth of skilled human capital. Messinis (2008) proposed that the increase of skilled human capital is conductive to technological advancement. In the theory of endogenous economic growth, human capital is considered as the main input factor of technological advancement, which will bring endogenous power to economic growth. Therefore, human capital can promote economic growth through technological advancement. At the same time, the difference in internal structure of human capital brings about its endogenous heterogeneity. Therefore, the increase of skilled human capital can promote the development of innovation departments, while the increase of unskilled human capital is related to non-innovative departments. The adjustment of internal heterogeneity of human capital can lead to the adjustment of industrial structure, and also promote the transformation of economy.

Secondly, making use of human capital can improve economic structure. Jiqiang Guo (2005) proposed that human capital structure and industrial structure are effective counterparts, which are the basic implicit conditions for the quantity and structure of human capital investment to effectively promote economic growth. This conclusion confirms the relationship between human capital structure and economic structure. Yifu Lin (2013) proposed that the optimization of human capital structure will promote the upgrading of technology structure and industrial structure. Yijun Yuan (2008) defined the development process of technology as original technology, primary technology, intermediate technology, advanced technology and highly advanced technology, and the corresponding industrial development process is labor intensive industry, labor-capital intensive industry, capital intensive industry, technology intensive industry and knowledge intensive industry. Through the structural adjustment of human capital, we can promote the transformation of original technology to highly advanced technology, so that the labor intensive industry will gradually upgrade to the knowledge intensive industry. Therefore, the upgrading of human capital structure will lead to the upgrading of economic structure. Relevant researches at home and abroad have proved that the stock of human capital is conductive to promoting the development of industry, and the difference in internal structure of human capital has different promoting effects on the upgrading of industrial structure. Acemoglu (2002) believed that the process of industrial transformation from labor intensive industries to knowledge intensive industries will also promote the adjustment of human capital. Therefore, the relationship between human capital structure and economic structure shows a two-way impact. Through this impact mechanism, it can ultimately promote the transformation and upgrading of economy.

At the same time, human capital is closely related to income distribution. Mincer (1957) first applied human capital to the study of income distribution, and constructed a human capital model based on income distribution, which is believed that the accumulation of human capital could be realized through school education. The workers with high human capital often have high income while worker with low human capital can only choose low-income jobs. So it will naturally lead to uneven income distribution. But the country regards "compulsory education" as a basic national policy, and is trying to expand the scope of compulsory education. This kind of public service provided by the society can greatly promote the accumulation of human capital, promote the level of human capital and promote technological advancement in the whole society, which will eventually lead to the equality of income distribution. Therefore, the improvement of human capital level plays a positive role in narrowing the income distribution gap.

Chapter 4

HUMAN CAPITAL IN CHINA

4.1. INTRODUCTION

Human capital can be analyzed from the perspective of its storage and structure. Human capital storage is related with demographic structure, input of education, staff training and other factors. The structure of human capital is about the differences in individual quality. This kind of difference is arisen from the education level in different communities. We will analyze human capital in China from these two perspectives above.

According to definition of National Bureau of Statistics of the People's Republic of China, the working-age population is who are over 16 years old and have the ability to participate in or be requested to participate in social activities. The working-age population includes employment population and unemployment population. From 1992, the number of working-age population is steadily increasing. The number of working-age population was up to 80.694 billion since 2016. The growth rate of this population is up to 20.83%. The large number of working-age population indicates that there is abundant human capital in China.

Table 4.1.1. Employment information in China from 1994 to 2018

Year	Unemployment population (Billion)	Employment population (Billion)	Unemployment rate (%)
1994	4.76	679.47	2.80
1995	5.20	679.47	2.90
1996	5.53	688.50	3.00
1997	5.70	696.00	3.10
1998	5.71	699.57	3.10
1999	5.75	727.91	3.10
2000	5.95	739.92	3.10
2001	6.81	744.32	3.60
2002	7.70	753.60	4.00
2003	8.00	744.32	4.30
2004	8.27	752.00	4.20
2005	8.39	758.25	4.20
2006	8.47	769.90	4.20
2007	8.30	774.80	4.10
2008	8.86	779.95	4.00
2009	9.21	761.05	4.20
2010	9.08	764.20	4.30
2011	9.22	785.79	4.10
2012	9.17	788.94	4.10
2013	9.26	793.00	4.05
2014	9.52	796.90	4.09
2015	9.66	800.91	4.05
2016	9.82	806.94	4.02
2017	9.72	806.86	3.90
2018	9.74	805.67	3.80

Source: China Statistical Yearbook from 1994 to 2019.

Unemployment population is often referred as housewife and specific people who are finding jobs. The reasons for unemployment are as follow:

1. Frictional unemployment

In reality, labor force has different preferences and abilities while job itself has its own characters. Human capital should meet specific requirements. Then the incomplete information exists between jobs seekers and head hunters. Meanwhile, the regional flow of human capital is not instant. Finding a job needs time and efforts, which will lead to the difficulty in finding a job. So, frictional unemployment is caused by the long process of job hunting.

2. Structural unemployment

Structural unemployment is caused by the mismatch between supply and demand in the labor market. The character of this kind of unemployment is the coexistence of unemployment and job vacancies. Because human capital does not have proper vocational skills or abilities, it cannot fill vacancies in existing positions. The basic reason of structural unemployment is the wage rigidity. The wage rigidity leads to the disequilibrium in labor market.

Most unemployment population relies on the financial support from government. Compared with working-age population, in order to find the economic-friendly factors, we should pay more attention on the number of employment population. This is the index which can indicate human capital much more effectively. Because the Chinese government limits the unemployment rate strictly, the growth rate of working-age population and employment population is roughly kept similar since the beginning of the 21th century and this trend will go on for a long time in the future. It is obvious that the storage of human capital in China has an absolute advantage.

Human capital has become a major production factors and its positive effect on economic growth and social development has become a consensus in mainstream society. From 1970, China's regional economic development gap is increasingly serious. Town economy surpasses rural economy far away and coastal provinces developed faster than central and western provinces. For example, in 2018, Shanghai's GDP is 32679.87 billion Yuan and its growth rate is up to 6.6% while Qinghai's GDP is 2865.32 billion Yuan and its growth rate is 9.1%. Shanghai's GDP is more than 10 times larger than Qinghai's. Generally, these gaps existed between provinces are common in China. So are the gaps between towns and rural areas.

Table 4.1.2. Gross Domestic Productivity of 31 Provinces in China in 2018 (Unit: Billon Yuan)

Province	GDP	Province	GDP	Province	GDP
Anhui	30006.82	Hubei	39366.55	Shanxi	24438.32
Beijing	30319.98	Hunan	36425.78	Shanghai	32679.87
Fujian	35804.04	Jilin	15074.62	Sichuan	40678.13
Gansu	8246.07	Jiangsu	92595.4	Tianjin	18809.64
Guangdong	97277.77	Jiangxi	21984.78	Xizang	1477.63
Guangxi	20352.51	Liaoning	25315.35	Xinjiang	12199.08
Guizhou	14806.45	Inner Mongolia	17289.22	Yunnan	17881.12
Hainan	4832.05	Ningxia	3705.18	Zhejiang	56179.15
Hebei	36010.27	Qinghai	2865.32	Chongqing	20363.19
Henan	48055.86	Shandong	76469.67		
Heilongjiang	16361.62	Shanxi	16818.11		

Source: China Statistical Yearbook 2018.

The factors contributing to China's regional economic development disparity vary. There is no doubt that human capital plays an important role. It is a matter about the difference of human capital between provinces. As a result, the most obvious feature of human capital in China is quality differences.

Actually, there is no doubt that China has a huge quantity of human capital. Every labor force completes the work in his or her position and creates value to realize the target of social welfare. When it comes to the human capital in China, we should pay attention to the storage, education level and average ages of human capital. So in this part, we try to get a description statistics on human capital in China. These parts are based on China Human Capital Report Series published by China Center for Human Capital and Labor Market Research Central University of Finance and Economics Beijing, China. This is a project funded by National Science Foundation of China and Central University of Finance and Economics, which was established in March 2008. It is an international project aimed at the study on human capital and labor markets, paying more attention to the situation in China. According to the result and reports published by this project, the major research includes the situation of human capital, human capital investment, human capital mobility, the relationship between human capital and education and other things concerning human capital. These reports provide a measure for us to know the measurement of human capital in China and, based on which, we can easily analyze the present situation of human capital in China.

As a result, in this chapter we will explain the trend of population and education distribution, the age and education of human capital, national human capital and the differences of human capital from the perspective of cross-province in China.

4.2. The Population and Education Distribution in China

China is a nation with the largest population in the world. Human capital, in fact, is based on population itself. Population growth for a nation includes the imputed population measured by educational attainment, age, sex, and spatial differences. With the development of economics and science, the total population in China is increasing gradually, from 54167 million in 1949 to 139538 million in 2018. Meanwhile, with the policy of revolution and openness in 1978, the urban population increased by 65892 million while the rural population decreased by 22613 million.

Figure 4.2.1 to Figure 4.2.5 show the changes on total, and population by gender classified with educational attainment. We can find that from 1998, the educational structure keeps upgrading. In 1998, the major population in china, which accounts for 39%, is the population with primary schooling. At that time, the average quality of labor force is relatively low, which cannot meet the needs of social development. With the policy of nine-year compulsory education, the average quality of labor force got promoted. The number of junior middle school students grew most among all education levels, which increased from 33% in 1998 to 43% in 2013. Senor middle school graduates increased from 10% in 1998 to 17% in 2013. However, we can find that in 2018, National Bureau of

Statistics of China divided the graduates with the schooling above senior middle school into junior vocational schooling, senior vocational schooling, bachelor schooling, and postgraduate schooling. This change on dividing standard reflects the trend of increasing of high quality talents.

Table 4.2.1. The population in China from 1949 to 2019 (Unit: Million)

Year	Total Population	Urban Population	Rural Population
1949	54167	5765	48402
1950	55196	6169	49027
1951	56300	6632	49668
1955	61465	8285	53180
1960	66207	13073	53134
1965	72538	13045	59493
1970	82992	14424	68568
1971	85229	14711	70518
1972	87177	14935	72242
1973	89211	15345	73866
1974	90859	15595	75264
1975	92420	16030	76390
1976	93717	16341	77376
1977	94974	16669	78305
1978	96259	17245	79014
1979	97542	18495	79047
1980	98705	19140	79565
1981	100072	20171	79901
1982	101654	21480	80174
1983	103008	22274	80734
1984	104357	24017	80340
1985	105851	25094	80757
1986	107507	26366	81141
1987	109300	27674	81626
1988	111026	28661	82365
1989	112704	29540	83164
1990	114333	30195	84138
1991	115823	31203	84620
1992	117171	32175	84996
1993	118517	33173	85344
1994	119850	34169	85681
1995	121121	35174	85947
1996	122389	37304	85085

Year	Total population	Urban population	Rural population
1997	123626	39449	84177
1998	124761	41608	83153
1999	125786	43748	82038
2000	126743	45906	80837
2001	127627	48064	79563
2002	128453	50212	78241
2003	129227	52376	76851
2004	129988	54283	75705
2005	130756	56212	74544
2006	131448	58288	73160
2007	132129	60633	71496
2008	132802	62403	70399
2009	133450	64512	68938
2010	134091	66978	67113
2011	134735	69079	65656
2012	135404	71182	64222
2013	136072	73111	62961
2014	136782	74916	61866
2015	137462	77116	60346
2016	138271	79298	58973
2017	139008	81347	57661
2018	139538	83137	56401

Source: China Statistical Yearbook from 1949 to 2018.

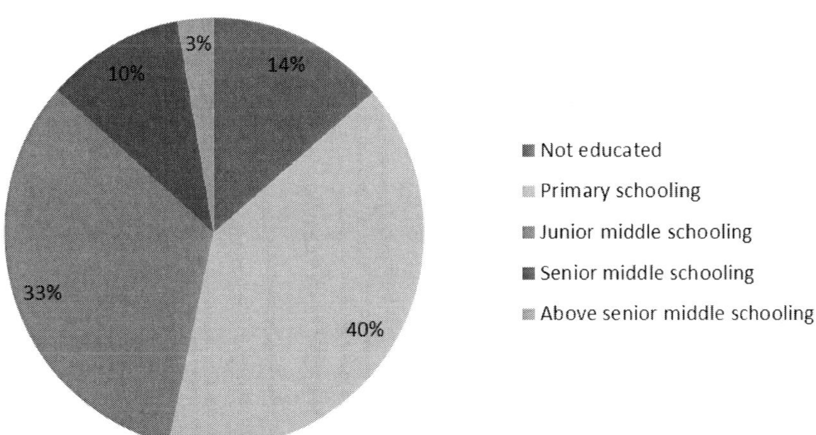

Source: China Statistical Yearbook.

Figure 4.2.1. Total Population by education attainment in China in 1998.

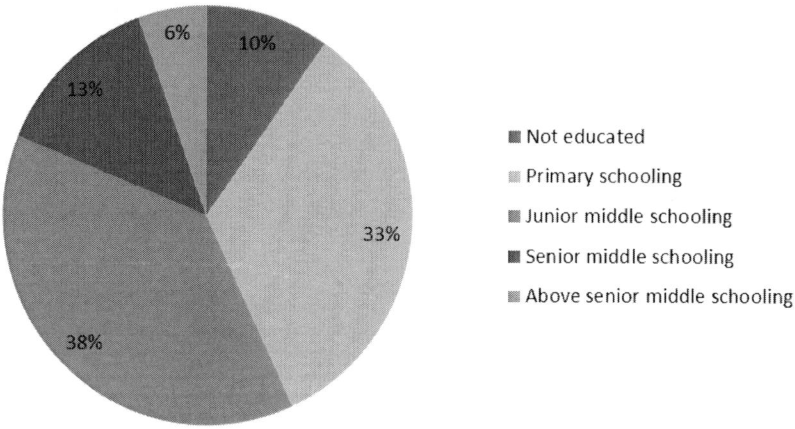

Source: China Statistical Yearbook.

Figure 4.2.2. Total Population by education attainment in China in 2003.

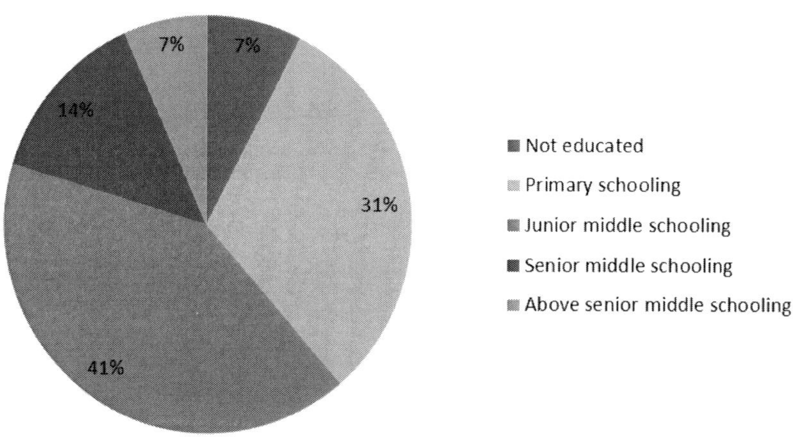

Source: China Statistical Yearbook.

Figure 4.2.3. Total Population by education attainment in China in 2008.

Figure 4.2.6 to 4.2.10 show the population of education attainment by gender in the year of 1998, 2003, 2008, 2013, and 2018. In 1998, among the five education levels, the proportion of the population and those just receiving primary education dominated the distribution. At the same time, we can also find the gender differences in education attainment. Actually, we can find that female labor force has fewer opportunities to get higher education in the past time. However, with the development of society, female education attainment has increased relative to that of males. And also we can find that the gender gap at high education levels also shrank considerably.

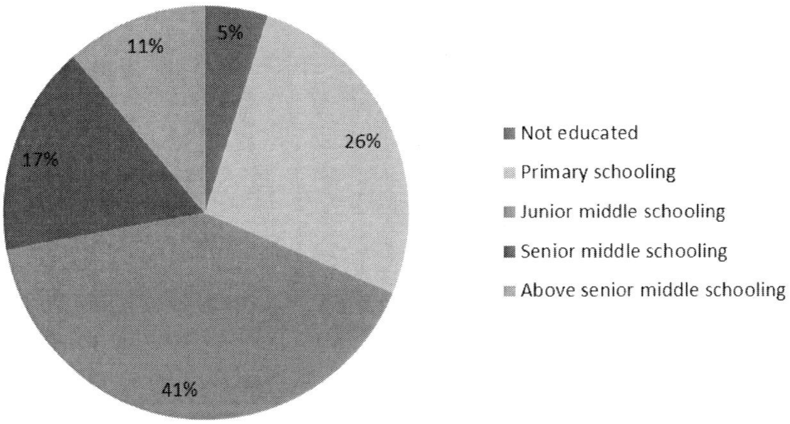

Source: China Statistical Yearbook.

Figure 4.2.4. Total Population by education attainment in China in 2013.

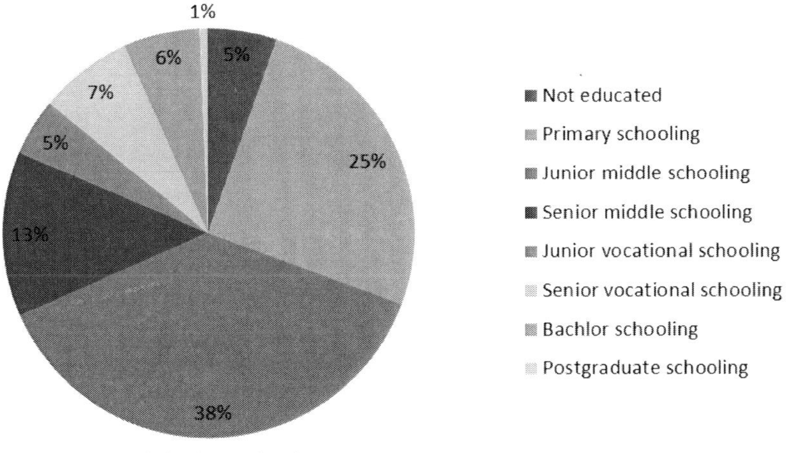

Source: China Statistical Yearbook.

Figure 4.2.5. Total Population by education attainment in China in 2018.

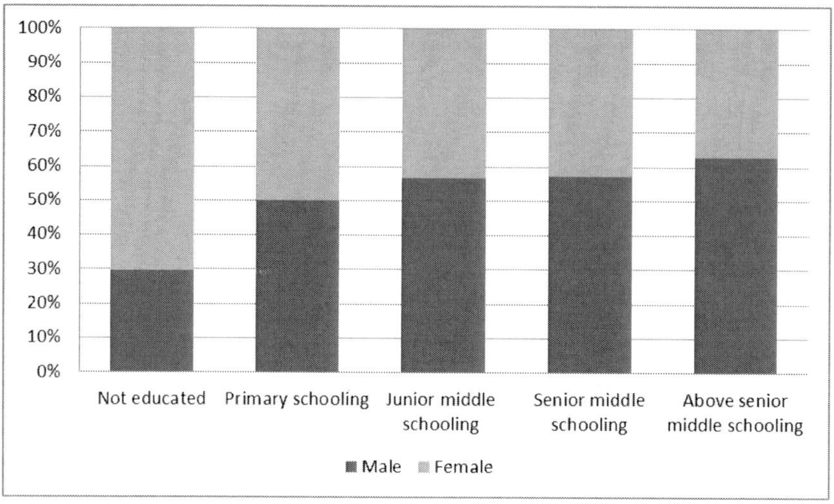

Source: China Statistical Yearbook.

Figure 4.2.6. Population by education attainment in China in 1998.

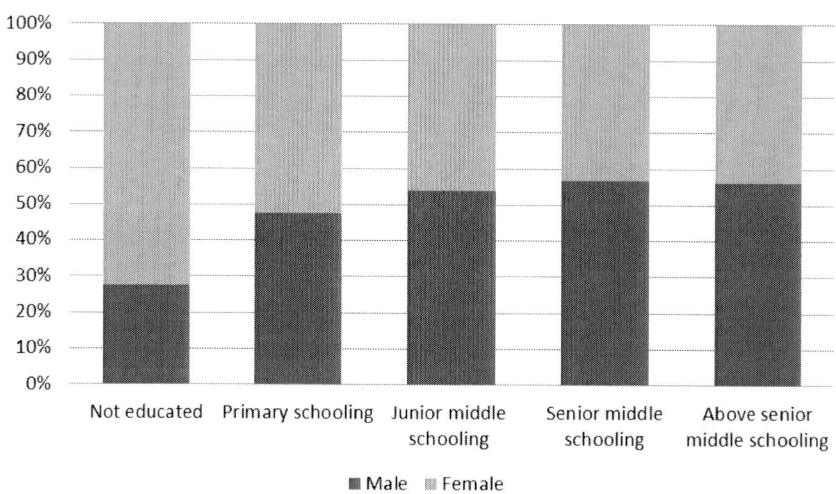

Source: China Statistical Yearbook.

Figure 4.2.7. Population by education attainment in China in 2003.

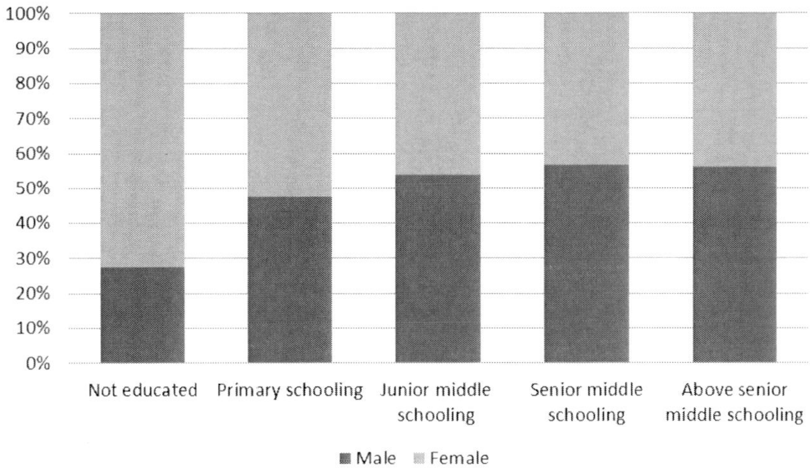

Source: China Statistical Yearbook.

Figure 4.2.8. Population by education attainment in China in 2008.

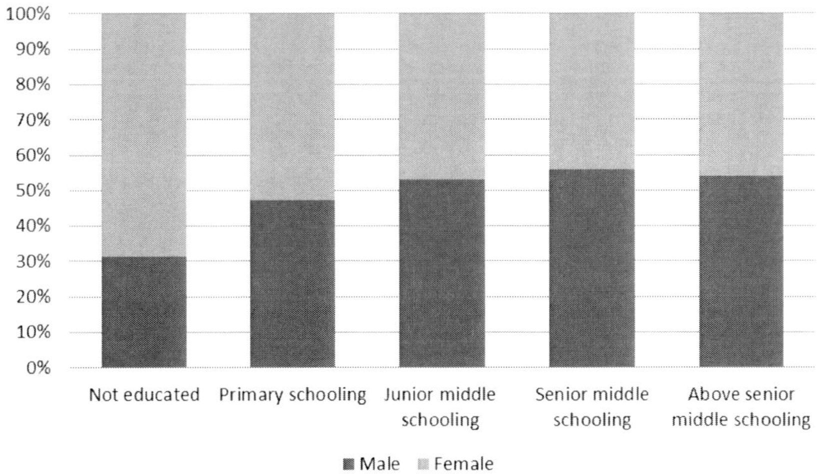

Source: China Statistical Yearbook.

Figure 4.2.9. Population by education attainment in China in 2013.

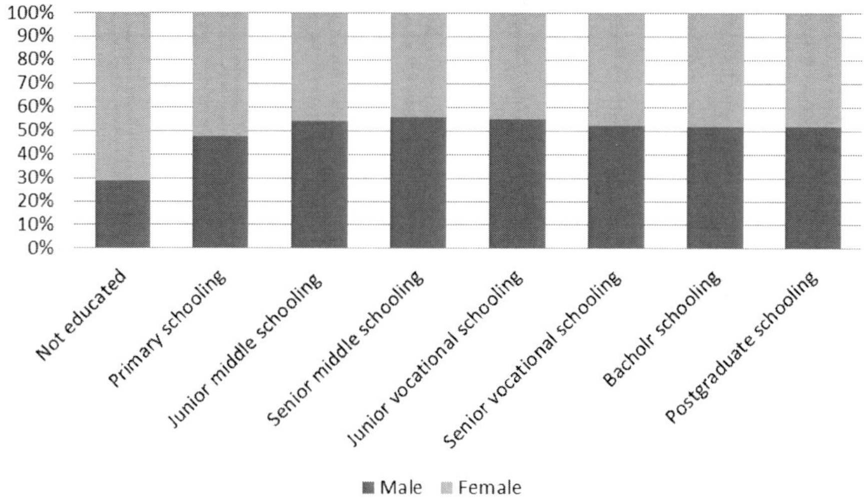

Source: China Statistical Yearbook.

Figure 4.2.10. Population by education attainment in China in 2018.

Above all, we can find that the population and education distribution keep promoting. No matter the storage and quality of human capital in China are in the trend of perfection.

4.3. Educational Attainment of Human Capital in China

We can find that the storage and quality of human capital in China are getting gradual promotion. At the same time, as for human capital, the age and education of it are important factors that should be considered. As a result, in this part, we try to site calculations of degree of population aging, education status and higher education penetration of labor force in China.

First of all, we should talk about the definition of the labor force again, which we had referred to in Chapter 3. Generally speaking, male labor force means the population out of school, whose age is from 16 years old to 59 years old, while female labor force means the population out of school, whose age is from 16 years old to 54 years old. According to the calculations presented in China Human Capital Report Series published by China Center for Human Capital and Labor Market Research Central University of Finance and Economics Beijing, China, levels of education attainment are showed in Table 4.3.1 and Table 4.3.2.

Table 4.3.1. Levels of education attainment before 2000 in China

Level	Illiterate	Primary School	Junior Middle School	Senior Middle School	College and Above
Years of Schooling	0	6	9	12	15

Table 4.3.2. Levels of education attainment since 2000 in China

Level	Illiterate	Primary School	Junior Middle School	Senior Middle School	College	University and Above
Years of Schooling	0	6	9	12	15	16

Based on this calculation, we can distinguish labor force and divide them into different kinds of level of education attainment. First of all, let's talk about the average age of the national labor force. Here are the data of national labor force from 1985 to 2017 in Mainland China shown in Table 4.3.3. We can find that the average age of labor force is increasing gradually and the average age is about 35 years old, which means that the human capital in China is in a good condition. Meanwhile, due to rural-urban labor force immigration, the average age of the labor force in rural areas fell beneath that in urban areas.

In order to find the tendency of average age of labor force in Mainland, China, we can draw the line chart. Figure 4.3.1 shows the upward trend of average age of labor force from 1985 to 2017 in mainland China. No matter the average age in urban areas and that in rural areas are increasing in a stable pace. And this kind of tendency is under control and good for economic development.

Table 4.3.3. Average age of the national labor force from 1985 to 2017 (Unit: Year (of age))

Year	Average Age of the Labor Force		
	Total	Urban	Rural
1985	32.21	33.42	31.82
1986	32.17	33.34	31.78
1987	32.13	33.21	31.76
1988	32.14	33.12	31.79
1989	32.17	33.07	31.84
1990	32.18	33.01	31.88
1991	32.36	33.20	32.04
1992	32.62	33.51	32.38
1993	32.78	33.37	32.55
1994	33.12	33.82	32.85
1995	33.41	34.06	33.16
1996	33.67	34.11	33.49
1997	33.95	34.19	33.85
1998	34.15	34.20	34.12
1999	34.45	34.39	34.49
2000	34.70	34.59	34.76
2001	35.02	35.18	34.92
2002	35.12	35.30	35.01
2003	35.25	35.55	35.04
2004	35.52	36.04	35.14
2005	35.71	36.26	35.29
2006	35.83	36.39	35.38
2007	36.02	36.49	35.63
2008	36.16	36.50	35.85
2009	36.25	36.46	36.05
2010	36.35	36.43	36.28
2011	36.58	36.71	36.46
2012	36.78	36.93	36.61
2013	37.04	37.24	36.80
2014	37.29	37.52	37.03
2015	37.52	37.73	37.27
2016	37.70	37.93	37.40
2017	37.80	38.09	37.42

Source: China Human Capital Report Series.

When it comes to the average of the labor force in mainland China, Hong Kong region, and Taiwan region, we can fine that the average age of the labor force in Hong Kong region increased from 34.11 in 1985 to 39.13 in 2017, which increased by 5.02 years. And the average age of the labor force in Taiwan region increased from 33.01 in 1985 to 38.15, which increased by 5.14 years. At the same time, the average age of the labor force in Mainland increased from 32.21 in 1985 to 37.80 in 2017, which increased by 5.59 years.

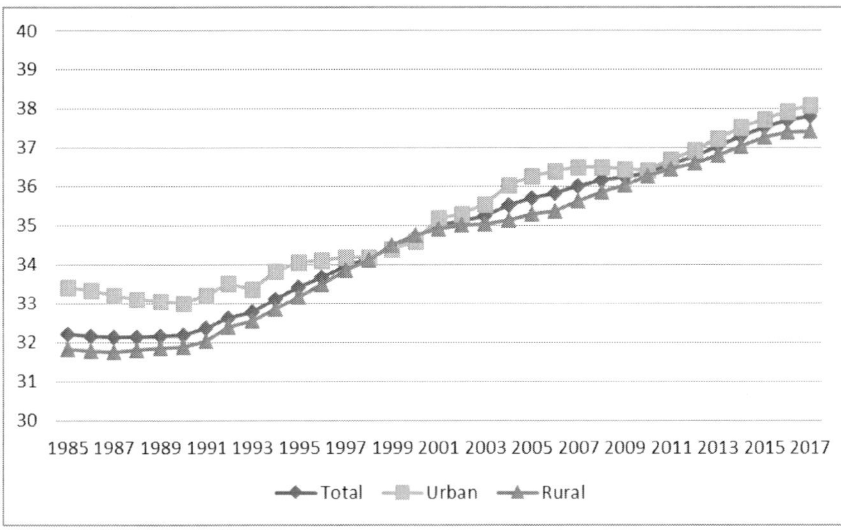

Source: China Human Capital Report Series.

Figure 4.3.1. Average age of the national labor force from 1985 to 2017.

Figure 4.3.2 shows an upward trend of the average age of the labor force in Mainland, Hong Kong region, and Taiwan region from 1985 to 2017. We can find that the average age of the labor force of Hong Kong region is significantly bigger than that of Mainland and Taiwan region. However, until 2017, the average age of the labor force in these three areas in China are almost the same, which is around 38 years old.

The average years of education for human capital are also an important factor related with human capital storage. Since 1985, the average years of education for both urban human capital and rural human capital increase dramatically. The average years of education for all human capital increase from 6.23 in 1985 to 10.09 in 2017. The increasing rate is up to 61.6%, which is higher than the growth rate of employment population. That is to say, the promotion of average skill for labor force contributes more to the

Table 4.3.4. Average age of the national labor force in Mainland China, the Hong Kong region, and the Taiwan region from 1985 to 2017 (Unit: Year (of age))

Year	Average Age of the Labor Force		
	Mainland	Hong Kong	Taiwan
1985	32.21	34.11	33.01
1986	31.17	34.37	33.26
1987	32.13	34.47	33.31
1988	32.14	34.63	33.38
1989	32.17	34.80	33.53
1990	32.18	34.83	33.75
1991	32.36	35.15	33.86
1992	32.62	35.33	33.92
1993	32.78	35.41	34.00
1994	33.12	35.65	34.10
1995	33.41	35.92	34.16
1996	33.67	36.07	34.27
1997	33.95	36.29	34.39
1998	34.15	36.50	34.49
1999	34.45	36.74	34.77
2000	34.70	37.07	35.12
2001	35.02	37.25	35.51
2002	35.12	37.46	35.85
2003	35.25	37.72	36.08
2004	36.52	37.97	36.29
2005	35.71	38.33	36.57
2006	35.83	38.45	36.83
2007	36.02	38.53	36.95
2008	36.16	38.69	37.15
2009	36.25	38.80	37.44
2010	36.35	38.91	37.46
2011	36.58	38.93	37.60
2012	36.78	39.08	37.73
2013	37.04	39.36	37.86
2014	37.29	39.37	37.91
2015	37.52	39.36	37.99
2016	37.70	39.15	38.08
2017	37.80	39.13	38.80

Source: China Human Capital Report Series.

increase of human capital than the optimization of demographic structure in China. From 1985 to 2017, the average years of education for urban human capital has increased by 2.93 years, and for rural human capital, it has increased by 3.37 years. However, there is a gap of the average year of education between urban and rural capital. The average year of education for human capital in China has increased in a fast speed. It also means that China has accumulated much human capital during this period.

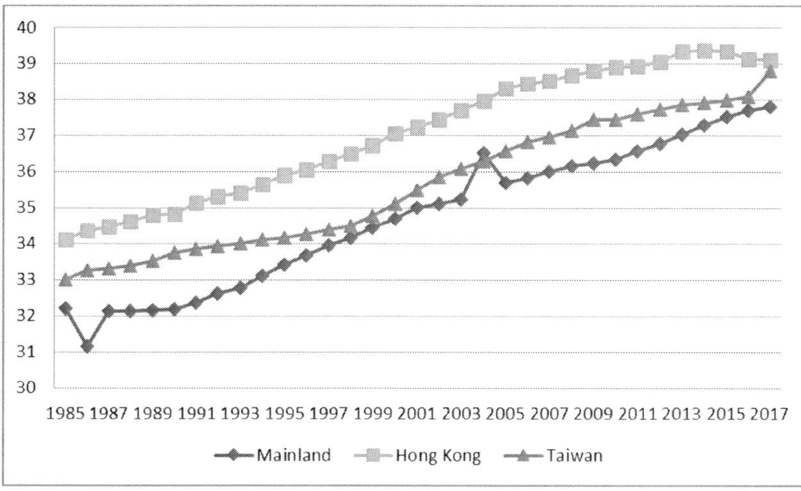

Source: China Human Capital Report Series.

Figure 4.3.2. Average age of the labor force in Mainland, Hong Kong region, and Taiwan region in China from 1985 to 2017.

Both the line chart and the table show the trends of average years of schooling of the labor force in urban areas and rural areas. When it comes to the data in Mainland, Hong Kong region, and Taiwan region, we can find in these three areas of China, the average years of schooling of the labor force is increasing. The average years of schooling of the labor force in Hong Kong region increased from 8.68 years in 1985 to 12.35 years in 2017, which increased by 3.67 years while that in Taiwan region increased from 8.89 years in 1985 to 13.64 years in 2017, which increased by 3.67 years. Compared with Hong Kong region and Taiwan region, it is obvious that the average years of schooling of the labor force in Mainland is quite shorter. Until 2017, the average years of schooling are only 10.19. However, we can find that in the recent year, with more attention and effort paid to the education field, government tries to push forward the development of vocational education and tertiary education, the quality of labor force will be promoted in the future.

Table 4.3.5. Average years of schooling of the national labor force from 1985 to 2017
(Unit: Year)

Year	Average Years of Schooling		
	Total	Urban	Rural
1985	6.23	8.18	5.59
1986	6.36	8.29	5.71
1987	6.51	8.42	5.85
1988	6.66	8.54	5.99
1989	6.80	8.64	6.13
1990	6.92	8.72	6.27
1991	7.08	8.84	6.40
1992	7.19	8.94	6.51
1993	7.30	9.06	6.61
1994	7.42	9.17	6.74
1995	7.55	9.30	6.87
1996	7.72	9.42	7.00
1997	7.88	9.52	7.13
1998	8.04	9.62	7.27
1999	8.20	9.69	7.40
2000	8.36	9.73	7.54
2001	8.45	9.78	7.61
2002	8.53	9.83	7.68
2003	8.62	9.88	7.74
2004	8.74	10.01	7.81
2005	8.85	10.12	7.89
2006	8.96	10.19	7.98
2007	9.08	10.27	8.09
2008	9.20	10.34	8.20
2009	9.34	10.43	8.33
2010	9.48	10.50	8.45
2011	9.56	10.59	8.49
2012	9.65	10.67	8.56
2013	9.75	10.73	8.64
2014	9.85	10.80	8.73
2015	10.00	10.92	8.86
2016	10.09	11.02	8.91
2017	10.19	11.11	8.96

Source: China Human Capital Report Series.

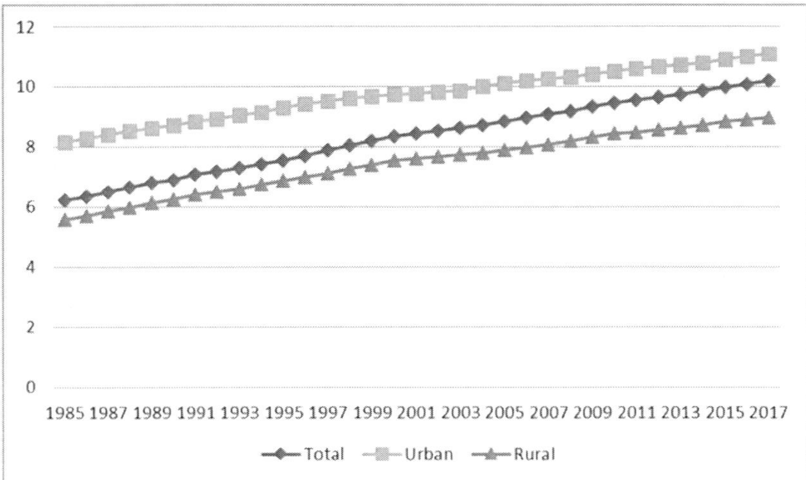

Source: China Human Capital Report Series.

Figure 4.3.3. Average years of schooling of the national labor force from 1985 to 2017.

According to the tables and charts, we can find that at present, the average labor force in China has got a senior high school education. However, currently, the competition between nations is the completion on science and technology. The speed and efficiency of innovation and creation decides the economic growth of an economy. In this way, we must pay more attention to the national proportions of high school and above of the labor force. Here is the data from 1985 to 2017.

We can find a significant increase on the total proportions of high school and above of the labor force, which increases from 11.40% in 1985 to 37.51% in 2017 (Table 4.3.7). It means that the total quality of labor force in China has been promoted during these years. At the same time, we can find that the differences between rural areas and urban area on proportions of high school and above of the labor force have become more and more clear. The proportions in urban areas increases from 24.68% in 1985 to 50.33% in 2017 while the proportions in rural areas increases from 7.04% in 1985 to 20.50% in 2017.

Table 4.3.6. Average years of schooling of the labor force from 1985 to 2017
(Unit: Year (of age))

Year	Average Age of the Labor Force		
	Mainland	Hong Kong	Taiwan
1985	6.23	8.68	8.89
1986	6.36	8.84	9.03
1987	6.51	9.00	9.17
1988	6.66	9.11	9.32
1989	6.80	9.23	9.51
1990	6.92	9.40	9.64
1991	7.08	9.58	9.76
1992	7.19	9.75	9.86
1993	7.30	9.88	9.98
1994	7.42	10.01	10.09
1995	7.55	10.15	10.19
1996	7.72	10.33	10.28
1997	7.88	10.39	10.37
1998	8.04	10.43	10.31
1999	8.20	10.46	10.59
2000	8.36	10.51	10.88
2001	8.45	10.62	11.14
2002	8.53	10.73	11.40
2003	8.62	10.81	11.96
2004	8.74	10.91	12.09
2005	8.85	11.02	12.21
2006	8.96	11.18	12.34
2007	9.08	11.28	12.48
2008	9.20	11.36	12.60
2009	9.34	11.45	12.69
2010	9.48	11.56	12.84
2011	9.56	11.72	12.97
2012	9.65	11.80	13.09
2013	9.75	11.86	13.22
2014	9.85	11.97	13.33
2015	10.00	12.10	13.43
2016	10.09	12.28	13.54
2017	10.19	12.35	13.64

Source: China Human Capital Report Series.

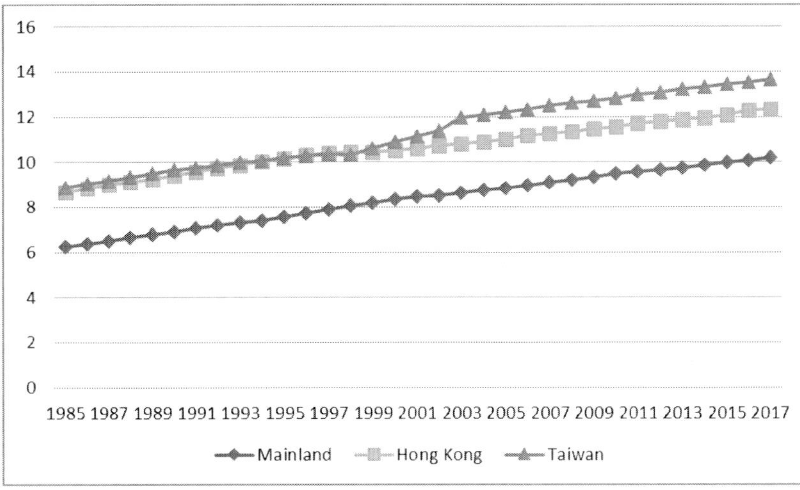

Source: China Human Capital Report Series.

Figure 4.3.4. Average years of schooling of the labor force from 1985 to 2017.

Table 4.3.7. National proportions of high school and above of the labor force from 1985 to 2017 (Unit: %)

Year	Proportions of High School and Above		
	Total	Urban	Rural
1985	11.40	24.68	7.04
1986	11.50	25.20	6.88
1987	11.64	25.77	6.75
1988	11.73	26.15	6.64
1989	11.82	26.26	6.52
1990	11.63	26.04	6.40
1991	12.20	27.01	6.49
1992	12.51	27.94	6.54
1993	12.92	28.95	6.65
1994	13.41	30.30	6.86
1995	14.05	31.92	7.08
1996	14.97	33.17	7.30
1997	15.91	34.22	7.55
1998	16.92	35.28	7.86
1999	17.94	35.95	8.20
2000	18.79	36.12	8.53
2001	19.19	36.16	8.56

Table 4.3.7. (Continued)

Year	Proportions of High School and Above		
	Total		Total
2002	19.59	36.29	8.57
2003	20.07	36.53	8.63
2004	21.29	38.38	8.78
2005	22.12	39.17	9.08
2006	22.87	39.53	9.57
2007	23.90	40.14	10.30
2008	25.07	41.00	11.15
2009	26.45	41.89	12.15
2010	27.85	42.52	13.11
2011	29.04	43.84	13.70
2012	30.29	44.84	14.57
2013	31.67	45.65	15.92
2014	33.41	46.70	17.74
2015	35.69	48.29	19.93
2016	36.64	49.34	20.38
2017	37.51	50.33	20.50

Source: China Human Capital Report Series.

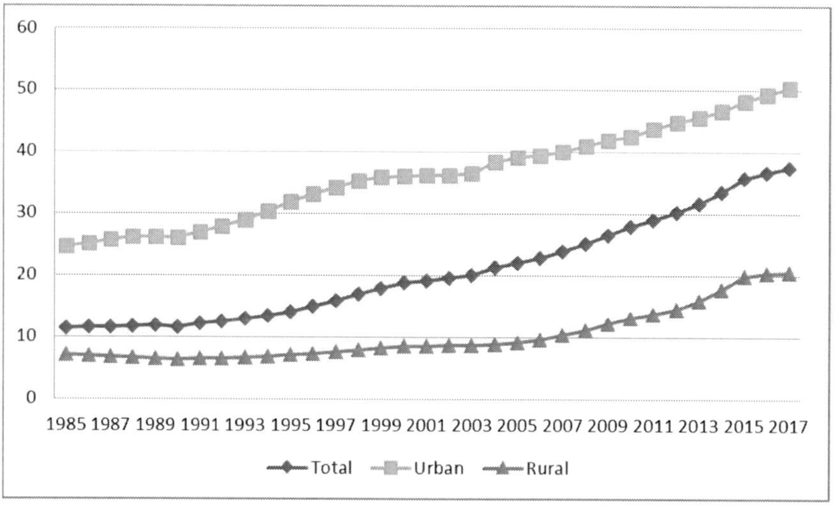

Source: China Human Capital Report Series.

Figure 4.3.5. National Proportions of High School and Above of the Labor Force from 1985 to 2017.

Table 4.3.8. Proportions of High School and Above of the Labor Force from 1985 to 2017
(Unit: %)

Year	Proportions of High School and Above		
	Mainland	Hong Kong	Taiwan
1985	11.40	37.64	39.83
1986	11.50	39.87	41.50
1987	11.64	41.48	43.53
1988	11.73	42.31	45.06
1989	11.82	43.42	46.31
1990	11.63	45.20	47.65
1991	12.20	46.40	49.14
1992	12.51	48.44	50.34
1993	12.92	49.91	51.17
1994	13.41	51.31	51.63
1995	14.05	52.89	51.95
1996	14.97	54.84	51.79
1997	15.91	55.67	51.56
1998	16.92	56.03	50.23
1999	17.94	56.49	53.96
2000	18.79	57.17	58.05
2001	19.19	58.41	61.77
2002	19.59	59.73	64.65
2003	20.07	60.32	71.48
2004	21.29	61.02	72.88
2005	22.12	61.94	74.13
2006	22.87	63.27	75.48
2007	23.90	64.66	76.82
2008	25.07	65.62	77.90
2009	26.45	66.70	78.95
2010	27.85	67.88	80.33
2011	29.04	69.37	81.58
2012	30.29	70.55	82.67
2013	31.67	71.21	83.86
2014	33.41	72.38	84.98
2015	35.69	73.67	85.93
2016	36.64	75.50	87.02
2017	37.51	76.47	87.92

Source: China Human Capital Report Series.

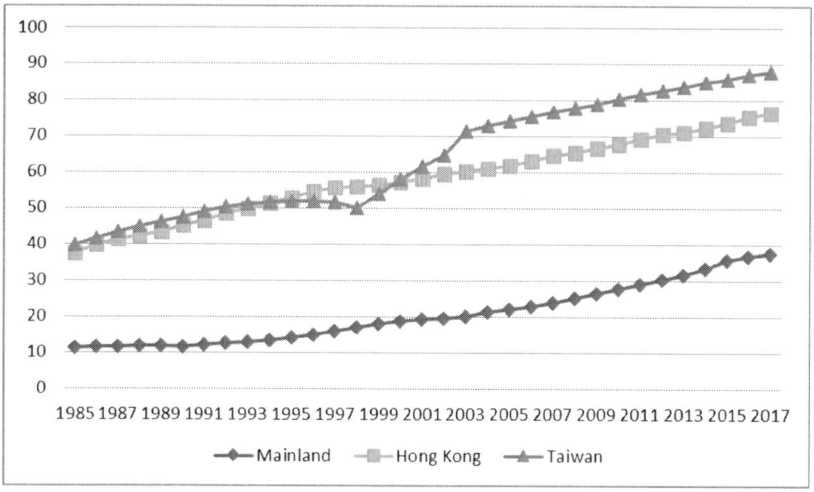

Source: China Human Capital Report Series.

Figure 4.3.6. Proportions of high school and above of the labor force from 1985 to 2017.

Compared with rural areas, urban areas have much more advanced education system. The national proportions of high school and above of the labor forces in urban areas are much higher than that in rural areas. At present, more than half of the labor force in urban areas has got well educated, which can cater to the need of social development.

Table 4.3.8 shows proportions of high school and above of the labor force from 1985 to 2017 in Mainland, Hong Kong region, and Taiwan region. The total qualities of labor force in these three parts in China are getting promoted gradually. The proportions of high school and above of the labor force in Hong Kong region increase from 37.65% in 1985 to 76.47% in 2017 while the proportions in Taiwan region increase from 39.83% in 1985 to 87.92% in 2017. There is no doubt that the education in Hong Kong region and Taiwan region is much better than that in Mainland. And the proportion in Hong Kong region is greater than that in Taiwan region before 2001, but smaller since 2001.

Table 4.3.9 shows the national proportions of college education and above of the labor force from 1985 to 2017. We can find that in 1985, only 1.30% of the labor force in China got college education. At that time,

4.65% of the urban residents and 0.20% of the rural residents got college education. With the reform of college education, the situation is getting better. Until 2017, 26.69% of the urban residents and 5.46% of rural residents got college education and above.

Table 4.3.9. National proportions of college education and above of the labor force from 1985 to 2017
(Unit: %)

Year	Proportions of College Education and Above		
	Total	Urban	Rural
1985	1.30	4.65	0.20
1986	1.47	5.18	0.22
1987	1.62	5.63	0.23
1988	1.75	5.99	0.25
1989	1.87	6.24	0.26
1990	1.91	6.42	0.27
1991	2.14	6.91	0.30
1992	2.32	7.45	0.33
1993	2.46	7.81	0.37
1994	2.67	8.47	0.42
1995	2.89	9.10	0.47
1996	3.20	9.52	0.53
1997	3.46	9.74	0.59
1998	3.70	9.87	0.65
1999	3.98	10.03	0.72
2000	4.26	10.16	0.77
2001	4.68	10.85	0.81
2002	5.04	11.36	0.87
2003	5.53	12.09	0.98
2004	6.39	13.56	1.14
2005	7.27	15.00	1.35
2006	7.99	15.94	1.63
2007	8.65	16.58	2.00
2008	9.21	17.05	2.36
2009	9.85	17.58	2.69
2010	10.68	18.31	3.01
2011	11.52	19.57	3.19
2012	12.50	20.74	3.60
2013	13.47	21.72	4.19
2014	14.53	22.75	4.84
2015	15.90	24.25	5.46
2016	16.71	25.51	5.44
2017	17.57	26.69	5.46

Source: China Human Capital Report Series.

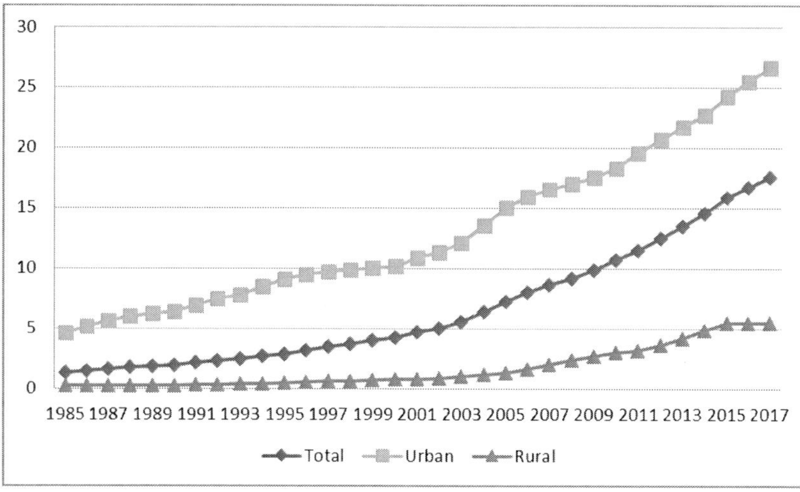

Source: China Human Capital Report Series.

Figure 4.3.7. National proportions of college education and above of the labor force from 1985 to 2017.

Table 4.3.10. National proportions of college education and above of the labor force from 1985 to 2017 (Unit: %)

Year	Proportions of College Education and Above		
	Mainland	Hong Kong	Taiwan
1985	1.30	7.70	11.32
1986	1.47	8.06	11.65
1987	1.62	8.94	11.98
1988	1.75	9.95	12.52
1989	1.87	10.73	13.52
1990	1.91	11.38	13.80
1991	2.14	12.78	14.27
1992	2.32	13.80	14.90
1993	2.46	14.84	15.43
1994	2.67	15.63	16.11
1995	2.89	16.32	16.46
1996	3.20	17.47	16.66
1997	3.46	17.82	17.13
1998	3.70	18.27	17.96
1999	3.98	18.43	19.77
2000	4.26	18.44	22.33
2001	4.68	18.98	25.20
2002	5.04	20.62	27.73

Year	Proportions of College Education and Above		
	Mainland	Hong Kong	Taiwan
2003	5.53	22.29	33.05
2004	6.39	23.90	34.58
2005	7.27	25.51	35.84
2006	7.99	27.63	37.21
2007	8.65	28.62	38.92
2008	9.21	30.02	40.33
2009	9.85	31.27	41.30
2010	10.68	32.31	43.14
2011	11.52	33.96	44.84
2012	12.50	34.82	46.60
2013	13.47	36.17	48.44
2014	14.53	37.96	50.00
2015	15.90	39.99	51.48
2016	16.71	42.24	53.02
2017	17.57	43.01	54.54

Source: China Human Capital Report Series.

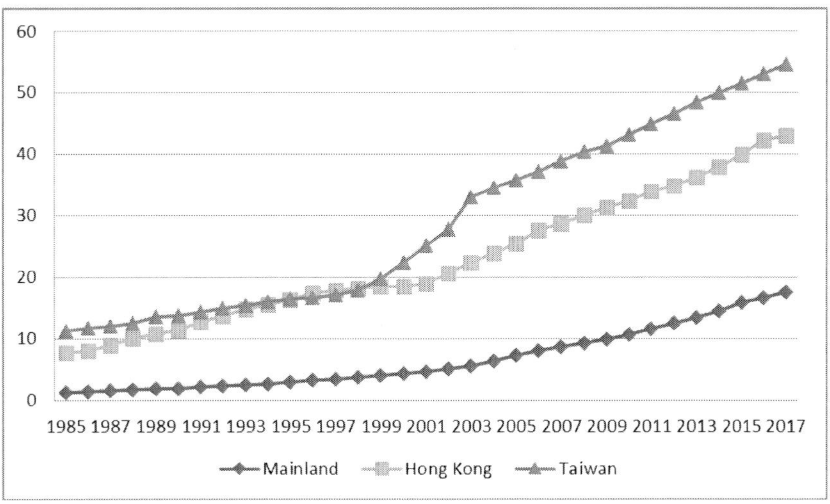

Source: China Human Capital Report Series.

Figure 4.3.8. National Proportions of College Education and Above of the Labor Force from 1985 to 2017.

The tables and figures all show the structure of human capital. The key point of human capital structure is the difference in individual quality. The quality includes education level, vocational skills, the mobility of labor force and some other factors that will influence the value of human capital.

According to the education level, we can divide human capital into different groups as follows:

1) Human capital without education experience.
2) Human capital with primary school education.
3) Human capital with junior middle school education.
4) Human capital with senior middle school education.
5) Human capital with college education or above.

With the popularization of free and compulsory education, the people who have not been educated are almost nowhere to see in China. Meanwhile, the number of the people who merely get primary school education is decreasing while the number of people who get middle school education or above is increasing rapidly. The number of children who have not got education has decreased by 159 billion. The decreasing rate is up to 48%, which we could call a miracle of educational intervention. These amazing data does not mean that children in China stop receiving education but mean that this kind of people are very likely to get higher level education. The number of people receiving middle school education continuously increasing and this truth reveals the improvement of human capital.

4.4. The Provincial Perspective

In fact, the quantity and quality of human capital is decided by the condition of labor force. In this part, we will know the average age and education level of labor forces in China from the perspective of provinces.

First of all, we present some features of Chinese population growth from the perspective of provinces in 2017. Generally speaking, the average age of the labor force at provincial level is between 34 and 40 years of age in 2017. The average of the labor force in west provinces of China is younger than that in other places, and the average age of the labor force in Tibet is the youngest, which is only 34.38 years of age.

Table 4.4.1. Average age of the labor force at provincial level in 2017 (Unit: Year (of age))

Rank	Province	Average Age		
		Sub-Total	Urban	Rural
1	Liaoning	39.51	39.78	38.95
2	Jilin	39.29	39.74	38.81
3	Heilongjiang	39.28	39.43	39.06
4	Chongqing	39.15	38.54	38.41
5	Hunan	38.57	39.12	37.98
6	Zhejiang	38.48	38.15	39.18
7	Inner Mongolia	38.24	37.98	38.64
8	Shanghai	38.23	38.23	-
9	Sichuan	38.23	38.69	37.77
10	Jiangsu	38.20	38.08	38.45
11	Shandong	38.00	37.76	38.24
12	Hebei	37.95	37.99	37.91
13	Tianjin	37.82	37.75	38.17
14	Hubei	37.80	37.82	37.77
15	Jiangxi	37.75	38.43	37.06
16	Fujian	37.71	37.69	37.74
17	Henan	37.31	37.98	36.72
18	Guangxi	37.22	37.71	36.82
19	Shannxi	37.22	36.94	37.54
20	Gansu	37.21	37.78	36.80
21	Qinghai	37.14	38.60	35.77
22	Ningxia	36.90	36.77	37.64
23	Beijing	36.90	38.11	35.43
24	Anhui	36.83	36.43	37.64
25	Shanxi	36.76	36.94	36.56
26	Yunnan	36.74	37.45	36.20
27	Guangdong	36.38	36.75	35.56
28	Guizhou	36.07	37.65	35.56
29	Hainan	36.04	36.74	35.30
30	Xinjiang	35.97	36.79	35.30
31	Tibet	34.38	35.54	34.11

Source: China Human Capital Report Series.

Table 4.4.2. Average years of schooling of the labor force at provincial level in 2017 (Unit: Year)

Rank	Province	Average Years of Schooling		
		Sub-Total	Urban	Rural
1	Beijing	12.84	13.23	10.44
2	Shanghai	11.86	11.86	-
3	Tianjin	11.04	11.37	9.38
4	Jiangsu	10.81	11.35	9.64
5	Liaoning	10.76	11.63	8.99
6	Shannxi	10.55	11.64	9.34
7	Hunan	10.64	11.36	9.50
8	Hubei	10.37	11.39	9.01
9	Guangdong	10.34	10.76	9.38
10	Shanxi	10.27	11.31	9.06
11	Zhejiang	10.15	10.60	9.23
12	Heilongjiang	10.12	11.22	8.62
13	Jilin	10.12	11.39	8.75
14	Chongqing	10.12	10.79	8.85
15	Hebei	10.11	11.00	9.17
16	Shandong	10.09	11.33	8.84
17	Inner Mongolia	10.09	11.03	8.63
18	Hainan	10.06	10.80	9.26
19	Henan	10.01	10.87	9.25
20	Fujian	9.95	10.53	8.87
21	Jiangxi	9.92	10.76	9.07
22	Xinjiang	9.89	11.56	8.50
23	Ningxia	9.71	10.91	8.26
24	Anhui	9.69	10.83	8.46
25	Sichuan	9.69	10.89	8.53
26	Guangxi	9.62	10.75	8.67
27	Gansu	9.43	11.33	8.11
28	Yunnan	8.95	10.41	7.82
29	Guizhou	9.79	10.11	8.02
30	Tibet	8.18	9.93	6.52
31	Qinghai	5.72	9.26	4.91

Source: China Human Capital Report Series.

The average age reveals a part of quality of human capital and the education attainment of labor force is a more important part for the quality of human capital in China. Table 4.4.2 shows the provincial rankings of average years of schooling of the labor force in China in 2017, which indicates the educational attainment of labor force. In this table, we can find that Beijing takes the lead in the average years of schooling, which is about 12.84 years. And then the following ranks are Shanghai, Tianjin, and Jiangsu. At the same time, the average years of schooling of Guizhou is only 8.79 years, Tibet is 8.18 years and Qinghai rank at the bottom in terms of educational attainment. Meanwhile, there is a significant difference on average years of schooling between urban areas and rural areas in provinces. However, in different areas, the gap between urban areas and rural areas varies. As for developed areas, the gap will be huger. For example, the urban-rural differential in Tibet is 4.35 while the gap in Beijing is only 2.79.

Table 4.4.3 shows the proportion of high school education and above of the labor force from the perspective of provincial level in 2017. We can find that Beijing, Shanghai, Tianjin, and Jiangsu have the highest proportion of high school education and above, which are 71.44%, 58.54%, 47.76%, and 45.85% respectively. At the same time, Guizhou and Tibet rank in the bottom of tables, which are only 23.13% and 13.01%. It is significant that the regional differences are a big problem. As for Tibet, the gap on the proportion of high school education and above between urban areas and rural areas is up to 31.66%.

Table 4.4.4 shows the proportion of college education and above of the labor force from the perspective of provincial level in 2017 in China. The data is similar to the data of the proportion of high school education and above of the labor force in the last table. However, we can find the rank change a little that Liaoning ranks the fourth. And some provinces like Jiangsu rank lower in the proportions of college graduates than of the high school graduates. This atmosphere may be explained by the education factors such as the quality and quantity of universities and regional education oriented policies in the specific provinces.

Table 4.4.3. The proportion of high school education and above of the labor force at provincial level in 2017 (Unit: %)

Rank	Province	The Proportion of High School Education and Above		
		Sub-Total	Urban	Rural
1	Beijing	71.44	76.28	41.49
2	Shanghai	58.54	58.54	-
3	Tianjin	47.76	53.31	19.84
4	Jiangsu	45.85	53.65	28.85
5	Hunan	42.61	55.98	28.22
6	Shannxi	41.70	56.24	25.33
7	Liaoning	41.26	54.88	13.36
8	Guangdong	40.73	47.32	25.83
9	Hubei	38.60	54.43	17.52
10	Chongqing	38.12	47.70	20.08
11	Zhejiang	37.30	42.95	25.58
12	Inner Mongolia	36.68	50.72	14.93
13	Ningxia	36.60	50.57	19.60
14	Shanxi	36.38	53.33	16.48
15	Fujian	36.05	43.29	22.73
16	Jilin	34.50	54.71	12.62
17	Gansu	34.47	56.18	19.33
18	Hainan	33.97	46.55	20.49
19	Jiangxi	33.89	45.86	21.61
20	Henan	33.75	47.52	21.57
21	Hebei	33.52	47.79	18.24
22	Shandong	33.43	52.73	14.05
23	Heilongjiang	33.38	50.33	10.04
24	Sichuan	33.05	48.34	18.21
25	Xinjiang	32.61	58.01	11.59
26	Anhui	29.77	46.87	11.18
27	Guangxi	28.31	44.55	14.79
28	Qinghai	25.93	41.34	11.37
29	Yunnan	25.66	42.18	13.01
30	Guizhou	23.13	37.71	14.59
31	Tibet	13.01	38.79	7.13

Source: China Human Capital Report Series.

Table 4.4.4. The proportion of college education and above of the labor force at provincial level in 2017 (Unit: %)

Rank	Province	The Proportion of College Education and Above		
		Sub-Total	Urban	Rural
1	Beijing	50.55	55.95	17.09
2	Shanghai	37.40	37.40	-
3	Tianjin	25.58	29.22	7.29
4	Liaoning	22.90	32.09	4.07
5	Shannxi	22.61	35.34	8.27
6	Jiangsu	22.54	28.80	8.90
7	Zhejiang	19.85	25.16	8.86
8	Ningxia	19.59	30.20	6.68
9	Xinjiang	18.48	36.33	3.71
10	Hubei	18.43	29.14	4.17
11	Fujian	17.41	23.43	6.31
12	Inner Mongolia	17.18	25.18	4.77
13	Heilongjiang	16.65	26.51	3.07
14	Gansu	16.39	31.45	5.89
15	Hunan	16.18	26.14	5.47
16	Jilin	16.08	27.21	4.02
17	Chongqing	16.07	22.06	4.78
18	Shandong	15.80	28.88	2.66
19	Shanxi	15.75	26.76	2.83
20	Sichuan	15.19	25.74	4.96
21	Guangdong	15.10	19.56	5.03
22	Hebei	14.57	24.18	4.27
23	Hainan	13.66	20.56	6.27
24	Anhui	13.49	23.56	6.27
25	Jiangxi	13.38	21.57	4.99
26	Qinghai	13.25	22.68	4.34
27	Yunnan	12.64	23.96	3.98
28	Guangxi	11.91	21.98	3.52
29	Henan	11.84	20.53	4.16
30	Guizhou	10.65	21.40	4.36
31	Tibet	6.97	25.21	2.81

Source: China Human Capital Report Series.

4.5. Descriptive Statistics of Human Capital in China

Human capital, in essence, is decided by the human being. That is to say, all the things concerning citizens in China, such as gender, population distribution, education condition, are related with the quality and quantity on human capital. As a result, it is meaningful to find the change and trends of real value of human capital stock than the nominal value.

Among all variables gender and population distribution are the most important and intuitive aspects when we evaluate the human capital in China. Table 4.5.1 shows the national real human capital by gender and region. We can find that from 1985 to 2017, human capital increased from 37459 billion to 388554 billion of 1985 Yuan. The total increasing rate is up to 937.27% and the annual growth rate it more than 7%. However, we can find that the annual growth rate of human capital is lower than that of national economic growth rate. Based on this phenomenon, it is reflected that although the economic growth and human capital promotion are prosperously booming in China, the exit of the aging low-educated population from the labor market and entrance of younger individuals with higher expected education and higher income. That is to say, the promotion of human capital is not completely balanced with the growth of macroscopic economic growth.

As for the gender distribution of national real human capital in China, we can find that in 1985, male human capital is about 19372 billion while female human capital is about 18087 billion of 1985 Yuan. During these 40 years, both male and female human capital keep increasing and in 2017, the male human capital is up to 260809 billion while female human capital is up to 127745 billion of 1985 Yuan. When comparing the data of male human capital and female human capital, we can find with the stock of national real human capital keeping booming, the difference between male human capital and female human capital keeping significant. The gap of

Table 4.5.1. National real human capital by gender and region (Unit: Billions of 1985 Yuan)

Year	National	Male	Female	Urban	Rural
1985	37459	19372	18087	14310	23149
1986	41209	22571	18638	16989	24220
1987	44437	25036	19400	19040	25396
1988	44409	25602	18807	19571	24838
1989	44065	25906	18160	20529	23536
1990	48989	29236	19753	23415	25575
1991	55871	33863	22008	27442	28429
1992	61875	38431	23444	31549	30326
1993	63745	40351	23394	33825	29920
1994	60402	38911	21491	33218	27183
1995	58356	37619	20738	32441	25916
1996	63961	41701	22260	37656	26305
1997	70324	45877	24447	42389	27935
1998	82152	53975	28178	51607	30546
1999	97581	63992	33588	63989	33592
2000	112149	72632	39517	75590	36559
2001	122474	78868	43607	82845	39629
2002	131734	85352	46382	89951	41783
2003	142749	92592	50158	98976	43774
2004	150261	96890	53371	105877	44384
2005	160513	103332	57180	114583	45930
2006	181055	117272	63784	130862	50194
2007	191399	124270	67129	140823	50576
2008	201835	131174	70661	150777	51058
2009	224166	146186	77980	168967	55199
2010	236026	153934	82092	178575	57451
2011	254980	166726	88255	197490	57490
2012	272150	178940	93210	213473	58676
2013	299988	198610	101378	239467	60521
2014	321488	213323	108166	257819	63669
2015	341940	228809	113131	273531	68409
2016	364976	244717	120259	296631	68345
2017	388554	260809	127745	316129	72425

Source: China Human Capital Report Series.

male human capital and female capital in 1985 is about 1285 billion while the gap in 2017 is up to 133064 billion of 1985 Yuan. Male human capital is the double of female human capital. In recent year, with the development of education equality, both boys and girls can have the same right to get educated. More and more women can enter the workplace. So actually, the significant gap also indicates that the gender is still a sensitive variable.

When it comes to the regional distribution of national real human capital in China, we can find that both urban real capital and rural real human capital keep increasing from 1985 to 2017. The urban real human capital increases from 14310 billion to 316129 billion of 1985 Yuan while the rural real human capital increases from 23149 billion to 72425 billion of 1985 Yuan. Different from the gender distribution of human capital, the gap of human capital between urban areas and rural areas is always here. In 1985, the real human capital in rural areas is almost the double of that in urban areas. With the development of economics and the process of urbanization, the gap between rural areas and urban areas become wider. However, in the future, with the policies concerning rural revitalization, this kind of gap will be controlled in a proper range.

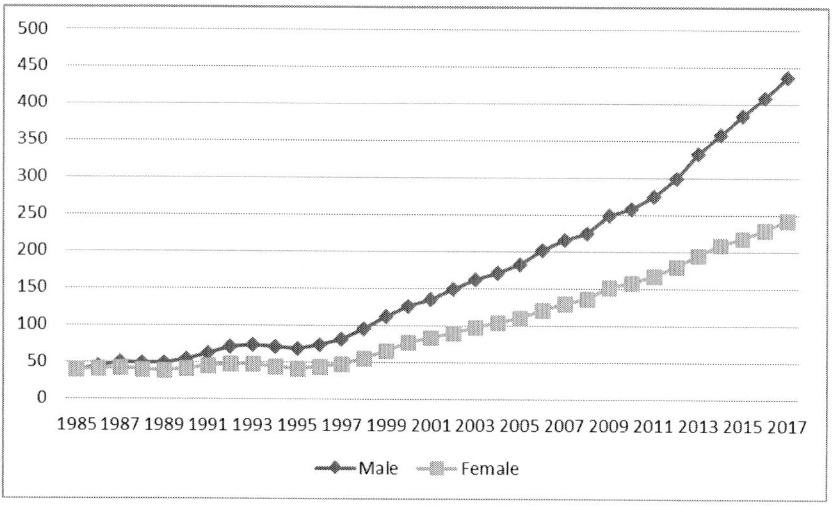

Source: China Human Capital Report Series.

Figure 4.5.1. National real human capital by gender.

Figure 4.5.1 shows the trend of national real human capital by gender and region. We can find that the rural real human capital had little difference with urban real human capital before 1998. And since 1998, the difference of real human capital in rural areas and urban areas become much more significant. This phenomenon can be explained by several reasons for the more rapid growth of the urban than that of the rural human capital stock. First of all, this kind of change is a result of the rapid urbanization during the process of economic transformation. It is common that during the process of economic transformation, there must be a large scale rural-urban migration. With the large scale rural-urban migration, more labor force in urban areas will have more chance to get the education and skill vocation. And then here comes the education gap. Urban areas usually have a higher proportion of educated population than rural areas.

Next, Table 4.5.2 shows the human capital index (1985=100) by gender and region.

The trends of national real human capital implies the total condition of human capital in China, which is caused by a number of factors, such as population growth, demographic changes, region migration and the process of urbanization. To understand the changes on real human capital, we need to pay attention on the national real human capital per capita by gender and region. Table 4.5.2 shows the concerning data from 1985 to 2017.

We can find that the national real human capital per capita in 1985 is about 39.78 thousand, and in 2017 it has increasing to 345.79 thousand of 1985 Yuan. The growth rate of national real human capital per capita is up to 344.79% with an average annual growth rate of 7.13%. There is no doubt that since 1985, the growth speed of real human capital per capita in China is very fast. It may be caused by the rapid growth of economy, the expansion of education and the improvement of market economy.

When it comes to the real human capital per capita by gender, we can find that in 1985, the female human capital per capita is higher than that of male. Since 1985, both male real human capital per capita and female real human capital per capita keep increasing. From 1986, the data of male exceeds and the growth speed is much faster than that of female. And now, there is a significant gender gap of human capital per capita.

Table 4.5.2. National real human capital index by gender and region (1985=100)

Year	National	Male	Female	Urban	Rural
1985	100	100	100	100	100
1986	110.01	116.52	103.05	118.73	104.63
1987	118.63	129.24	107.26	133.06	109.71
1988	188.56	132.16	103.98	136.77	107.30
1989	117.64	133.73	100.40	143.46	101.67
1990	130.78	150.92	109.21	163.63	110.48
1991	149.15	174.81	121.68	191.77	122.81
1992	165.18	198.39	129.62	220.48	131.00
1993	170.17	208.30	129.34	236.38	129.25
1994	161.25	200.86	118.82	232.14	117.43
1995	155.79	194.20	114.65	226.71	111.95
1996	170.75	215.27	123.07	263.15	113.63
1997	187.74	236.83	135.16	296.23	120.67
1998	219.31	278.63	155.79	360.65	131.95
1999	260.50	330.34	185.70	447.18	145.11
2000	299.39	374.94	218.48	528.25	157.93
2001	326.96	407.13	241.09	578.95	171.19
2002	351.68	440.60	256.44	628.61	180.49
2003	381.08	477.98	277.31	691.68	189.09
2004	401.14	500.17	295.08	739.91	191.73
2005	428.51	533.42	316.14	800.74	198.41
2006	483.35	605.38	352.65	914.51	216.83
2007	510.96	641.51	371.14	984.12	218.48
2008	538.82	677.15	390.67	1053.68	220.56
2009	598.43	754.64	431.13	1180.80	238.45
2010	630.10	794.64	453.87	1247.95	248.18
2011	680.70	860.67	487.94	1380.13	248.35
2012	726.53	923.72	515.34	1491.83	253.47
2013	800.85	1025.26	560.50	1673.48	261.44
2014	858.25	1101.21	598.03	1801.73	275.04
2015	912.85	1181.16	625.48	1911.53	295.51
2016	974.34	1263.28	664.89	2072.96	295.24
2017	1037.29	1346.35	706.28	2209.22	312.86

Source: China Human Capital Report Series.

When it comes to changes on urban and rural human capital per capita, the urban real human capital per capita is significantly higher than rural real human capital per capita with a widening gap. It is known to all that human capital is an important contributing factor to economic development. From 1997, the rural human capital become less than the urban stock, the rural per capita stock has also been accelerating.

Table 4.5.3. National real human capital per capita by gender and region (Unit: Thousands of 1985 Yuan)

Year	National	Male	Female	Urban	Rural
1985	39.78	39.14	40.50	66.79	31.83
1986	43.31	45.20	41.22	76.34	33.22
1987	46.28	49.82	42.39	82.10	34.87
1988	44.93	49.30	40.10	79.54	33.46
1989	43.92	48.96	38.29	79.23	31.62
1990	48.34	54.59	41.33	87.94	34.23
1991	54.07	62.11	45.08	99.64	37.51
1992	59.96	70.66	48.04	112.88	40.31
1993	61.26	73.66	47.48	118.32	39.65
1994	57.63	70.72	43.16	114.03	35.92
1995	55.08	67.88	41.04	108.18	34.12
1996	59.18	73.55	43.33	115.69	34.83
1997	65.60	81.21	48.21	123.35	38.36
1998	76.29	94.96	55.42	141.74	42.86
1999	90.26	112.00	65.89	166.58	48.20
2000	102.96	126.05	77.02	186.46	53.46
2001	111.03	135.49	83.69	194.02	58.61
2002	121.18	148.92	90.24	204.98	64.45
2003	131.73	162.25	97.78	217.68	69.60
2004	139.41	171.37	104.15	225.93	72.86
2005	148.56	182.67	111.08	234.04	77.74
2006	163.55	201.65	121.39	253.98	84.82
2007	174.97	215.21	129.97	268.45	88.83
2008	183.46	225.00	136.64	278.55	91.36
2009	203.25	249.15	151.08	304.38	100.77
2010	211.94	258.86	158.18	312.35	106.01
2011	224.66	274.63	167.19	332.05	106.43
2012	243.98	299.68	179.81	355.64	113.89
2013	269.11	332.67	195.82	389.92	120.90
2014	289.13	358.58	209.22	411.76	131.07
2015	307.09	384.08	218.50	428.12	144.15
2016	325.18	409.01	229.47	449.39	147.83
2017	345.79	436.40	242.85	467.89	161.66

Source: China Human Capital Report Series.

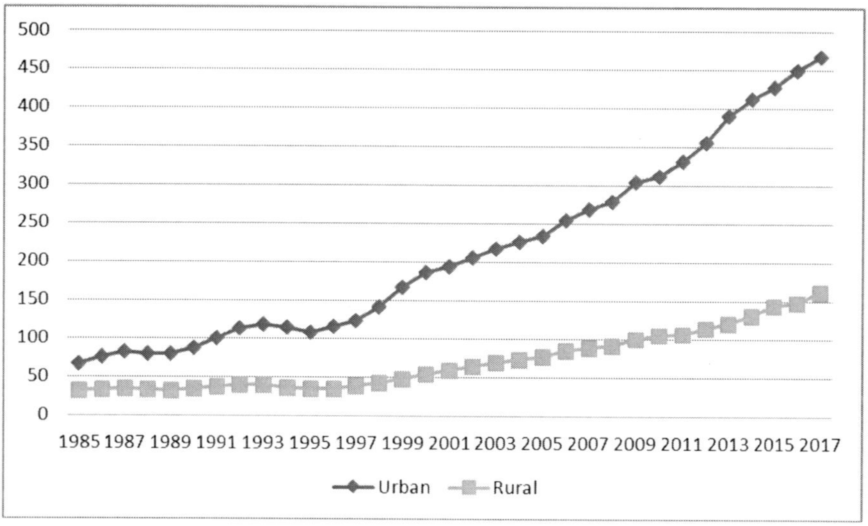

Source: China Human Capital Report Series.

Figure 4.5.2. National Real Human Capital by Gender.

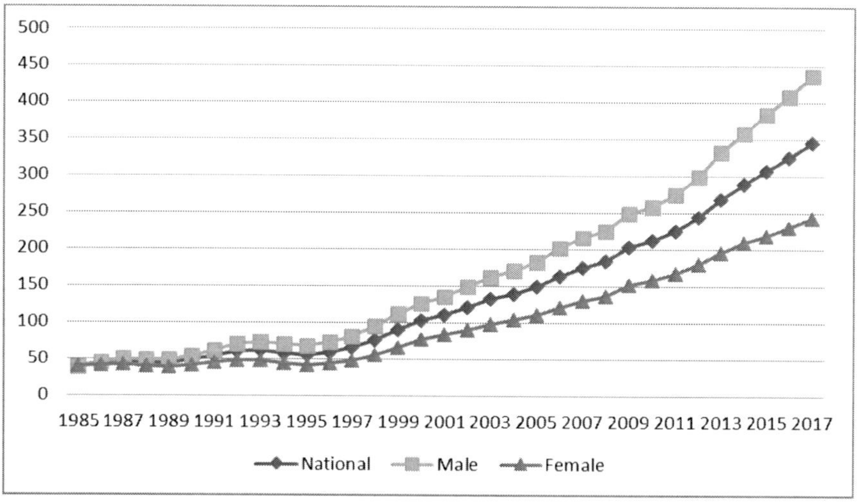

Source: China Human Capital Report Series.

Figure 4.5.3. National real human capital per capita by gender.

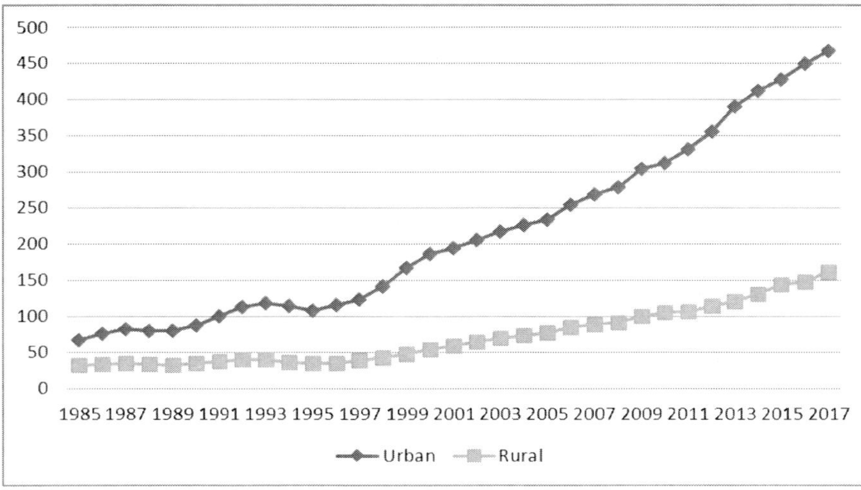

Source: China Human Capital Report Series.

Figure 4.5.4. National real human capital per capita by region.

Chapter 5

LABOR-FORCE HUMAN CAPITAL

Among all labor force, the human capital of the population that is over 15 years old, non-retired and out of school is the most active labor force in economic development. As a result, we often regard this kind of human capital as labor force human capital. In this chapter, we will discuss the labor force human capital in China to find more about the relationship between human capital and economic development and transformation.

5.1. NATIONAL LABOR FORCE HUMAN CAPITAL

According to the China Human Capital Report, the national labor force human capital can be calculated by deflating the nominal values with the CPI using 1985 as the base year. Table 5.1.1 shows the national nominal and real labor force human capital and nominal GDP.

Table 5.1.1 shows the changes on nominal labor force human capital and nominal GDP in China. When we pay attention to the ratio of GDP to labor force human capital, we can find that the ratio increases from 0.06 in 1985 to 0.11 in 2017. The increasing in this ratio means that the level of nominal labor force human capital is much higher than that of nominal

GDP. Figure 5.1.1 depicts the changing trend on the ratio of GDP to labor force human capital.

Table 5.1.1. National nominal and real labor force human capital and nominal GDP

Year	Nominal labor force human capital (Billions of Yuan)	Real labor force human capital (Billions of 1985 Yuan)	Nominal GDP (Billions of Yuan)	Ration of GDP to labor force human capital
1985	15433.80	15433.80	909.89	0.06
1986	18010.21	16917.00	1037.62	0.06
1987	21315.29	18657.96	1217.46	0.06
1988	25740.03	18949.53	1518.04	0.06
1989	30472.41	19000.07	1717.97	0.06
1990	35845.07	21687.22	1887.29	0.05
1991	41656.57	24330.20	2200.56	0.05
1992	47089.72	25831.62	2719.45	0.06
1993	53362.10	25499.31	3567.32	0.07
1994	60285.32	23199.55	4863.75	0.08
1995	68729.50	22551.20	6133.99	0.09
1996	79722.18	24102.32	7181.36	0.09
1997	90633.30	26597.22	7971.50	0.09
1998	104816.50	30932.97	8519.55	0.08
1999	120512.81	35969.28	9056.44	0.08
2000	141031.74	41785.35	10028.01	0.07
2001	155200.51	45607.73	11086.31	0.07
2002	167424.14	49519.49	12171.74	0.07
2003	183166.46	53495.71	13742.20	0.08
2004	199299.83	55934.12	16184.02	0.08
2005	224015.27	61631.27	18731.89	0.08
2006	260795.62	70681.89	21943.85	0.08
2007	290542.73	75079.81	27009.23	0.09
2008	327467.45	79241.67	31924.46	0.10
2009	367467.45	90149.89	34851.77	0.09
2010	426573.10	101149.77	41211.93	0.10
2011	475738.81	106934.46	48794.02	0.10
2012	506008.22	110780.44	53858.00	0.11
2013	545261.06	118487.20	59296.32	0.11
2014	587955.40	124802.74	64128.06	0.11
2015	647933.19	135552.07	68599.29	0.11
2016	684284.44	140309.49	74006.08	0.11
2017	725273.09	146432.28	82075.43	0.11

Source: China Human Capital Report Series.

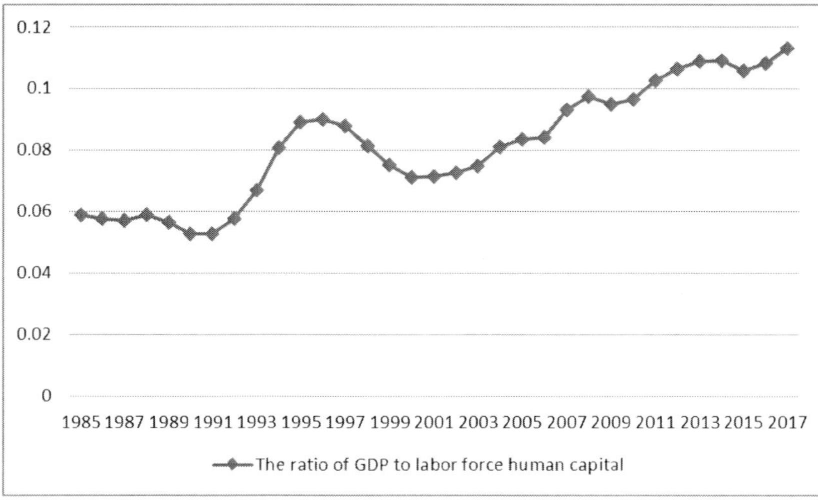

Source: China Human Capital Report Series.

Figure 5.1.1. The ratio of GDP to labor force human capital from 1985 to 2017.

According to Figure 5.1.1, it is clear that the ratio's growth rate gradually slows down in the recent year which means that the contribution made by labor force human capital becomes stable.

5.2. Real Labor Force Human Capital by Gender and Region

Gender is an important variable in learning human capital. So Table 5.2.1 shows the labor force human capital by gender.

As Table 5.2.1 shows, it is clear that both national nominal and real labor force human capital increase in the past 40 years, especially from the year of 1998. As for the gender difference, we can find that male real labor force human capital was about 8112 billion while female real labor force human capital was about 7321 billion of 1985 Yuan. Since 1985, both male real labor force human capital and female labor force human capital keep increasing. The growth rate of male real labor force human capital is significantly higher than that of female real labor force human capital. Till

2017, male real labor force human capital is almost the double of female labor force human capital.

Table 5.2.1. National nominal and real labor force human capital by gender

Year	Nominal labor force human capital (Billions of Yuan)			Real labor force human capital (Billions of 1985 Yuan)		
	National	Male	Female	National	Male	Female
1985	15434	8112	7321	15434	8112	7321
1986	18010	9882	8129	16917	9274	7643
1987	21351	12090	9225	18658	10554	8104
1988	25740	14992	10748	18950	10992	7957
1989	30472	18124	12349	19000	11279	7721
1990	35845	21741	14104	21687	13152	8535
1991	41657	25637	16020	24330	14960	9370
1992	47090	29399	17691	25832	16107	9724
1993	53362	33817	19545	25499	16147	9352
1994	60285	38568	21717	23200	14844	8356
1995	68729	44294	24435	22551	14547	8005
1996	79722	52065	27657	24102	15764	8339
1997	90633	60165	30468	26597	17687	8911
1998	104817	70239	34577	30933	20774	10159
1999	120513	80909	39604	35969	24217	11752
2000	141032	95343	45688	41785	28337	13448
2001	155201	104804	50396	45608	30902	14706
2002	167424	113419	54005	49519	33651	15868
2003	183166	123948	59218	53496	36307	17189
2004	199230	134029	65201	55934	37727	18208
2005	224015	150259	73757	61631	41432	20200
2006	260796	175960	84835	70682	47785	22897
2007	290543	196279	94263	75080	50798	24282
2008	324931	219508	105423	79242	53588	25653
2009	367467	248452	119016	90150	60993	29157
2010	426573	288382	138191	101150	68402	32748
2011	475739	322691	153048	106934	72531	34404
2012	506008	344233	161775	110780	75339	35441
2013	545361	371688	173572	118487	80741	37746
2014	587955	402315	185640	124803	85339	39463
2015	647933	444685	203248	135552	92938	42614
2016	684284	466576	217709	140309	95538	44772
2017	725273	492278	232995	146432	99203	47229

Source: China Human Capital Report Series.

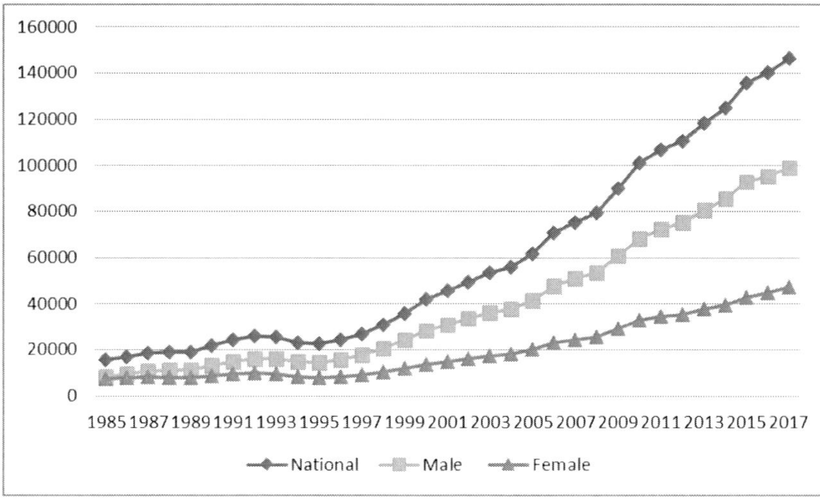

Source: China Human Capital Report Series.

Figure 5.2.1. National real labor force human capital by gender.

Table 5.2.2 shows the nominal and real labor force human capital for urban and rural regions respectively. The same as the changing trends by gender, both the national nominal and real labor human capital keep increasing from 1985 to 2017. However, we can find an interesting phenomenon, although the national real labor force human capital for urban and rural areas both exhibit positive trends, the urban real labor force human capital exceeds its rural counterpart for the first in 1998. In 2017, the regional gap becomes much clearer. In 1985, the regional gap is about 3342 billion of 1985 Yuan. And in 2017, the regional gap is about 60045 billion of 1985 Yuan, which is about 20 times of that in 1985.

Figure 5.2.2 shows the trends of real labor force human capital for urban areas and rural areas respectively. Before 1998, the real labor force human capital for the rural regions was higher than that for urban areas. After 1998, the real labor force human capital in urban areas increased more rapidly than that for rural areas, which resulted in an increasing regional gap between rural areas and urban areas.

Table 5.2.2. National nominal and real labor force human capital by region

Year	Nominal labor force human capital (Billions of Yuan)			Real labor force human capital (Billions of 1985 Yuan)		
	National	Urban	Rural	National	Urban	Rural
1985	15434	5946	9488	15434	5946	9288
1986	18010	7285	10725	16917	6808	10109
1987	21315	9090	12225	18658	7808	10850
1988	25740	11277	14463	18950	8025	10924
1989	30472	13805	16668	19000	8447	10553
1990	35845	16655	19190	21687	10061	11626
1991	41657	19466	22191	24330	11188	13142
1992	47090	22099	24990	25832	11696	14136
1993	53362	25165	28197	25499	11471	14028
1994	60285	28714	31571	23200	10471	12728
1995	68729	33369	35360	22551	10491	12132
1996	79722	40252	39471	24102	11551	12551
1997	90633	47673	42960	26597	13270	13328
1998	104817	57375	47442	30933	16067	14866
1999	120513	68859	51654	35969	19536	16433
2000	141032	84529	56503	41785	23792	17994
2001	155201	94022	61179	45608	26280	19328
2002	167424	102873	64551	49519	29044	20475
2003	183166	113896	69270	53496	31870	21626
2004	199230	126413	72817	55934	34242	21692
2005	224015	147364	76651	61631	39288	22343
2006	260796	171890	88905	70682	45150	25532
2007	290543	193433	97109	75080	48621	26459
2008	324931	218291	106640	79242	51959	27283
2009	367467	250970	116498	90150	60252	29898
2010	426573	299660	126914	101150	69710	31439
2011	475739	227455	138284	106934	74552	32383
2012	506008	361414	144594	110780	77746	33035
2013	545261	390795	154466	118487	84154	34333
2014	587955	433382	165573	124803	88651	36151
2015	647933	468534	179400	135552	96885	38668
2016	684284	492759	191525	140309	99798	40511
2017	725273	518412	206861	146432	103239	43194

Source: China Human Capital Report Series.

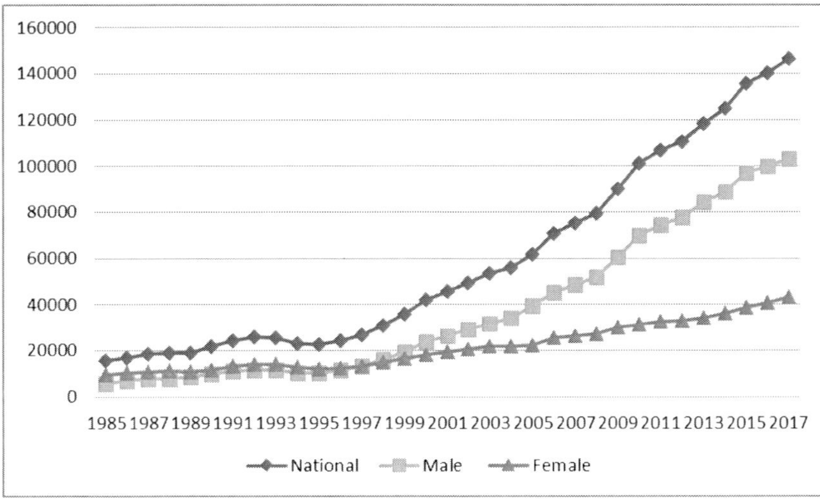

Source: China Human Capital Report Series.

Figure 5.2.2. National real labor force human capital by region.

5.3. AVERAGE LABOR FORCE HUMAN CAPITAL

In the two parts above, we discuss the national labor force human capital from the perspective of gender and region. In order to learn the dynamic trends of the national labor force human capital, we should pay attention to the average labor force human capital. The definition of the average labor force human capital is national labor force human capital divided by the number of the population that are over 16 years old, non-retired and out of school.

Table 5.3.1 shows the average labor force human capital in nominal and real terms. As is shown in the table, we can find that both nominal and real average labor force human capital increase dramatically. However, we can find a huge difference between nominal and real average labor force human capital. This reveals that during these years, the inflation does exist and has an important influence on economic development.

Table 5.3.1. National nominal and real average labor force human capital

Year	Nominal average labor force human capital (Billions of Yuan)	Real average labor force human capital (Billions of 1985 Yuan)
1985	28.05	28.05
1986	32.08	30.13
1987	36.89	32.29
1988	42.53	31.31
1989	48.89	30.49
1990	56.10	33.94
1991	63.21	36.92
1992	70.84	38.86
1993	79.37	37.93
1994	88.88	34.21
1995	99.60	32.68
1996	113.03	34.17
1997	129.14	37.90
1998	147.84	43.63
1999	167.86	50.10
2000	192.44	57.02
2001	209.32	61.51
2002	227.95	67.42
2003	248.61	72.61
2004	271.27	76.16
2005	301.27	82.89
2006	340.13	92.18
2007	382.06	98.73
2008	424.70	103.57
2009	476.28	116.84
2010	539.17	127.85
2011	591.90	133.05
2012	646.07	141.44
2013	698.56	151.80
2014	756.34	160.55
2015	824.64	172.52
2016	879.38	180.31
2017	943.98	190.59

Source: China Human Capital Report Series.

Table 5.3.2. National nominal and real labor force human capital by gender

Year	Nominal average labor force human capital (Billions of Yuan)			Real average labor force human capital (Billions of 1985 Yuan)		
	National	Male	Female	National	Male	Female
1985	28.05	28.05	28.05	28.05	28.05	28.05
1986	32.08	33.58	30.43	30.13	31.51	28.62
1987	36.89	40.11	33.38	32.29	35.01	29.33
1988	42.53	47.18	37.39	31.31	34.59	27.68
1989	48.89	55.10	41.96	30.49	34.29	26.23
1990	56.10	64.25	46.93	33.94	38.87	28.40
1991	63.21	73.71	51.47	36.92	43.01	30.10
1992	70.84	84.08	56.15	38.86	46.07	30.86
1993	79.37	95.89	61.14	37.93	45.79	29.26
1994	88.88	109.05	66.91	34.21	41.97	25.74
1995	99.60	123.68	73.62	32.68	40.62	24.12
1996	113.03	141.75	81.82	34.17	42.92	24.67
1997	129.14	163.64	91.18	37.90	48.10	26.67
1998	147.84	188.58	102.75	43.63	55.77	30.19
1999	167.86	214.22	116.39	50.10	64.12	34.54
2000	192.44	246.80	131.84	57.02	73.35	38.81
2001	209.32	269.41	143.00	61.51	79.44	41.73
2002	227.95	294.95	154.33	67.42	87.51	45.35
2003	248.61	322.20	168.20	72.61	94.38	48.82
2004	271.27	351.42	184.68	76.16	98.92	57.57
2005	301.27	390.12	205.79	82.89	107.57	56.36
2006	340.13	440.03	231.24	92.18	119.50	62.41
2007	382.06	491.13	261.25	98.73	127.11	67.30
2008	424.70	542.32	292.57	103.57	132.40	71.19
2009	476.28	605.37	329.57	116.84	148.61	80.74
2010	539.17	681.43	375.56	127.85	161.63	89.00
2011	591.90	749.25	410.25	133.05	168.41	92.22
2012	646.07	818.89	445.85	141.44	179.22	97.68
2013	698.56	886.86	480.23	151.80	192.65	104.43
2014	756.34	965.17	514.90	160.55	204.73	109.94
2015	824.64	1055.49	557.74	172.52	220.59	116.94
2016	879.38	1123.80	599.80	180.31	230.11	123.35
2017	943.98	1202.20	694.32	190.59	242.27	131.62

Source: China Human Capital Report Series.

Table 5.3.2 shows the national nominal and real labor force human capital by gender and from 1985 to 2017, the nominal and real average labor force human capital exhibit upward trends. The same as the analysis above, we can find that the gap between male and female labor force human capital become wider and in 2017, the male real average labor force human capital is almost the double of female real average labor force human capital.

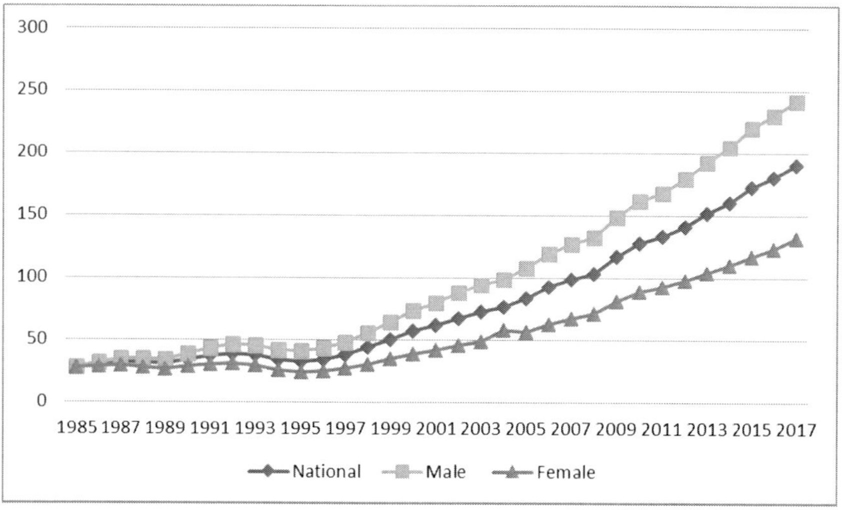

Source: China Human Capital Report Series.

Figure 5.3.1. National nominal and real labor force human capital by gender.

Table 5.3.3 reports the national nominal and real average labor force human capital by region. From 1985 to 2017, the nominal and real average labor force human capital exhibit upward trends. The growth for urban region is much higher than that for rural and the regional gap between urban areas and rural areas widens significantly. The average labor force human capital for urban areas was always higher than that for rural area from 1985 to 2017.

Table 5.3.3. National nominal and real average labor force human capital by region

Year	Nominal average labor force human capital (Billions of Yuan)			Real average labor force human capital (Billions of 1985 Yuan)		
	National	Male	Female	National	Male	Female
1985	28.05	43.91	22.91	22.91	43.91	22.91
1986	32.08	32.08	25.51	30.13	48.36	24.05
1987	36.89	60.91	28.51	32.29	52.32	25.30
1988	42.53	70.46	32.46	31.31	50.14	24.52
1989	48.89	80.97	36.78	30.49	49.55	23.28
1990	56.10	93.23	41.63	33.94	56.32	25.22
1991	63.21	105.27	46.74	36.92	60.51	27.68
1992	70.84	118.34	52.22	38.86	62.63	29.54
1993	79.37	133.76	58.17	37.93	60.97	28.94
1994	88.88	150.21	64.70	34.21	54.78	26.08
1995	99.60	167.97	71.78	32.68	52.45	24.63
1996	113.03	188.48	80.07	34.17	54.09	25.46
1997	129.14	230.45	89.60	37.90	64.14	27.80
1998	147.84	264.00	100.16	43.63	73.93	31.39
1999	167.86	296.78	110.92	50.10	84.20	35.29
2000	192.44	306.80	122.75	57.02	86.35	39.09
2001	209.32	209.32	134.21	61.51	91.16	42.40
2002	227.95	349.66	145.83	67.42	98.72	46.26
2003	248.61	374.99	159.06	72.61	104.93	49.66
2004	271.27	401.92	172.18	76.16	108.87	51.29
2005	301.27	437.87	186.55	82.89	116.74	54.38
2006	340.13	487.75	212.81	92.18	128.12	61.12
2007	382.06	542.19	238.71	98.73	136.28	65.04
2008	424.70	596.85	264.84	103.57	142.07	67.76
2009	476.28	662.40	293.50	116.84	159.03	75.32
2010	539.17	745.85	321.52	127.85	173.51	79.65
2011	591.90	814.28	350.38	133.05	179.89	82.05
2012	646.07	875.39	384.37	141.44	188.31	87.82
2013	698.56	931.14	421.36	151.80	200.51	93.66
2014	756.34	987.10	464.14	160.55	207.18	101.34
2015	824.64	1051.96	514.03	172.52	217.53	110.79
2016	879.38	1108.54	561.05	180.31	224.51	118.67
2017	943.98	1168.07	626.63	190.59	232.61	130.84

Source: China Human Capital Report Series.

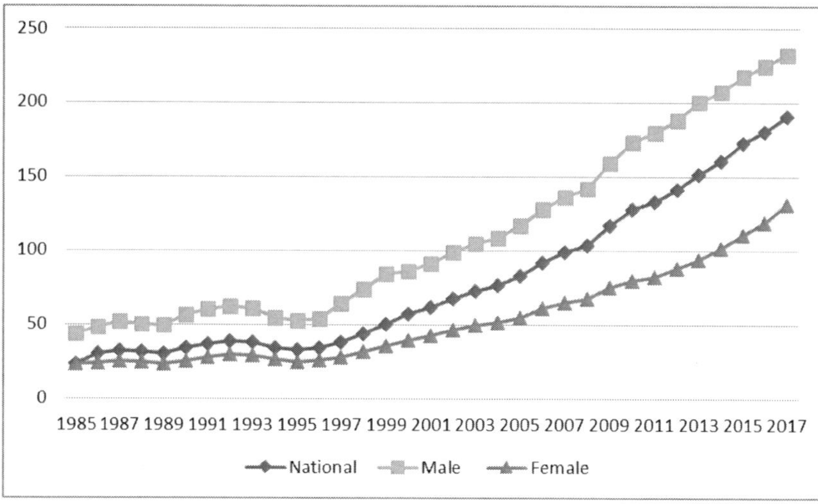

Source: China Human Capital Report Series.

Figure 5.3.2. National nominal and real average labor force human capital by region.

5.4. Human Capital and Employment

Human capital is the output and input of population. It plays an important role in economic development and transformation. As a result, we can find that the growth rates of human capital and GDP have the same changing trends. With the development of science and technology, human capital will play much more important role in promoting the quality of economic development. It can significantly promote the level of national economics. Compared with physical capital, human capital has more potential. With more attention paid on human capital, the structure of employment can be promoted. Table 5.4.1 shows the trends of employment in China concerning the number of employees in different kinds of industries and different regions.

At the time that New China was just founded, most of the employees work in the primary industry and now the employment structure has become more mature. This is an intuitive description of the role of human capital.

Table 5.4.1. The trends of Employment in China (Unit: Ten thousand)

Year	Total number of employees	The number of employees				
		The primary industry	The secondary industry	The tertiary industry	Urban	Rural
1952	20729	17317	1531	1881	2486	18243
1953	21364	17747	1715	1902	2754	18610
1954	21832	18151	1882	1799	2744	19088
1955	22328	18592	1913	1823	2802	19526
1956	23018	18544	2468	2006	2993	20025
1957	23771	19309	2142	2320	3205	20566
1958	26600	15490	7076	4034	5300	21300
1959	26173	16271	5402	4500	5389	20784
1960	25880	17016	4112	4752	6119	19761
1961	25590	19747	2856	2987	5336	20254
1962	25910	21276	2059	2575	4537	21373
1963	26640	21966	2038	2636	4603	22037
1964	27736	22801	2183	2752	4828	22908
1965	28670	23396	2408	2866	5136	23534
1966	29805	24297	2600	2908	5354	24451
1967	30814	25165	2661	2988	5446	25368
1968	31915	26063	2743	3109	5630	26285
1969	33225	27117	3030	3078	5825	27400
1970	34432	27811	3518	3103	6312	28120
1971	35620	28397	3990	3233	6868	28752
1972	35854	28283	4276	3295	7200	28654
1973	36652	28857	4492	3303	7388	29264
1974	37369	29218	4712	3439	7687	29682
1975	38168	29456	5152	3560	8222	29946
1976	38834	29443	5611	3780	8692	30142
1977	39377	29340	5831	4206	9127	30250
1978	40152	28318	6945	4890	9514	30638
1979	41024	28634	7214	5177	9999	31025
1980	42361	29122	7707	5532	10525	31836
1981	43725	29777	8003	5945	11053	32672
1982	45295	30859	8346	6090	11428	33867
1983	46436	31151	8679	6606	11746	34690
1984	48197	30868	9590	7739	12229	35968
1985	49873	31130	10384	8359	12808	37065
1986	51282	31254	11216	8811	13292	37990
1987	52783	31663	11726	9395	13783	39000
1988	54334	32249	12152	9933	14267	40067
1989	55329	33225	11976	10129	14390	40939
1990	64749	38914	13856	11979	17041	47708
1991	65491	39098	14015	12378	17465	48026

Table 5.4.1. (Continued)

Year	Total number of employees	The number of employees				
		The primary industry	The secondary industry	The tertiary industry	Urban	Rural
1992	66152	38699	14355	13098	17861	48291
1993	66808	37680	14965	14163	18262	48546
1994	67455	36628	15312	15515	18653	48802
1995	68065	35530	15655	16880	19040	49025
1996	68950	34820	16203	17927	19922	49028
1997	69820	34840	16547	18432	20781	49039
1998	70637	35177	16600	18860	21616	49021
1999	71394	35768	16421	19205	22412	48982
2000	72085	36043	16219	19823.38	23151	48934
2001	72797	36399	16234	20164.77	24123	48674
2002	73280	36640	15682	20958.08	25159	48121
2003	73736	36204	15927	21604.65	26230	47506
2004	74264	34830	16709	22724.78	27293	46971
2005	74647	33442	17766	23439.16	28389	46258
2006	74978	31941	18894	24142.92	29630	45348
2007	75321	30731	20186	24404	30953	44368
2008	75564	29923	20553	25087.25	32103	43461
2009	75828	28890	21080	25857.35	33322	42506
2010	76105	27931	21842	26332.33	34687	41418
2011	76420	26594	22544	27282	35914	40506
2012	76704	25773	23241	27690	37102	39602
2013	76977	24171	23170	29636	38240	38737
2014	77253	22790	23099	31364	39310	37943
2015	77451	21919	22693	32839	40410	37041
2016	77603	21496	22350	33757	41428	36175
2017	77640	20944	21824	34872	42462	35178
2018	77586	20258	21390	35938	43419	34167
2019	77471	19445	21305	36721	44247	33224

Source: CSMAR Database.

Having learning the definition and situation of economic transformation, human capital, and labor force human capital, we will discuss more parts about human capital in the following chapters, such as the relationships between human capital and technology diffusion, structure change, development strategies, spatial inequality and so on.

Chapter 6

TECHNOLOGY DIFFUSION

6.1. INTRODUCTION

In the era of knowledge economy, science and technology are advancing rapidly. The deepening of economic globalization makes technological innovation and technological progress play an increasingly important role in promoting economic growth, which leads to the adjustment and upgrading of industrial structure, and ultimately promotes the transformation and upgrading of a country's economy. The decision of economic transformation and upgrading is not only the invention or creation of technology, but also the diffusion of new technology. Through technology diffusion, technology can be continuously spread and applied in economy and geographical space. Technology diffusion has become an important way to promote industrial technology progress. As Schoitz, an American economist, once said, "Without proliferation, innovation cannot have an impact on the economy."

Nowadays, the world's industrial technology is complex and the global competition is increasingly fierce, which determines that the source of industrial innovation technology cannot all rely on endogenous R&D. Generally, an industry has a life cycle. Therefore, for an industry with advanced technology, while maintaining its own technological advantages, it should constantly develop new technologies. And at the same time, it can also spread backward or standardized technologies. The ultimate goal is to seek the greatest economic benefits. For the industries with backward technology, we can improve their own technology level through the technology diffusion of advanced industries and the introduction of advanced technology, so as to avoid the repeated labor and high technology cost caused by their independent development. Therefore, technology diffusion can extend the life cycle of industrial technology, and industry can use its leading position in technology to spread its new technology to technology users and potential users through technology diffusion, and the life cycle of industrial technology can continue at the same time of spatial diffusion. Industrial technology diffusion is a continuous and slow process. It makes new technology spread, popularize and apply among potential users. It is of great significance to promote the industrialization of scientific achievements, enhance the industrial independent innovation ability and industrial technology level, and improve the economic benefits and competitiveness of the industry. Industrial technology diffusion is not only related to the realization of your own value of technological achievements, but also plays an important role in rationalizing and upgrading the industrial structure, improving the economic benefits of scientific and technological investment, effectively spreading technology to industries, departments or other fields, and promoting economic development and social progress.

At the same time, whether it is technological innovation or technological diffusion, it is always in urgent need of talents. Enterprises or companies are the main subjects of technological innovation and technological diffusion, while talents are the core factors within enterprises or companies. The quality of human capital has a direct impact on many aspects of technology diffusion. The way and process of technology innovation and technology diffusion are often dominated by human capital. The improvement and flow of talent quality can promote the speed of technology innovation and technology diffusion.

6.2. The Essence of Technology

In order to understand the meaning of technology advancement, we should firstly know the definition of technology.

6.2.1. The Definition of Technology

Technology, which is widely used in our daily life, has no widely accepted definition. An Unabridged, Comprehensive Dictionary (Cihai) defines technology as the sum of labor tools and skills, and emphasizes that technology is a system of experience, knowledge, skills and material means used by people in the process of production or service. According to the explanation of Encyclopedia of Great Britain, the word Technology was originally composed of Greek words "techne" (art, handicraft) and "logos" (speech), which means that technology focuses on the practicability of and emphasizes the usability and ease of use. Aristotle regarded technology as "the wisdom of making." In the Roman Empire, practical technology developed rapidly, and people not only paid attention to the process of technological creation, but also underlined the knowledge form of technology. At the end of the 18th century, Diderot, a French scientist, added the concept of "technology" to encyclopedia, and pointed out that technology is a kind of tool and rule system for a certain purpose, which is a relatively complete definition of technology.

With the development of economy and society, the meaning of technology becomes more and more abundant. From the 20th century, the word technology has been widely used in production and daily life. Soviet scholar defined technology as the means and objects of labor created by people. According to the World Intellectual Property Organization (WIPO), technology refers to the systematic knowledge of manufacturing a product, generally refers to the adopted technology or services provided, and it can refer to an invention, a shape design, a utility model, a new species of animals and plants, technical information or skills, etc. In 1983, the National Science Foundation of the United States quoted Schorn's definition that technology is any tool or skill to expand human capabilities, including tangible equipment or intangible working methods. In addition, Ferreira believes that technology refers to the ability of a reproducible method or means that can lead to the improvement of products, processes and services. OECD believes that technology is the knowledge applied in the whole process from product research and development to sales.

In general, firstly, technology is a kind of human ability with strong subjective initiative. Secondly, technology is the synthesis of tools or means of labor to achieve a certain purpose. Thirdly, technology is a kind of scientific applied knowledge, which is all the knowledge and experience accumulated by human beings in using natural laws to conform to nature and using nature. Fourth, technology is the synthesis of ability, means and knowledge, which is a very comprehensive definition.

6.2.2. The Factors of Technology

Due to the vague understanding of technical concepts, we need to look into the average range of related technologies from the perspective of set. Technological elements include the basic components of technology, the concrete forms of technological essence, and the sources of technological essence. Because people discover the world following the law of movement from simple to complex, from one-sided to comprehensive, from low to high, so as the object of people's understanding. Technical elements have also experienced a process from shallow to deep, and the understanding of technical elements has been constantly improved with the development of economy and society. In different periods, people interpret the elements of technology from different perspectives, which can be summarized as the following representative theories:

1. The skill theory of technical elements

In ancient times, people thought that technology was skill itself. In the era of low productivity, the tools corresponding to technology are relatively insufficient, and technological activities mainly rely on the experience accumulated in human daily life. Technology is mainly based on human carriers. At this time, people's understanding of technical elements is mainly focused on the subjective factors of technical summary, and technology is regarded as the subjective ability to complete relevant work obtained through repeated operation on the basis of experience.

2. Technical elements and tools

Entering the time of large-scale machine production, technology plays a more important role in production and daily life. Driven by the industrial revolution, the power was upgraded by the revolution of tools and machines, and the era of large-scale machines was officially brought about. As a result, what can be achieved by the skills formed by long-term experience accumulation in the past can be easily realized by means of tools, and the tools can further strengthen and improve people's skills. The technical elements have acquired the material form of tools, which take the physical objects as the carrier, can be separated from the active subjects and exist independently, and are not dependent on the subjects' survival. At this time, the role of skills is relatively weakened, and the role of tools is enhanced. At this time, technology pays more attention to tools, equipment and other objective factors.

3. Knowledge theory of technical elements

Since the 1940s, because of the increasingly comprehensive requirements of production on technology, relying merely on experience technology has been unable to satisfy the needs of technological development. Only with the empirical knowledge of natural science, the evaluative knowledge of social science and the planning knowledge of technical science, can we use technology with the help of machinery and equipment. Without such background knowledge, modern technology will no longer exist. Therefore, technology begins to attach importance to both subject and object factors, and then the scope of technology has become more extensive, and gradually become a comprehensive concept.

With the development of market economy, technology has gradually become a commodity that can circulate in the market. The use value of technology is to improve production efficiency and economic benefits through its continuous progress. At the same time, the value of technology is generally far higher than that of ordinary goods. Technology is a special kind of commodity, and its right of use and ownership can be traded in the market. Therefore, it is also an important driving force to promote the economic development, transformation and upgrading of a country.

6.3. Theories About Technology Advancement

Generally speaking, the process of technological progress can be divided into three parts: technological learning activity, technological innovation activity and technological imitation activity. Technology imitation activities include technology chasing and technology diffusion. When a country has been well developed and the education level and R&D expenditure are relatively higher, its technological innovation activities will increase, and generally it will be able to become an economy with advanced technology. At this time, if free trade exists, countries with backward technology tend to have more technology learning activities and technology imitation activities.

6.3.1. Technology Learning

Amsden (1989) believed that technological learning is a process in which enterprises in developing countries strive to acquire technological capabilities through learning. Linsukim (1997) understood technology learning as the ability to acquire technology. Hobday (1995) defined technology learning as the whole activity for enterprises to acquire technology knowledge. Generally speaking, it is believed that technology learning is the process or ability to acquire technology, which refers to the process of improving technical ability or skill. That is to say, in order to improve technical ability, it is the process of actively requiring learning behavior and thinking mode of acquiring technology, and finally acquiring knowledge and skills.

According to the theory of technology learning, technology is essentially a combination of knowledge needed to master a certain method and understand a certain method, and is also the combination of this knowledge which is supported by other external factors and influenced by other intangible assets. Therefore, when learning technology, enterprises must have certain background knowledge in order to learn and develop relevant technological changes. The technological ability of enterprises depends on the cost of learning and acquiring technological changes. Therefore, the theory of technology learning holds that the improvement of enterprise's technology ability is the result of conscious technology learning.

Technology learning can be generally divided into the following two categories.

1. The imitation mode

The technology learning mode of the introduction mode generally refers to the technology imitation strategy adopted by the countries or enterprises with backward technology in their economic development, which is to introduce the technological invention and technological innovation that they think they need from the advanced countries or enterprises. And then the countries or enterprises with backward technology apply them into their own production after digestion, absorption, improvement, so as to improve their own technology ability and level. From the perspective of a nation, the technology learning mode of introducing imitation is mainly aimed at the technology provided by the developed countries for the backward countries, and provides learning and imitation opportunities for the technological progress of the developing countries. From the perspective of industry, introduction and imitation can quickly obtain technology learning opportunities, shorten the cycle of technology research and development, quickly reach the level of imported technology through rapid digestion and absorption, promote the improvement of industrial technology capacity, and even carry out higher-level innovation. From the perspective of enterprises, the capital investment of technology imitation is small, and new products can be launched quickly. The launch cycle of new products of imitation learning is shorter than that of new products of independent research and development, so that the life cycle of new products is longer. In the end, more product profits can be obtained.

2. The autonomous mode

The learning mode of independent invention and innovation technology usually refers to the process of independent research and development of technology based on its own technology accumulation and innovation ability, thus promoting the industrialization and commercialization of technological achievements. By using the technological advantages brought by technological innovation, economics of scales can be formed. At the national level, the self-invented and innovative technology learning mode is the purpose and means to achieve a country's comprehensive national advantages and sustainable development, which can promote the rapid development of national economy, and even promote the economic transformation and upgrading. From the industrial point of view, relying on the late development advantage, a nation can accelerate the realization of part of the technological development stage, or open up new technological inventions, through the independent innovation technology learning process. The industrial technology can reach the leading level. The technology learning mode of independent invention and innovation can also make enterprises form and maintain the dominant position in the same industry, and maintain the rapid growth of development speed.

6.3.2. The Theory of Technology Innovation

Schumpeter first put forward the concept of technological innovation in his book *The Theory of Economic Development* in 1912. Schumpeter believed that innovation refers to the process that entrepreneurs introduce new combinations of production factors and conditions into the production system to obtain excess profits. He summarized the contents of innovation into five parts including introducing new products, adopting technologies, exploring new sources of supply of materials, discovering new target markets and adopting new management methods. Schumpeter pointed that entrepreneurs are the main undertakers of innovation behavior. This view is consistent with Marx's analysis of the relationship between technological invention and innovation, which means that science and technology are important driving forces for the development of social economy and productivity. Conversely, social economy determines the development of science and technology, which are interdependent dialectical development processes.

Different scholars have different understanding of the connotation of technological innovation. Someone defined technological innovation as a non-continuous behavior with novelty and it has the potential to succeed. Someone believed that technological innovation is a comprehensive activity, including the selection of inventions, the guarantee of capital investment, the establishment of organizations, the formulation of plans, the recruitment of talents and the development of markets. Mansfield believed that when an invention is first applied into reality, it can be called as a kind of technological innovation. Japanese economists generally believe that technological innovation is different from a technological invention, rather, it is an innovation through technology, and technology itself does not need to undergo revolutionary changes. The basis of measuring technological innovation lies in whether the promotion of technology has opened up new markets, stimulated economic development and promoted social transformation and upgrading. Chinese scholars believe that technological innovation is not only means the achievements of technological innovation itself, but also means the promotion, diffusion and application process of the achievements.

To sum up, the understandings of domestic and foreign scholars on the connotation of technological innovation are summarized as follows:

Firstly, technological innovation is regarded as the commercial application of technology or invention. This view emphasizes the commercial application and economic value of invention, which is the process of commercialization and manufacture of scientific and technological achievements.

Secondly, technological innovation is regarded as the whole process of forming productive forces which can enter the technology market successfully. Technological innovation includes the whole process of scientific invention, introduction of achievements into the market and commercialization.

Thirdly, technological innovation is understood as the organic combination of technology and economic society. This point of view clarifies that technological innovation is a process of combination of technological invention and economic society. The invention of technology has its own specific purpose and needs to meet the requirements of social development and transformation.

At present, there have been four theoretical schools in the study of technological innovation abroad, which are neoclassical school, new Schumpeter school, new institutional innovation school and national innovation system school.

The neoclassical school of technological innovation holds that technological innovation is the endogenous variable of economic growth and the basic factor of economic growth. When the market of technological innovation fails, the government should take macroscopic policies to reasonably intervene in technological innovation activities, promote technological progress and economic development.

Schumpeter's innovation theory holds that innovation can create new value through the application of new tools and methods. He believes that innovation is an endogenous variable, which can promote economic development.

The main point of the new institutional school emphasizes that institutional innovation determines the improvement of technological innovation efficiency, while technological innovation will also change the potential profits and operating costs brought by institutional arrangements.

The national innovation system is an evaluation framework that links the institutional arrangement with the national technological and economic development. The purpose is to guide science and technology into the process of economic growth, and pay more attention to explore the relationship between innovation and national development from a macroscopic perspective.

6.3.3. The Theory of Technology Transfer

The concept of technology transfer was put forward in the 1960s, and its theoretical research is still developing. Technology transfer refers to the transfer of systematic knowledge about the manufacturing of products, the application of production methods or the provision of services, but does not include the simple sale or lease of goods. At present, there are many definitions of technology transfer, which can be generally divided into two categories, including a broad sense and a narrow sense.

The broad sense of technology transfer is also called vertical technology transfer, which means that various forms of technology and related elements of knowledge have changed from common areas to more specialized areas. In a narrow sense, technology transfer is also called horizontal technology transfer, which refers to the transfer of technology as a production factor from one application environment to another. Academic circles tend to explain transfer technology in a narrow sense, especially for international technology transfer.

Technology transfer can be generally divided into three forms. The first form is the transfer of advanced technology in products, that is, technology transfer is realized through product trade. The second form is through licensing. The third from is through the way of contracted construction.

In the late 1970s, with the rise of reform and opening up, the concept of technology transfer began to be introduced into China. After entering the new century, the research on technology transfer has gradually deepened, and the theoretical circle has basically reached a consensus on the concept of technology transfer. It is believed that technology transfer is the diffusion process of technology in geospatial or different fields. The process of technology forming industry is also the process of technology transfer and diffusion in the industry.

6.3.4. The Theory of Technology Diffusion

So far, there is no widely accepted definition of technology diffusion. The more influential one was put forward by Rogers in 1983. He regards technology diffusion as a process in which innovative technology is accepted by the whole society through various channels over time. Rogers believes that the process of technology diffusion consists of four key factors, including innovative technology, time, communication channels and social systems. Technology diffusion is considered as the subsequent stage of technology innovation, so technology diffusion is also called technology innovation diffusion in the market.

Generally speaking, technology diffusion mainly includes three levels:

The first level is the diffusion among enterprises, that is, the process of new technological achievements spreading among enterprises in the industry.

The second level is the internal diffusion of enterprises, that is, the process of expanding the application scope of new technological achievements in enterprises.

The third level is the overall diffusion, that is, the superposition of the diffusion between enterprises and the diffusion within enterprises, represents the overall change process in which new technological achievements are adopted in the industry.

In general, technology diffusion is a kind of unconscious technology diffusion, and its recipients can be multiple. Only when all potential adopters stop using the technology, the technology diffusion will stop. So in general, the technology diffusion shows a strong passivity.

The development of technology diffusion theory can be roughly divided into three stages. The first stage is the early technology diffusion theory with Vernon and Krugman as the main representatives. They mainly study the results of international technology transfer in North-South trade, which lays the foundation for the development of international technology diffusion theory. The second stage is represented by Jason, Saisby and other scholars, who study the mechanism of technology diffusion through the process of technology innovation, diffusion and transfer. These studies mainly use the local equilibrium analysis method. The third stage focuses on the general equilibrium analysis under the condition of open economy, which makes up for the deficiency of the previous theory.

6.4. Technology and Human Capital

According to endogenous growth theory, the impact of human capital on technological progress is reflected in two aspects: innovative knowledge (Technology) and accelerating the absorption and diffusion of technology. First of all, human capital is an important source of knowledge innovation and technology development. Romer (1990) pointed out that knowledge (technology) can produce "spillover effect" due to its non-competitiveness, so any individual's knowledge production can improve the productivity of the whole society. Secondly, human capital is a necessary point for technology application. Under certain conditions, the larger the stock of human capital, the better the technology absorption and diffusion are, and the higher the production efficiency of material capital is. Technological progress mainly includes technological innovation and application. Technological innovation means the extrapolation of production possibility boundary, while technological application is embodied in the optimization of internal resource allocation towards production possibility boundary. Under the condition of open economy, technology application also includes the catching up of transnational technology. The changes of efficiency brought about by technological progress, including technological changes and technological efficiency changes. The former represents the change of technological innovation level, that is, the efficiency change caused by the improvement of technological level when the input factors remain unchanged, and the latter represents the change of technological application efficiency, that is, the change caused by the improvement of factors' utilization efficiency when the technological level remains unchanged.

Scholars usually divide human capital into skilled human capital and unskilled human capital based on the education level. The former is generally the labor force with higher education. In order to distinguish human capital more clearly, we can divide human capital into primary education human capital, secondary education human capital and higher education human capital. From the perspective of technological progress, according to the different nature of activities, technological progress can be divided into technological innovation activities and technological imitation activities. The influence of human capital structure on technological change and technological efficiency change is different. Meanwhile, according to previous scholars' research, higher education resources are often regarded as the key input elements of technological progress. Compared with the application of technology, technological innovation needs more input of skills, so it requires human capital to have more labor skills or higher education level. Therefore, the human capital of higher education has a greater impact on technological innovation. In addition, primary education human capital and secondary education human capital can be introduced into production activities as direct labor input. When the level of technology remains unchanged, the role of both in production activities is mainly reflected in the application of technology. It is worth noting that for the human capital of secondary education, it will have a certain impact on technological innovation and application because it includes both general education and vocational education. In the past, when analyzing the impact of different types of human capital on technological progress, the main research objects are technological innovation and technological imitation. Benhabib (1994), Spiegle (2005),

Dowrik & Rogers (2002) found that the improvement of human capital level is not only conducive to technological innovation, but also to technological diffusion and technological catch-up. However, the subject of their analysis is the overall human capital stock, where human capital is not distinguished from the type of human capital. Vandenbussche (2006) assumes that technological innovation activities are skill intensive compared with technological imitation activities, and constructs an endogenous growth model at one time. Combined with empirical analysis, it is pointed out that the more advanced the technology, the more obvious the growth rate of skilled labor. If the technology is not well developed, factories need to use much more unskilled labor to engage in technological imitation activities. So we can conclude that the main driving force to improve the total factor productivity of the society is technology progress. Messinis & Ahmed (2008) used the empirical analysis and found that skilled labor is conducive to technological innovation and technological diffusion. Ang (2011) further expanded the sample range based on the analysis of Vandenbussche (2006). In fact, the analysis results show that primary education and secondary education are conducive to technological imitation, while higher education is conducive to technological innovation. With the high-end technology in middle and high-income countries, the growth effect of higher education on technological progress will gradually increase. Basu & Mehar (2014) explored the different roles of different types of human capital by constructing endogenous growth models in different types of technological progress, and found that skilled human capital had obvious growth effects in the growth mode of "technological imitation technological innovation" and "technological innovation," while unskilled human capital only played a promoting role in "technological imitation."

To sum up, we can summarize the following:

1) The increase of the total amount of human capital can significantly affect the overall rate of technological progress
2) The effect of different human capital on technological progress is heterogeneous.

3) Skilled human capital mainly promotes technological innovation, while unskilled human capital mainly promotes technological learning, technological imitation and technological catch-up.

Chapter 7

STRUCTURAL CHANGE

7.1. INTRODUCTION

Human capital has an influence on the optimization and upgrading of industrial structure through market demand mechanism. The essential reason is that the macroscopic economy is always in need of the realization of dynamic balance between total demand and total supply in the long term. Human capital investment is not only conductive to the accumulation of human capital stock but also conducive to the adjustment of internal structure of human capital. The optimization of the internal structure of human capital will cause the change of the market demand structure, and then transmit it to the supply side, and eventually promote the industry in supply side to develop in the direction of higher quality. Actually, on the one hand, through investment, we can realize the advancement of human capital, and consequently, realizing the continuous development of high-quality service industries such as medical treatment, finance and education, With investment of human capital, industrial structure can be advanced. On the other hand, the internal structure optimization of human capital promotes the upgrading of demand structure, so as to achieve the effect of industrial structure upgrading.

Besides, human beings are both producers and consumers of technology. The increase of human capital quantity and the improvement of its quality can obviously promote the progress of technology. The neoclassical growth model with technological factors considers that in addition to physical capital, science and technology are the fundamental reason to promote economic growth. The endogenous economic growth model considers that knowledge and technology can bring endogenous growth to the economy. Technological progress can make capital overcome the law of diminishing marginal returns. As a result, there is a common sense that technological progress rather than factor endowment is the primary productivity to economic growth and transformation.

Meanwhile, human capital can form different human capital abilities through differential investment, within which the most important ability is resource allocation. The resource allocation ability of human capital enables human capital to do adjustment quickly according to the changes of social economy, which can make the production factors flow fully in the market, improve the utilization efficiency of various resources as much as possible, make reasonable arrangement for distribution, and in the end to achieve Pareto Optimality. In a country's market economy system, human capital can participate in the allocation of resources, and combine with various factors of production to derive different types of division on labor, which makes the industrial sectors more specialized. Generally speaking, the higher the investment cost of human capital, the stronger the ability of resource allocation it has. Therefore, high-level human capital has a strong ability of rational allocation of resources and efficient integration of elements. By investing in human capital to cultivate talents and attract professionals, we can provide talents reserve for the development and transformation of economy.

7.2. Human Capital and the Market Demand Mechanism

Human capital influences industrial structure through market demand mechanism, and finally influences economic development and transformation by means of human capital investment and internal structure optimization of human capital.

The formation of human capital ability mainly depends on human capital investment, which is also an important reason for the formation of human capital heterogeneity. The increase of human capital investment demand will promote the supply of corresponding industries. For example, the demand for health investment will promote the development of health care industry, the demand for body & beauty investment will promote the development of health beauty industry, the demand for education investment will promote the development of training and social practice related industries, and the demand for migration investment will promote the development of transportation, communication, IT and some other related industries. It is not difficult to find that these industries driven by human capital investment, such as medical, beauty, education, transportation and other industries, which are all typical service industries. Therefore, there is no doubt that the investment of human capital will undoubtedly increase the proportion of service industry in the total social industry, promote the development of service industry in a country, and finally realize the adjustment and upgrading of industrial structure.

As for the study of industrial structure, there is a famous theory named industrial relevance theory, which can help us learn market demand mechanism. Industrial relevance theory mainly studies the relationship between intermediate input and intermediate output, which could well reflect the intermediate input and intermediate output of each industry. However, this is not the matter we should rest our eyes. Most important of all, the theory of industrial association is widely used in the research of the correlation degree of related industrial. Generally speaking, industrial association effect refers to the direct and indirect influence on other industries caused by the change of production scale, output value, technology and so on. It is usually divided into forward association effect and backward association effect. In order to understand the forward correlation effect and backward correlation effect better, we had better understand two groups of concepts:

A. Intermediate demand & final demand

The intermediate demand, also known as endogenous demand, is in the core position of input-output system, reflecting the dependence and trading relationship between industries in the process of reproduction in a certain period of time.

The final demand, also known as exogenous demand, reflects the destination of products and services produced by various industries. These products and services are called final products and services, and they can be used to calculate GDP, which can be divided into four parts: consumption, investment, government purchase and export.

B. Forward association & backward association

Forward association refers to that the products of the former industrial sector are the production factors of the latter industrial sector, which continues until the products (which we call them final products) of the last industry. The following industrial relations are as follows:

Mining industry – Steel industry – Machining industry – Assembly industry

Backward association refers to the direct consumption of products provided by subsequent industrial departments to the first industrial departments and the production of the first industrial departments. For example, the mining machinery and equipment produced by the mechanical processing industry are provided for the operation of the mining industry.

Therefore, we can conclude the definition of these two correlation effects. The forward correlation effect refers to the corresponding change of the forward correlation industry caused by the change of the scale, output value and technology of an industry. The backward correlation effect refers to the corresponding change of the backward correlation industry caused by the change of the scale, output value and technology of an industry.

According to this theory, we can find that industrial development is not carried out in a single sector, but will be affected by the forward and backward industrial sectors' development. The increase of human capital investment promotes the development of health care, education, communication and other industries, which will generate new demand for retail, accommodation, catering and other industries, bring more extensive development of non-agricultural sectors, and ultimately promote the upgrading of industrial structure. It proves that human capital is the driven force for economic development, transformation and upgrading.

Human capital investment is not only conductive to the accumulation of human capital stock, but also to the optimization of the internal structure of human capital, so as to promote the adjustment of industrial structure. In addition to the direct investment expenditure, human capital investment expense includes the opportunity cost abandoned to obtain the ability. The higher the ability of human capital, the higher the cost is. From the perspective of market theory, high cost investment requires high return on investment. Generally speaking, high-level human capital will get higher income level than primary and intermediate human capital. According to the theory of income elasticity of demand, the income elasticity of luxury goods is greater than that of necessities of life, which can also make the demand structure of society keep upgrading and appear the tendency to get into high level. At the same time, the supply and demand of the market requires to maintain a dynamic balance. According to the Cobweb Model, the supply in current period depends on the demand in the previous period. As a result, the optimization of the internal structure of human capital leads to the upgrading of demand structure, and finally promotes the development and upgrading of the industrial structure.

Firstly, the optimization of the internal structure of human capital can have a positive impact on the income level. Mincer (1958) did the research on the relationship between human capital and income distribution, and he pointed that the time spent on human capital investment would shorten the years of work experience. Under the assumption of equalization of present value of life-long income, the groups who obtained more human capital investment would obtain higher income. Through data analysis and relevant empirical analysis, it can also be found that the average wage of workers receiving more education is higher.

Secondly, the improvement of income level can promote the upgrading of demand structure. Keynes thought that consumption has a positive effect on income. Influenced by marginal propensity to consume, the consumption of citizens will increase with the increase of income level. In addition, the increase of income level will also cause the change of consumption structure. Generally speaking, due to the different demand income elasticity of different commodities, the income elasticity of luxury goods is greater than unity, the income elasticity of necessities is between zero and unity and the income elasticity of inferior goods is less than zero. Consequently, the increase of income will increase demand for luxury goods and necessities, and reduce the demand for inferior goods. Meanwhile, the improvement of income level can promote the upgrading of demand structure. From the perspective of real life, when the income level continues to improve, with the most basic needs met, people tend to be willing to use the increased income for the purchase of products in higher demand level, and finally realize the upgrading of demand structure.

Finally, the upgrading of demand structure can promote the upgrading of industrial structure. From a macroscopic perspective, the supply and demand of the whole society are in a dynamic balance. The upgrading of the demand structure will affect the supply structure by means of the input-output model. Because of it, the upgrading of the demand structure is very important in the upgrading of the advanced industrial structure. From the microscopic point of view, supply chain requires enterprises to stand in customers' shoes. That is to say, the enterprises should determine the adjustment of production according to the change of customer demand. This operation mode can meet the different needs, which can greatly benefit the sales volume and profits. These two aspects both reflect the great effect of demand upgrading on industrial structure upgrading.

To sum up, the investment of human capital can affect the industrial structure through the market demand mechanism. On the one hand, the demand for human capital investment will promote the development of service industry and then upgrade a country's industrial structure. On the other hand, human capital investment leads to the optimization of the internal structure of human capital, which can improve the consumption level of a country's residents and optimizes the demand structure, so that the industrial structure can be adjusted according to the changes of the market consumption structure. The combination of the two eventually makes the industrial structure of a country advanced due to the investment of human capital.

7.3. Human Capital and the Market Innovation Mechanism

The increase of human capital stock can promote the progress and technology, which can further promote the development of leading industries to a higher level, so as to promote the upgrading of industrial structure. This is what we called the market innovation mechanism. Rostow (1988) held the view that modern economic growth is the result of sector growth. Without the analysis of industrial sector, it cannot explain the reason of economic growth. Based on this, we can find the following three points. Firstly, the advanced technology is always related to the development of industrial sectors. The industrial sector is the first demander of labor, capital, knowledge and other factors in production. Making good use of certain technology, sectors can organically combine human capital and physical capital to improve the efficiency. Secondly, technology is a concrete and abstract concept. Technology can be used in average production, or it can be used to get added value through learning and creating. Thirdly, technology innovation can bring dynamic benefits, so that the development of the industrial sector is not static and it can be a driving force for the change of industrial structure in a complex way. In a word, economic growth is the result of the change of leading industrial sectors, which is always accompanied by the shrinking of inefficient industrial sectors and the rise of emerging industrial sectors. The diffusion effect of leading industrial sectors can drive the development of other sectors and ultimately promote economic development.

The process of leading industries' replacement can also be considered as the process of industrial structure upgrading. In different periods of economic development, the leading sectors in human society are agriculture, manufacturing industry, service industry and information & technology industry. The upgrading of industrial structure is such a kind of change. Therefore, human capital can promote the upgrading of industrial structure through scientific innovation mechanism, and its development logic can be described as follows.

The increase of human capital stock can significantly promote the progress of science and technology, so as to cause the orderly replacement of leading industrial sectors, so as to achieve a much more reasonable industrial structure.

The increase of human capital stock can promote technological progress, improve labor productivity and change the relative cost between different sectors. The change of relative cost will lead to the redistribution of production factors among different sectors, and then push forward the upgrading of industrial structure. The relative cost can also reflect the cost of production factors in different industries. Due to the different speed of technological advancement in each sector, the efficiency of the sector with rapid technological advancement is faster than that of other sectors, so that the relative cost of such sector is lower than that of other sectors. At the same time, the sectors with lower cost can attract more production factors in that price plays an important role in the flow direction of factors. On the contrary, the production efficiency of sectors with slow technological advancement is improved slowly, resulting in low cost of sectors and factors tend to flow out, which eventually leads to the decline of the sectors. Based on this, we can find that the factors flow from the low efficiency sectors to the high efficiency sectors, which will benefit the efficiency of resource utilization and enhances the coordination between different sectors. This kind of process is definitely the process of industrial upgrading.

To sum up, human capital can influence the change of industrial structure through the mechanism of scientific and technological innovation. From the perspective of stock, the accumulation of human capital stock is conductive to promoting technological advancement. From the perspective of the internal structure of human capital, the transformation efficiency of high-level human capital innovation is higher, and the role of technological innovation is stronger. On the one hand, technological advancement can promote the transformation of leading industries and the evolution of industrial structure towards the direction of upgrading. On the other hand, it can change the relative costs between sectors, lead to the reallocation of factors, and ultimately promote the development and upgrading of industries.

7.4. Human Capital and the Resource Allocation Mechanism

Different from the influence of human capital on the upgrading of industrial structure caused by market demand mechanism and innovation mechanism, resource allocation mechanism means that the ability of resource allocation plays a role in the adjustment of industrial structure. The role of human capital's resource allocation is reflected in two aspects, includes factor aggregation effect and factor replacement effect.

Factor aggregation effect means that the increase of human capital stock in sectors will make other production factors, which are mainly physical capital and others, gather to some specific sectors. This is because the promotion of human capital in a sector will make the physical capital relatively scarce. In order to make good use of all factors, the sector needs to increase investment and improve its physical capital level. Schumpeter's creative destruction theory emphasizes that the entrepreneur's ability, as a kind of human capital, plays an important role in the redistribution of other factors. It underlines the ability of human capital's resource allocation which enables entrepreneurs to destroy the market equilibrium, so as to obtain excess profits. Due to the ability to allocate resources, high-level human capital can reduce the risk of material capital investment to a certain extent. As a result, the factor aggregation effect of high-level human capital is extremely stronger, which is manifested in that more physical capital flows into the industry intensive in high-level human capital and then promotes the development of advancement industrial structure.

The factor replacement effect refers to the substitution of high-level human capital for intermediate and primary human capital. The higher the level of human capital, the stronger the ability of resource allocation is. When more high-level human capital flows into the sectors to combine with physical capital, the surplus physical capital will be reduced. And the demand of human capital matching with the physical capital will also be reduced. Consequently, high-level human capital gradually replaces primary and intermediate human capital. The resource allocation ability of human capital influences the upgrading of industrial structure dependent on the effect of factor aggregation and factor replacement.

7.5. Findings and Interpretations

In this part, we will rest our eyes on the statistics on human capital in China. According to China Human Capital Report Series 2019 published by China Center for Human Capital and Labor Market Research of Central University of Finance and Economics, both urban real human capital and rural real human capital increased from 1985 to 2017. Table 5.5.1 shows that urban real human capital increases from 14310 billion Yuan to 316129 billion Yuan while rural real human capital increases from 23149 billion Yuan to 72425 billion Yuan. The annual growth rates of urban human capital are up to 10.31% while those of rural are 3.74%. Before 1992, the stock of rural human capital is much bigger than that of urban human capital. With the trend of urbanization, urban human capital exceeds that in rural areas.

Table 7.5.1. National real human capital by region from 1985 to 2017 (Unit: Billions of 1985 Yuan)

Year	National	Urban	Rural
1985	37459	14310	23149
1986	41209	16989	24220
1987	44437	19040	25396
1988	44409	19571	24838
1989	44065	20529	23536
1990	48989	23415	25575
1991	55871	27442	28429
1992	61875	31549	30326
1993	63745	33825	29920
1994	60402	33218	27183
1995	58356	32441	25916
1996	63961	37656	26305
1997	70324	42389	27935
1998	82152	51607	30546
1999	97581	63989	33592
2000	112149	75590	26559
2001	122474	82845	39629
2002	131734	89951	41783
2003	142749	98976	43774
2004	150261	105877	44384
2005	160513	114583	45930
2006	181055	130862	50194
2007	181399	140832	50576
2008	201835	150777	51058
2009	223166	168967	55199
2010	236026	178575	57451
2011	254980	197490	57490
2012	272150	213473	58676
2013	299988	239467	60521
2014	321488	257819	63669
2015	341940	273531	68409
2016	364976	296631	68345
2017	388554	316129	72425

Source: China Human Capital Report Series.

An increase in real human capital can be caused by a variety of reasons, such as population growth, the size of retirement group, region migration, urbanization, higher education attainment, higher rates of return to education and higher rates of return to on-the-job training. These reasons are all related to human capital itself. We can consider these factors as the process of individual improvement. In order to further understand the role of human capital in economic transformation, we should calculate real human capital per capita.

Table 7.5.1 shows the real human capital per capita and we can easily find that it has grew by 8.69 times, from 37.78 thousand Yuan in 1985 to 345.79 thousand Yuan in 2017, with an average annual growth rate of 7.13%. Compared with the growth rate of rural human capital per capita, which is about 607.9%, the growth rate of urban human capital per capita is up to 800.5% during the past 20 years. No matter the quantity and quality, urban human capital per capita has got an amazing promotion. There is no doubt that the rapid growth rate is resulted from the expansion of education and the improvement of market economy, and it has become a strong driving force for economy transformation.

The rapid growth of China's human capital stock, on the one hand, comes from the improvement of human capital quality, on the other hand, comes from the improvement of China's population structure. Figure 7.5.1 reveals that the total amount of human capital is rising significantly, but the stock of human capital between urban and rural areas also shows a certain difference. The difference is not only because the city has mature education system and training resources, but also is inseparable with the transfer of population between urban and rural areas, which leads the situation that the stock of urban real human capital definitely exceeds the rural real human capital.

Figure 7.5.1 shows the contribution rate to GDP of different industries, including primary industry, secondary industry and tertiary industry. We can find that except the year 1990, the contribution made by primary industry is stable, about 10%. The proportion of secondary industry keeps decreasing while tertiary industry develops rapidly. In 2017, the contribution rate of tertiary industry has been up to 59.6%, more than the half of GDP.

Table 7.5.2. National real human capital per capita by region from 1985 to 2017 (Unit: Thousands of 1985 Yuan)

Year	National	Urban	Rural
1985	39.78	66.79	31.83
1986	43.31	76.34	33.22
1987	46.28	82.10	34.87
1988	44.93	79.54	33.87
1989	43.92	79.23	31.62
1990	48.34	87.94	34.23
1991	54.07	99.64	37.51
1992	59.96	112.88	40.31
1993	61.26	118.32	39.65
1994	57.62	114.03	35.92
1995	55.08	108.18	34.12
1996	59.18	115.69	34.83
1997	65.60	123.35	38.36
1998	76.29	141.74	42.86
1999	90.26	166.58	48.20
2000	102.96	186.46	53.46
2001	111.03	194.02	58.61
2002	121.18	204.98	64.45
2003	131.73	217.68	69.60
2004	139.41	225.93	72.86
2005	148.56	234.04	77.74
2006	163.55	252.98	84.82
2007	174.97	268.45	88.83
2008	183.46	278.55	91.36
2009	203.25	304.38	100.77
2010	211.94	312.35	106.01
2011	224.66	332.05	106.43
2012	243.98	355.64	113.89
2013	269.11	389.92	120.9
2014	289.13	411.76	131.07
2015	307.09	428.12	144.15
2016	325.18	449.39	147.15
2017	345.79	467.89	161.66

Source: China Human Capital Report Series.

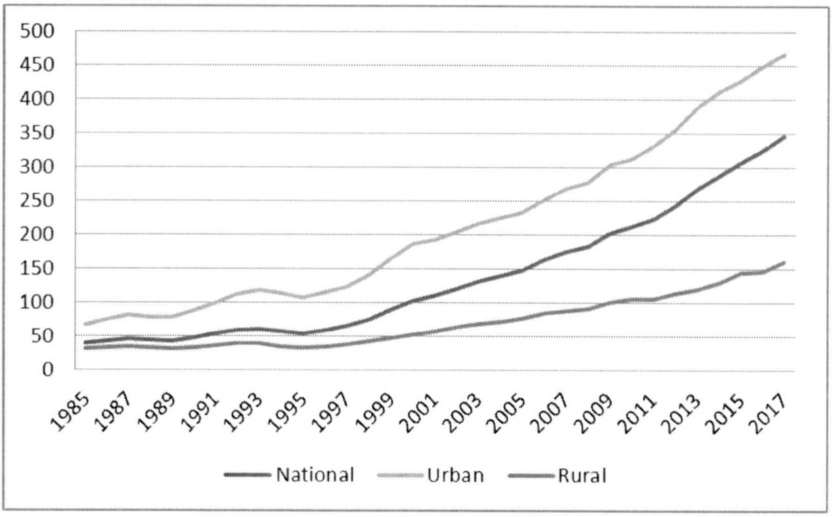

Source: China Statistical Yearbook.

Figure 7.5.1. National real human capital per capita by region.

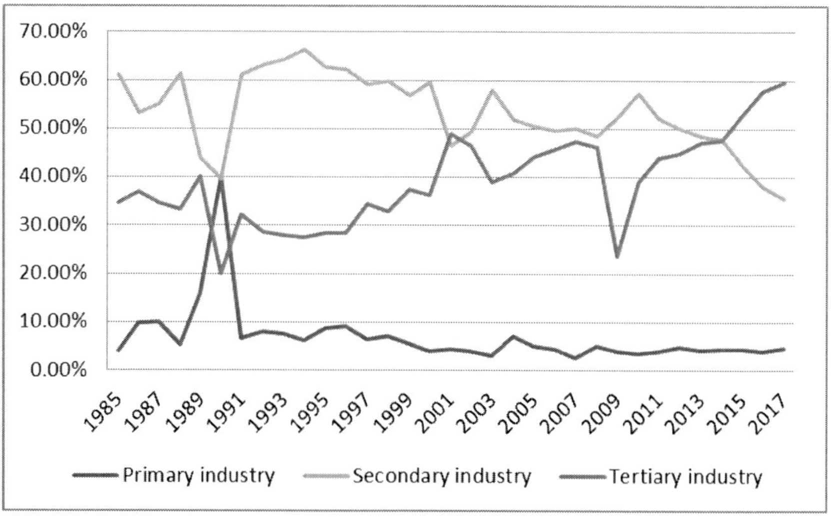

Source: China Statistical Yearbook.

Figure 7.5.2. Contribution Rate to GDP in China by Industries.

According to the Theory of Social Capital Reproduction proposed by Marx, one of the general laws of industrial structure change is that all industrial sectors in the national economy should maintain a certain proportion. It includes two aspects. Firstly, rationalization of industrial structure is the coordination among industries based on existing technology. It involves the coordination of various relations among industries, such as a reasonable proportion of production scale in an economy, the improvement of the degree in inter-industry association, and is also about the coordination of output value structure, technical structure, asset structure and intermediate element structure. Secondly, the optimization of industrial structure means that the industrial structure develops from the low level to the high level according to the historical and logical sequence of economic development. A beneficial structure change includes the evolution from the dominant proportion of the primary industry to the dominant proportion of the secondary industry and then tertiary industry. Also, it includes the evolution from a structure with dominant proportion of the labor-intensive industry to that with the dominant proportion of capital-intensive industry and then the technology & knowledge-intensive industry. In addition, it can include the evolution from the dominant proportion of industry manufacturing primary products to the dominant proportion of the industry manufacturing intermediate products and final product. An important sign of improvement is to promote the development of tertiary industry and maintain a reasonable proportion of all industries.

Analyzing the relevant data of human capital and industries from 1985 to 2017, we can find that with the continuous increase of human capital stock, the economic contrition rate to economy of tertiary industry is becoming larger and larger. At the same time, the economic structure has been constantly optimized and has a trend for rationalization and upgrading. Therefore, it is not difficult to find that the increase of human capital stock promotes the upgrading of economic structure.

Besides, the internal structure of human capital plays an important role in the improvement of industrial structure. Generally speaking, definitions of educational attainment levels are shown in Table 7.5.3 and Table 7.5.4.

Table 7.5.3. Levels of educational attainment before 2000 (Unit: Year)

Level	Illiterate	Primary School	Junior Middle School	Senior Middle School	College and Above
Years of Schooling	0	6	9	12	15

Source: China Human Capital Report Series.

Table 7.5.4. Levels of educational attainment since 2000 (Unit: Year)

Level	Illiterate	Primary School	Junior Middle School	Senior Middle School	College	University and Above
Years of Schooling	0	6	9	12	15	16

Source: China Human Capital Report Series.

Table 7.5.5. Proportions of human capital by industry since 2008 in China (Unit: %)

Year	Primary Human Capital	Secondary Human Capital	Advanced Human Capital
2008	38.7	54.6	6.7
2009	37.2	55.5	7.3
2010	42.3	53.4	4.3
2011	33.1	56.9	10.1
2012	32.2	57.2	10.6
2013	31.4	57.3	11.3
2014	31.6	56.9	11.5
2015	31.9	54.8	13.3
2016	31.3	55.7	12.9
2017	26.9	49.1	24.0

Source: China Human Capital Report Series.

According to the definitions of educational attainment levels, we can divide human capital into three types, including primary human capital, secondary human capital and advanced human capital. Among them, primary human capital refers to the people whose years of schooling are less than 6. Secondary human capital refers to the people whose years of schooling are between 7 and 12. Advanced human capital refers to those whose years of schooling are above 15. In order to discover the relationship between human capital structure and industrial structure, here are the proportions of different human capital and industries.

Table 7.5.6. Proportions of the three industries since 2008 in China (Unit: %)

Year	Primary Industry	Secondary Industry	Tertiary Industry
2008	5.20	48.60	46.20
2009	4.00	52.30	23.70
2010	3.60	57.40	39.00
2011	4.10	52.00	43.90
2012	5.00	50.00	45.00
2013	4.20	48.50	47.20
2014	4.60	47.90	47.50
2015	4.50	42.50	53.00
2016	4.10	38.20	57.70
2017	4.80	35.70	59.60

Source: China Human Capital Report Series.

We can find that since 2008, the proportion of advanced human capital in China has kept rising, from 6.7% in 2008 to 24% in 2017, and its growth rate is quite amazing. At the same time, the secondary and tertiary industries are developing rapidly, and the technology & knowledge-intensive industries as well as Internet industries are rising dramatically. In order to explore the relationship between them, we use the data of internal structure of human capital and industrial structure to find out the correlation. As a result, we establish the covariance matrix of internal structure of human capital and industrial structure.

Table 7.5.7. Covariance matrix between human capital and industry

Variety Name	Primary Industry	Secondary Industry	Tertiary Industry
Primary Human Capital	0.3587	0.4536	0.3258
Secondary Human Capital	0.1060	0.7810	0.6736
Advanced Human capital	0.3487	0.8629	0.7138

From the perspective of the primary industry, the correlation index between different kinds of human capital and the primary industry are 0.3587, 0.1060 and 0.3487 respectively. The primary human capital has the highest correlation with the primary industry which shows its core role in the development of primary industry. This is closely related to the widespread of compulsory education and the process of urbanization in China.

From the perspective of the secondary industry, secondary human capital plays the most significant role in its development. And as for the tertiary industry, it is in need of more advanced human capital for better service and higher technology. That is to say, advanced human capital is an important force to promote China's industries transformation and upgrading.

To sum up, human capital can influence the upgrading of industrial structure through market demand mechanism, scientific innovation mechanism and resource allocation. Among them, human capital investment is not only conducive to the accumulation of human capital stock, but also conducive to the optimization of the internal structure of human capital. On the one hand, human capital investment can promote the development of service industry and promote the upgrading of industrial structure through market demand mechanism. On the other hand, the optimization of internal structure of human capital will become a driving force to improve income level, promote the upgrading of demand structure and then upgrade industrial structure. At the same time, the increase of human capital stock can significantly promote technological progress. Technological progress can not only promote the change of leading industries, promote the upgrading of industrial structure, but also change the relative costs between different industrial sectors. It is beneficial to balance the development of various industries, and eventually realize the transformation of an economy.

Chapter 8

Development Strategies

8.1. Introduction

Economic development has always been the key point of economic research. Different economists have different views on the causes of economic development. Adam Smith believed that specialization and exchanging can bring about the improvement of production efficiency, and then increase social welfare. Harold Domar thought that the root of economic growth lies in the accumulation of material capital, and increasing investment can promote economic growth. Solow believed that technological progress is the reason of economic growth, and then he first introduced the concept of human capital into the research field of economic growth. Schultz's human capital accumulation theory comprehensively underlined the concept and importance of human capital. Subsequently, economists began to pay attention to the concept of human capital and applied it to the research of manufacturing industry development, international trade and enterprise micro research.

In recent years, with the rapid development of China's industrialization, the problems such as the surplus of medium and low-end products, insufficient supply of high-end products, low manufacturing efficiency and low resource utilization rate have gradually emerged. At the same time, modern service trade has gradually become a new economic growth point for a country's economy. The modern service industry also begins to transform from the traditional extensive service trade based on natural resources and labor force to the modern service trade dominated by human capital and technology. Under the promotion of information technology, the emerging service trade gradually focuses on improving the added value of services, which is closely related to the technological progress and innovation of service industry. This means that countries with high-quality human capital have more comparative advantages in the field of production and trade. At the same time, China's economy has also changed from high-speed development to medium high-speed development. Facing the background of the rise of artificial intelligence, how to maintain economic growth in the increasingly fierce international competition, promote economic development, and obtain competitive advantage in international trade has become a particularly important issue.

8.1.1. The Global Background

With the rapid change of the global economy, the revolutionary change has taken place in the development mode and value creation mode of the whole world economy. It also has a profound impact on China's economic development.

The new industrial revolution not only brings revolutionary changes to the world's industrial chain, but also brings a huge impact on China's traditional manufacturing industry. The essence of the industrial revolution is the rapid improvement of the productive capacity of the whole society. From the invention of steam engine and the use of electricity to the popularity of computers, it relies on the improvement of social production efficiency that causes great changes in the industry. With the continuous application of artificial intelligence, big data, cloud computing, and other up to date concepts, it can lead to the innovation of agriculture, manufacturing and service industry, and cause great changes in the whole value chain. Developed countries are leading the fourth scientific and technological revolution and hope to seize the opportunity to be the pioneers of industrial transformation. Nowadays, in the period of vigorous development of the Internet, China is facing great changes in which it is necessary to combine the Internet and traditional industries closely to create new production methods, management methods and marketing methods, so as to adapt to the increasingly fierce market competition. At the same time, the new production mode reduces the production cost rapidly, which makes the manufacturing advantage in China gradually lose. With the process of industrial transfer, China's status as a world factory is gradually facing threats. Therefore, we must pay more attention to the market mechanism, set up the talent team and transform the innovation into the actual productivity. Under the background that demographic dividend has not completely disappeared and new advantages have not yet formed, we should look for the potential comparative advantages. All of these must accelerate the accumulation of human capital.

In addition, the shock of the financial crisis in 2008 makes developed countries begin to think about how to ensure the stability of a country's economic development. They began to consider the advantages and disadvantages of the real economy and the virtual economy, and began to consider the development of manufacturing and service industries. Through thinking and practice, they think that the development of the real economy is the foundation of the development of the virtual economy. The development of the real economy is the premise of the development of the service industry, and the basis for the healthy development of the economy. It is the maintenance of the core competitiveness. Therefore, developed countries led by the United States began to take the plan of manufacturing return to protect their economic development. For example, the United States put forward the "industrial Internet" strategy to integrate information technology and manufacturing industry. Germany proposed the "Industry 4.0" strategy and accelerated the layout of intelligent manufacturing. Some emerging economies have also strengthened the relocation of manufacturing industry and actively joined the global industrial chain. As a big processing and manufacturing country, China provides raw materials and processing services for the world industrial chain, and is on the way to the development of high-quality manufacturing industry. At this time, the trend of Reindustrialization makes the competition of processing and manufacturing industry in the world industry chain become more and more fierce, which also brings great pressure on China's manufacturing industry.

At the same time, countries all over the world pay more and more attention to human capital and education, and begin to pay attention to the accumulation of human capital and the introduction of talents. At present, all countries in the world try to improve the overall quality of domestic labor force by increasing education investment, and reserve talents for economic development and transformation. It reflects the strategic value of human capital to a country's economic development.

8.1.2. The Domestic Background

China's economic development has always been faced with the severe international competition. At the same time, there are also a series of development bottlenecks in China, such as extensive growth mode, low product quality, low labor productivity and insufficient human capital.

Since the reform and opening up from 1978, China's economy has been an example in the world. In terms of GDP growth rate and scale, it is in the leading position in the world. China's strong manufacturing capacity has promoted the sustained and rapid development of China's economy. With the world economy entering the post industrialization stage, the industry economic development relies on has gradually changed from manufacturing industry to service-oriented manufacturing industry. As for manufacturing industry, it has changed from general manufacturing industry to advanced manufacturing industry. China's economic growth mainly depends on the development of physical manufacturing industry. China needs both advanced manufacturing industry and traditional manufacturing industry to improve efficiency and promote industrial transformation and upgrading. It requires higher manufacturing capacity, more advanced technical skill. Developed countries have experienced the early industrialization, and now they are experiencing reindustrialization and orderly evolves industrial structure. But for China, a big manufacturing country, the industrialization stage for transformation and upgrading is insurmountable. At present, China's economic growth depends on the low-cost and high-energy consumption growth model, and this growth model is no longer feasible. Overcapacity, rising labor costs and lack of competitiveness have seriously hindered the development of China's economy there. Some enterprises have some problems too, such as difficulties on heading hunting, high turnover rate and low labor productivity. From the perspective of global value chain, made in China plays the role of a processing plant, and the proportion of innovative manufacturing is very small. Therefore, China's economic development, especially the development of manufacturing industry, is facing great challenges in terms of continuous development, transformation and upgrading.

The research of the economic development in various countries shows that human capital has become the long-term driving force of economic growth. Enterprises can reduce the cost of production, improve the quality of products and shorten the cycle of production by adopting new technology, new materials, new production methods and new business models. This requires not only long-term accumulation of knowledge and skills, but also the improvement of knowledge and skills. It even requires the creation of new knowledge and skills. Therefore, we believe that the accumulation of human capital is a key strategy for a country's economic growth.

In terms of these problems, perhaps we can find feasible solutions from the perspective of human capital.

8.2. Human Capital Investment and Macroeconomic Development Strategies

For all countries in the world, the development of manufacturing industry and international trade is the main driving force for a country's macroeconomic growth. Therefore, this chapter will discuss human capital and macroeconomic development strategy from the perspective of manufacturing and international trade.

8.2.1. Human Capital and Manufacturing

In recent years, human capital has been widely concerned and has become the core factor of economic development. The accumulation of human capital can promote the skill level of employees, improve the output, promote technological progress, improve labor productivity, increase production income, promote social progress, and add economic and social benefits.

After the concept of human capital was put forward, economists found that because of the existence of human capital, the input of material capital lagged behind the economic growth rate. With the deepening of economists' research on the economic effect of human capital, it is found that the role of human capital on economic growth is greater than that of material capital, which is the decisive factor of economic development. Different from the material capital, human capital means a collection of various knowledge, experience, skills and quality. It has a strong innovation. Its marginal productivity is very high and the contribution rate to GPD is also very high. To a great extent, human capital can be used to overcome the negative externality problems in the world. After the reform and opening up, China has become a big industrial manufacturing country, with much more industrial population. With the fine division and mechanization of modern industry, the production process is more and more complex, and the industrial chain is longer and longer, which puts forward higher requirements for the skills of the industrial population. Therefore, it is particularly important to promote the accumulation of skilled human capital for China in the transformation period.

At the same time, China missed two industrial revolutions because of its late start, so the industrial system has a certain gap compared with the mature developed countries. After the reform and opening up, China gradually formed a market system of human capital accumulation in manufacturing industry. However, due to the characteristics of market capital profit driven, in recent years, the capital has gradually flowed to financial economy, real estate and other industries. Manufacturing industry presents the situation of insufficient investment and limited human capital accumulation. Therefore, in the face of the era of artificial intelligence, China needs not only to promote the development of manufacturing industry, train high-quality talents, but also to catch up with the international economy and gain competitive advantage.

After this period, China gradually catched up with the global developing trend. After the reform and opening up, China gradually polished up the market system of human capital accumulation in much more fields.

Now China has entered the key period of structural adjustment and transformation, which needs to change from extensive growth to intensive growth, which requires the accumulation of human capital as the basis to improve the quality of economic development. Therefore, human capital will be the factor that determines the future development of China's manufacturing industry. The accumulation and innovation of human capital has become a new driving force for the development of China's manufacturing industry and economy.

According to the law of diminishing marginal productivity, with the increase of input of production factors, the marginal productivity will decrease when the input of factors reaches a certain extent under the condition of constant technical level. But with the accumulation of human capital, if we can combine with material capital in a reasonable way, we can improve the technology used in the production process, thus hedging the negative growth of marginal productivity. In other words, under the appropriate conditions, the accumulation of human capital can achieve a long-term positive growth of marginal productivity. At the same time, human capital accumulation has multiplier effect to promote the transformation and upgrading of manufacturing industry. Similar to multiplier effect of material capital investment, with the accumulation of human capital and the progress of technology, the output of enterprises and the income of employees will increase. The improvement of the whole social consumption level can be promoted. If education investment increases, and human capital in the whole society can be accumulated further. Therefore, the accumulation of human capital can bring about the overall improvement of human quality and increase of output, and improve the quantity and quality of products. Compared with material capital, human capital has a greater multiplier effect because of its higher contribution level.

Today in China, demographic dividend and cost advantages are disappearing. The contribution of human capital accumulation to the economy is increasing gradually. The accumulation of human capital and the optimization of structure can improve the professional quality of workers. A worker with professional quality can learn new technology new technology and new methods better and faster and they can adapt to the new working environment and transform technology into productivity. At the same time, it can improve the ability of enterprise resource allocation and promote economic transformation and upgrading.

American economist Arrow first proposed to use externality to explain the role of spillover effect. He believes that the experience, knowledge and skills accumulated by employees in production can improve the ability to solve practical problems and improve the production efficiency of enterprises, which reflects the spillover effect of human capital accumulation. A person with a higher level of ability can have a strong impact on the people around him. He can improve the productivity of the people around him, but he may not get the corresponding benefits. This is an externality, that is, the spillover effect.

Generally speaking, according to the relevant analysis of economists, the spillover effects of human capital can be classified into the following 12 categories:

1) The improvement of children's comprehensive quality;
2) The improvement of the internal productivity of the family;
3) The improvement of the health status of the educated person;
4) The improvement of the health status of spouses and family members;
5) The reduction of fertility rate;
6) The improvement of consumer choice efficiency;
7) The improvement of labor market choice efficiency;
8) The more efficient marriage choice;
9) The high savings rate;
10) The increase of crime rate;
11) The improvement of social harmony;
12) The progress and dissemination of technology.

Because of the strong externality of human capital, human capital investment plays a greater role in promoting economic growth. At the same time, the spillover effect also further increases the investment in education, forming a good double-track influence mechanism. Nowadays, the problems faced by China's macroeconomic development cannot be solved only by fiscal and monetary policies, so we need to reform from the supply side. The focus of supply side reform is to improve the enthusiasm and productivity of workers, which is essentially a problem of human capital accumulation.

8.2.2. Human Capital and International Trade

The impact of human capital on international trade is mainly reflected in the impact on the international competitiveness of service trade.

According to the theory of National Competitive Advantage put forward by American economist Michael Porter, the domestic economic environment of a country has a great influence on the development of enterprises' competitiveness. The most direct factors are as follows:

1) Factors of production refer to the ability of a country to convert basic conditions into special advantages. Basic conditions generally include natural resources, human resources, infrastructure, etc. Porter further divided production factors into primary production factors and advanced production factors. Primary production factors refer to the natural resources and geographical location of a country, while advanced production factors refer to those created through social and personal investment and development. Porter believes that advanced production factors play a more obvious role in the formation of competitive advantage.
2) Demand conditions refer to the demand quantity and customer maturity of the products or services provided by the industry in the domestic market. In this regard, Porter emphasizes that domestic demand has a strong stimulating effect on national competitive advantage. Generally speaking, the degree of local customers' criticizing and satisfaction with products is very important to stimulate enterprises to improve their products.
3) Related and supporting industries refer to domestic suppliers with international competitiveness and related auxiliary industries. Only by forming an effective industrial group and the positive interaction between upstream and downstream industries and related industries, can the competitive advantage of industry develop sustainably.
4) Enterprise strategy, enterprise structure and horizontal competition refer to the conditions for the establishment, organization and management of enterprises and the degree of domestic competition. Porter believes that the existence of competitors plays

an important role in forcing domestic enterprises to constantly innovate, transform and upgrade.

In conclusion, from the perspective of production factors and demand conditions in the theory of national competitive advantage, we can analyze the impact of human capital on service trade.

From the perspective of production, advanced production factors have irreplaceable importance for international competitiveness. However, the advanced production factors are different from the primary production factors, which are difficult to obtain directly from the outside world. It needs a lot of investment and accumulation in the early period. As the core part of advanced production factors, human capital essentially improves the quality of labor through education investment and skill training, so as to meet the needs of production. In addition, human capital can not only affect the cost advantage of an industry, but also promote the development of industry to scale and innovation, thus affecting the quality of products. In addition, according to Rybczynski (1955) theorem, it can be deduced that human capital, as a kind of intensive use of production factors, can not only improve the technical level, health status and development potential of employees, but also improve the quality and output of service products through scale economy, so as to enhance the comparative advantage of service trade.

From the perspective of demand, demand factors have a significant pulling effect on industrial competitiveness. According to international experience, countries or regions with more abundant human capital stock will have higher per capita income level, and their demand and preference for services will be more diversified and hierarchical. Therefore, in the countries or regions where the proportion of service consumption is relatively large, people's nitpicking about the quality and output of service products can promote the structural adjustment of service industry and trade, and promote the refinement of service trade.

Human capital can influence the development of international trade, especially service trade through "spillover effect." Human capital investment in the long term can promote the improvement of production efficiency. And at the same time, it can drive the marginal production of other factors of production, such as capital, labor, and technology. Through training, education, experience sharing and other ways, the production efficiency of workers can be significantly improved, and the "learning by doing" effect can make the labor force learn from each other in the production process, resulting in the spillover effect of division of labor. In addition, the spillover effect of human capital is also reflected in the interrelated enterprises. For example, upstream and downstream enterprises can learn from each other and reduce costs through cooperation. In other words, the spillover effect of human capital can offset the diminishing marginal productivity brought by physical capital and enhance the competitive advantage of service industry.

Human capital can influence the service trade of multinational companies through the flow of talents. Human capital is a very valuable resource for both the country and enterprises. Therefore, both the government and enterprises will try their best to attract and introduce high-tech talents. This kind of transnational human capital investment behavior can cultivate a large number of talents for the country, and bring the experience matching with R&D, production and management. In addition, the international flow of human capital is bidirectional. For example, the parent company will assign high-quality human capital to overseas subsidiaries and the parent company's investment behavior is conducive to the improvement of the competitiveness of overseas subsidiaries. At the same time, technology and management enhance the profitability of the subsidiary, which in turn improves the competitiveness of the parent company. Therefore, the flow of human capital plays an important role in improving the overall level of international trade.

8.3. Human Capital Investment and Microeconomic Development Strategies

Human capital is valuable resource. It is very scarce and hard to imitate. It is the source of enterprise competitive advantage. Therefore, human capital has great strategic significance at the enterprise level.

1. Human capital and corporate culture

According to RAND Corporation, the competitiveness of enterprises is divided into three levels: the first level is the product level, that is, the ability to produce products and control their quality, the ability to service, the ability to control cost, the ability to market and the ability to develop technology. The second level is the system layer, that is, the structural platform caused by various operation and management elements, the relationship between internal and external people, environment, resource relations, enterprise operation mechanism, enterprise scale, brand, enterprise property rights system, etc. The third level is the core layer, that is, the corporate culture with corporate philosophy and corporate values, the internal and external consistent corporate image, enterprise innovation ability, differentiated and personalized enterprise characteristics, stable finance, excellent foresight and long-term global development goals. That is, they believe that the core competence is determined by corporate culture and philosophy.

Of course, corporate culture is not always conducive to competition. Some cultures help enterprises to compete more effectively, while others become barriers to corporations. To measure whether an enterprise culture is positive or negative, it mainly depends on the matching degree of organizational culture and group environment. So what kind of corporate culture is beneficial to the enterprise?

Obviously, the key to answer this question is enterprise human capital. First of all, how to establish a proper corporate culture is an integral part of corporate strategy, which requires entrepreneurs to make decisions based on their judgment. Generally speaking, the culture that can best adapt to the dynamic environment changes often needs to increase the decision-making authority of employees, strengthen the cooperation between departments, and make timely and accurate response to the environment. Secondly, how to create a culture that can adapt to the dynamic environment requires internal cooperation. In essence, it needs to be people-centered culture. A corporation need to value talents and use good talents. This reflects the important strategic position of human capital in corporate culture.

2. Human capital and accumulation learning

According to the theory of enterprise capability, organizational learning is the fundamental way to establish and continuously strengthen the core competence of an enterprise. The core competence comes from the collective learning of the enterprise organization, and comes from the transmission of experience. The accumulation of core competence should go through the accumulation and integration of internal resources, knowledge and technology. If the knowledge and experience acquired by individuals in the organization become the ability "gene," then the knowledge system formed by a team through learning in the enterprise organization constitutes a single core competence, and the different learning of the whole organization should integrate the single core competence to form a capability system, so as to form the core competitiveness of the enterprise. Generally speaking, through learning and knowledge sharing, the ability and knowledge of individuals can be transformed into the organizational ability and knowledge. As a result, enterprise human capital, and ultimately bring competitiveness and economic profits to enterprises.

3. Human capital and entrepreneurship

Entrepreneurship can be understood as the systematic innovation spirit widely existing in all fields of society, and it is the basis for enterprises to exist in the market. At the same time, there is no doubt that entrepreneurship is a kind of special human capital, which plays an important role in the development of enterprises.

The entrepreneur's position in the enterprise is the highest decision maker to make innovation decision. On the one hand, entrepreneurs' innovation decision-making needs to be based on the grasp of market opportunities and future development, so as to realize the source of cultivating new competitive advantages. On the other hand, the innovation decision-making of entrepreneurs also realizes the survival of the fittest in the market. For specific enterprises, the innovation decision-making of entrepreneurs must do some adjustments with the change of environment. Therefore, the essence of entrepreneurship is to obtain excess profits through innovation in the fierce market competition, which is the original power of enterprise organizational learning, and also the basis of enterprise survival and development.

Generally speaking, from the microscopic perspective, human capital is the real source of core competitiveness and value-added of enterprises, and it is also a crucial factor in the development strategy of enterprises.

8.4. Human Capital Investment Strategies in China

To accelerate the accumulation of human capital and adapt to the transformation and upgrading of a country's economy, the key point lies in improving the skills of human capital. It is important to form a division of labor, a cooperation system and a human capital structure suitable for the industrial development. Therefore, it is necessary to reform and explore a new path of human capital accumulation.

From the actual situation of China, it is very difficult to set up a group of talents who master the world up to date technology in the short term. Therefore, it is reasonable to be an imitative innovator or low-cost producer of successful products in the world market. Such economic transformation and upgrading urgently needs a large number of skilled, reasonable structure, production focused technical and skilled personnel, who undertake the task of transforming scientific research achievements into real productivity. Technical talents can carry out production process design, equipment debugging, product production and other related work, and can solve the sudden problems in production. However, there is a huge gap between the actual human capital and the needs. At the same time, the technological progress brought by the era of artificial intelligence has put forward higher requirements for human capital. In the face of such a form, we must choose the scientific path of human capital accumulation.

1. The state should speed up the macro planning of human capital accumulation in industrial transformation and upgrading

The accumulation of human capital needs the guidance of the government from a macro perspective. The government needs to improve the laws and regulations related to the accumulation of human capital, and amend and supplement the relevant laws and regulations on the design of human capital. For example, in the labor law, the definition of human capital accumulation needs to be more clear and detailed. "Vocational Education Law" should pay more attention to the provisions of vocational education funds. Through the construction of laws and regulations, the problem of insufficient investment in vocational education and on-the-job training caused by the incomplete competition of human capital market should be adjusted. To ensure that enterprises have sufficient resources to invest in on-the-job training, there must be some requirements for enterprises on the quality of human capital.

At the same time, we can consider and improve the security system arrangement of human capital accumulation, deepen the reform of intellectual property rights system, and clarify the ownership of property rights. For a long time, there is a big vacancy in the protection of intellectual property rights in China, and the protection of intellectual property rights has always been the most important institutional condition to stimulate enterprises to innovate and form a market environment of division and cooperation. Nowadays, most enterprises in China take technological imitation and technological innovation as the main development mode. The protection of intellectual property rights plays a decisive role in the production and development of these enterprises. Therefore, through the establishment and strengthening of intellectual property system, it is conducive to innovative enterprises to transform innovation and research into commercial products, and also can ensure that skilled human capital can obtain sufficient income, which can effectively mobilize innovation enthusiasm.

Finally, the country also needs to try to establish a relatively perfect labor market, so that enterprises can develop their own internal income distribution system. In this case, the price of labor market can accurately reflect the supply and demand of labor. The price orientation of labor market can not only determine the flow of existing talents among different industries, but also be the vane of talent reserve in the future. The mature labor market mechanism can not only play the role of price guidance and regulation of supply and demand, but also have a positive guidance on the price of scarce labor resources. To a certain extent, it can deal with the plight of shortage of technical and skilled human capital, which makes enterprises form a reasonable income distribution mechanism and form positive incentives.

2. The government should speed up the resource orientation of human resource accumulation

In terms of the accumulation of human capital, the government should play a guiding role, issue relevant government documents, and emphasize the system and environment construction of human capital accumulation. In the guidance process, it is necessary to plan the human capital system in line with economic development in advance, not blindly pursue high-quality and service-oriented talents for the development of emerging industries and tertiary industries, but to guide the accumulation of human capital based on the long-term economic development. In addition, the government should encourage the formation of enterprises as the theme to lead the path of industrial transformation and upgrading, and guide enterprises to increase human capital investment and innovation investment. The government can adopt comprehensive means to promote the scientific outlook on talents and employment, lead the social fashion of attaching importance to talents, and create a good social environment for human capital accumulation. Guided by culture, the core values of human capital accumulation should be formed through the combination of systems and policies. At the same time, we should improve the government incentive mechanism to form a social atmosphere conducive to the accumulation of skilled talents. Finally, the government needs to guide enterprises, families and individuals to play a leading role in the accumulation of human capital. On the one hand, we should deepen the market reform and speed up the formation of human capital market mechanism, so as to solve the problem of the surplus of middle and low-end talents and the shortage of skilled human capital. On the other hand, it is necessary to highlight the leading role of price in human capital market, so as to ensure that all kinds of human capital can obtain reasonable wage. At the same time, the government should also strengthen the construction of public information platform, improve the enthusiasm of social participation in human capital investment, and build learning organizations. Finally, we should pay attention to the positive impact of school enterprise linkage on human capital accumulation. In the current period of shortage and transformation of human capital, we need to pay attention to the supply market of human capital, that is, the education system. The government should promote the cooperation between schools and enterprises and try to reach the equilibrium of supply and demand in human capital market, so that schools can cultivate high-quality human capital suitable for market demand.

With the development and maturity of China's market economy, the state should pay more attention to the role of market in resource allocation. This idea also applies to the human capital market. Therefore, the main responsibility of the government is to create a system and environment that can promote the accumulation of human capital. Learning from the experience of developed countries, we should develop education, optimize the structure of education, encourage R&D and innovation of enterprises, support small and medium-sized enterprises to innovate, and cultivate local brands. At the same time, enterprises should be encouraged to cultivate the spirit of craftsmen and cultivate employees' sense of achievement and pride. In addition, we can consider starting from the demand of the labor market, focus on building a new education and training system, and improve the scale and quality of human capital as a whole.

Under the government's policy guidance and resource support, enterprises need to pay attention to training, education investment, and human capital management. Enterprises need to promote the transformation and long-term development of enterprises from multiple levels. Therefore, how to accelerate the accumulation of human capital and build a reasonable framework are the key issues that Chinese enterprises need to think about and deal with.

1. Manufacturing enterprises should make clear their development orientation and attach importance to the accumulation of human capital

The purpose of enterprises to define their own positioning is to understand the situation and future development direction of China's industrial development. According to the needs of enterprises' survival, development and the future trend of transformation and upgrading, under the premise of the government's formulation of human capital accumulation policy, enterprises need to recognize the situation according to actual needs, clarify their positioning and take action as soon as possible. Enterprises should deeply understand the importance of technological progress and human capital, and form a stable staff team with high professional quality, which is an important motivation for the development of enterprises.

Enterprises should establish a reasonable human capital structure. On the one hand, we should actively connect with schools, carry out professional talent training, reduce search costs, and participate in the work of school enterprise cooperation in talent training. Through school and enterprise cooperation, we can better improve the quality of personnel training, cultivate employees' loyalty, and support practical teaching. In addition, we should realize that human capital can increase value, bring wealth to enterprises, and increase income by sharing enterprise development, so as to better carry out self-investment and accumulate human capital. Enterprises can also increase the investment in human capital to obtain the benefits brought by the improvement of labor productivity, better play the main role in the process of human capital accumulation, and give full play to the learning by doing effect and spillover effect of human capital.

With the continuous development of the times, companies need to adopt new ways of human capital accumulation, such as providing platforms to encourage employees to innovate and start businesses. Faced with the Internet economy and industrial transformation, enterprises should seize the opportunity to tap the enthusiasm of existing employees in human capital accumulation. Some incentives can be used to provide the quality of existing human capital. Enterprises can encourage employees to participate in skills training to meet the requirements of technical progress and innovation to meet the needs of enterprise transformation and upgrading. Enterprises can encourage employees to consciously participate in multi skill on-the-job training, adapt to the flexibility of job rotation, and improve production efficiency. In addition, enterprises should adapt to the characteristics of the times, adjust the enterprise management mode, integrate Internet thinking, and strengthen the flexibility of enterprise management system, so as to meet the requirements of the times and achieve the purpose of encouraging talents.

2. Enterprises should consider reconstructing the incentive mechanism of human capital accumulation

According to the hypothesis of rational man and the theory of human capital, human capital has different levels of needs. Enterprises can not only start from the production needs, but also think more about human capital incentives from the internal stimulation of employees, reduce employee turnover, and maintain a stable talent team, so as to achieve long-term sustainable development. In view of the serious shortage of high skilled human capital, enterprises can consider providing long-term labor contracts for specialized human capital. The realization path of high skilled human capital in enterprises is mainly through school education, which is formed by the accumulation of long-term knowledge, experience and skills. Only when enterprises pay more attention to the establishment of human capital, provide employees with long-term labor contracts and stable working environment, and cultivate their sense of belonging, will employees be willing to invest in special skills for a long-term plan. Long term contract not only makes employees and enterprises closely linked together, but also brings a sense of security and belonging to employees, forming a psychological contract. Finally, it can promote the accumulation of skilled human capital and the industrial transformation and upgrading.

Chapter 9

STRUCTURE AND INEQUALITY

9.1. INTRODUCTION

Nowadays, China has entered a new stage of economic development, and economic growth has gradually changed from high-speed development to medium high-speed development. Since the reform and opening up, China has taken the pursuit of high economic growth rate as its main goal. However, sacrificing environment natural resource, the pursuit of economic growth rate has brought a series of problems, such as the widening of the income gap between residents, the imbalance of regional economic development, the huge difference between urban and rural economic development, and the imbalance of industrial structure. Among them, the most obvious problem is that the income gap of residents continues to expand, which is the reason for the imbalance regional development between urban and rural areas in China. Therefore, in today's society, how to solve the problem of the existence of income gap is a crucial issue. The Chinese government is also deeply aware of the problem and tries to solve the income gap between urban and rural areas, and has taken a series of measures to narrow the income gap between urban and rural areas, such as providing agricultural subsidies, increasing the construction of agricultural infrastructure, targeted poverty alleviation, giving tax incentives, and building a modern agricultural industrial system. Since 2009, China's urban-rural income gap has shown a downward trend, but the decline rate is relatively slow.

According to the definition of Lorenz curve, Gini, an Italian scholar in the early 20th century, set up an index to judge the fairness of annual income distribution, which is a proportional coefficient between 0 and 1. At this time, the smaller the value is, the more equitable the income distribution is, and the larger the value is, the more serious the polarization between the rich and the poor is. According to the relevant provisions of the United Nations on Gini coefficient:

- When Gini coefficient is lower than 0.2, income distribution is absolutely fair;
- When the Gini coefficient is between 0.2 and 0.3, the income distribution is relatively average;
- When the Gini coefficient is between 0.3 and 0.4, the income distribution is relatively reasonable;
- When the Gini coefficient is between 0.4 and 0.5, the income gap is large;
- When the Gini coefficient is higher than 0.5, the income gap is wide.

According to the data released by the National Bureau of statistics, China's Gini coefficient in 2017 was 0.407, which decreased by 16.94% compared with 2009. But it is undeniable that China's Gini coefficient has been maintained between 0.4 and 0.5, which means that the income gap is quite large.

Because of such unreasonable income distribution, the key point lies in the unbalanced allocation of capital, labor, technology and other elements between urban and rural areas. The essence of industrial structure optimization and upgrading is to reallocate capital and other production factors. From this perspective, industrial structure upgrading has the effect of urban and rural income distribution. Some scholars also pointed out that the adjustment and upgrading of industrial structure will indirectly affect the income of urban and rural residents by affecting the employment structure of urban and rural residents and the process of urban-rural integration. The practice of various countries also shows that the optimization and upgrading of industrial structure is an important reason affecting income distribution.

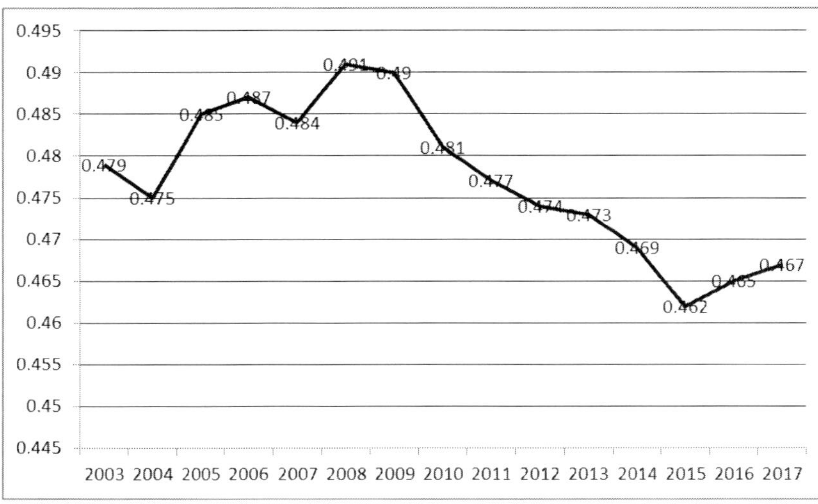

Source: China Statistical Yearbook from 2003 to 2017.

Figure 9.1.1. Gini coefficient in China from 2003 to 2017.

At the same time, with the progress of science and technology, the value of knowledge is gradually highlighted. Human capital, like labor and material capital, has become an important resource for economic growth. Nowadays, if China wants to realize economic transformation and upgrading, it cannot do without the investment of human capital. In other words, the competition between countries and regions is more about the competition for high-tech talents. The regional imbalance in China is precisely because of the large difference in human capital, which aggravates the income gap between urban and rural residents. In addition, human capital plays an important role in the optimization and upgrading of industrial structure. The upgrading of industrial structure needs coordination with human capital base. The quantity, structure and quality of human capital have a certain impact on the process of industrial structure optimization and upgrading, which determines the speed, direction and effect of industrial structure upgrading. In a word, the upgrading of industrial structure is inseparable from the matching quantity and structure of human capital. Human capital and the upgrading of industrial structure are important factors that affect the income gap and spatial imbalance between urban and rural areas and the upgrading of industrial structure cannot do without the matching human capital.

9.2. Upgrading Industrial Structure

In essence, the upgrading of industrial structure is the transformation from traditional low efficiency and low value-added labor-intensive industries to high efficiency and high-value-added capital, knowledge and technology intensive industries. The development of industry depends on the input of various resource elements. Therefore, with the rapid development of capital and technology intensive industry and service industry in China, capital, high-quality labor and technical factors have become the most important production factors in the new period. China is an economic system of distribution according to the factors of production. Under this system, the marginal reward of factor owners depends on the marginal productivity of each factor, and directly affects the income of factor owners. Therefore, with the upgrading of industrial structure, capital, high-quality labor and technology are relatively scarce, which, to a certain extent, improves the marginal productivity of these production factors, and thus determines the relative increase of the income level of the relevant factor owners.

From the perspective of urban-rural differences, with the continuous upgrading of industrial structure, the advantages of urban elements and resources are gradually highlighted, there is capital, technology and other resource agglomeration effects in urban areas, and promote the development of capital intensive industry and technology intensive industry. In this case, urban productivity is improved easier than rural productivity. Accordingly, urban residents occupy most of the welfare brought by the upgrading of industrial structure by virtue of their higher quality and labor skills, and the income of urban residents continues to increase.

However, with the upgrading of industrial structure in rural areas, the rural income has not increased but decreased for a long time. On the one hand, due to the lack of capital, technology and other production factors in rural areas, it is difficult to upgrade the rural industrial structure. Rural areas are still heavily reliant on the primary industry, with low production efficiency and low modernization level. Naturally, the agricultural income of rural residents cannot be very high. At the same time, with the upgrading of the industrial structure, the proportion of the primary industry in the national economy has been declining, and machine production has gradually replaced part of the labor force, which has gradually highlighted the problem of rural hidden unemployment This part of the labor force is not qualified with the work in the urban industrial sector due to their relatively low skills and quality. On the other hand, with the further development of capital intensive and technology intensive industries in cities and towns, the employment structure dominated by traditional labor-intensive industries will be changed, and better requirements for the quality of labor force will be put forward. This will make the rural labor force more unattractive in the labor market and lead to structural unemployment. Migrant workers that city can absorb some surplus labor from the countryside, but there are many obstacles to the rural labor force for their flowing to the city, such as the registered residence system in cities, the employment restriction of the peasant workers, and the discrimination in employment. Due to the existence of the law of factor flow, the rural high-quality or relatively rich labor force will be permanently transferred to cities and towns, resulting in the overflow of talents and funds in rural areas. This will not be conducive to the development of rural township enterprises, and the productivity of rural factors will continue to decline.

The result of the upgrading of industrial structure is that the tertiary industry dominated by service industry gradually occupies a dominant position. From the perspective of cities and towns, the development and accumulation of industrial industry has provided economic basis for the development of tertiary industry since the reform and opening up. At the same time, the tertiary industry has the characteristics of light assets. Its initial investment cost is relatively low. But it can absorb a large number of labor forces. As a result, the tertiary industry can get rapid development in the city, and create a large number of jobs. Within them, most of the jobs have relatively low requirements for labor quality. At this time, the rural surplus labor force, driven by the urban high income, will also timely adjust their quality and constantly transfer to the city. At this time, the upgrading of industrial structure will speed up the transfer of relatively high-quality rural labor force to the city, accelerate the urbanization of China and broaden the channels for rural labor to obtain non-agricultural income.

In addition, the implementation of a series of policies inclined to rural areas in the later stage of the country will help the labor force obtain higher income than that when working in the rural areas With the transfer of departments, the former unemployed residents in rural areas can get employment in rural areas, which can improve the rural agricultural productivity and increase farmers' income to a certain extent. With the development of urban industrial structure into a more mature period, capital intensive industries and technology intensive industries will show obvious spillover effect, which will play a leading role in the upgrading of rural industrial structure. Capital, technology and other factors of production began to transfer to rural areas, which will be conducive to the upgrading of rural industrial structure, improve the level of rural agricultural modernization, and ultimately increase the average income of rural residents.

To sum up, the upgrading of industrial structure mainly affects the income gap between urban and rural areas by affecting the income of urban and rural internal factor owners. The upgrading of industrial institutions in a region is often caused by the upgrading of urban industrial structure, which shows the flow of labor, capital, technology and other production factors from rural to urban areas. Due to the factor aggregation effect in urban areas, it will further promote the optimization and upgrading of urban industrial structure, and promote the large-scale development of related industries. Consequently, the income of urban residents will continue to increase. For rural residents, the impact of industrial structure upgrading on rural residents' income is periodic. With the upgrading of industrial structure, the further development of capital intensive industries in cities and towns will change the demand structure of the labor market. In the early stage, it will lead to serious problem of structural unemployment. At the same time, the income of rural residents is mainly from agricultural income. With the decline of rural productivity, farmers' agricultural income is also declining, thus widening the income gap with urban residents. After the upgrading of the industrial structure, the tertiary industry gradually occupies a dominant position and can absorb part of the rural force surplus labor force. At the same time, the state tends to support agriculture and guide rural residents to improve their own quality. Therefore, the upgrading of industrial structure in this stage will help to increase the non-agricultural income of rural residents. At the same time, the spillover effect of urban industrial structure will lead to the gradual increase of rural overall productivity and the agricultural income of rural residents. The income gap between urban and rural areas will gradually narrow.

Therefore, in the long run, the upgrading of industrial structure has a phased impact on the urban and rural income gap. In the early stage of industrial structure upgrading, the income gap between urban and rural areas gradually widened. With the gradual development of the tertiary industry, the income gap between urban and rural areas will gradually narrow.

9.3. Human Capital and Industrial Structure Upgrading

According to the relevant theories of human capital, human capital and labor quality are the important reasons that affect the income gap between urban and rural areas. Human capital influences economic growth, residents' income and industrial structure upgrading mainly through factor substitution and production effect, spatial agglomeration and spillover effect, resource allocation effect and technological progress effect.

1. Factor growth and production effect

With the development of economy, the traditional material capital is no longer the primary factor of modern production. At the same time, human capital has gradually become the most important factor of production in market competition. Human capital refers to the collection of all kinds of knowledge, labor, management skills and health quality of labor force. Different from the traditional factors of production, the output effect of human capital input has the characteristics of increasing returns to scale. The direct investment of human capital into production can improve the production efficiency of other production factors, and then improve its own labor productivity. This is because the material capital must be combined with people in order to have production capacity, and human capital as a factor of production has initiative, can improve the relationship between workers and other factors of production. In other words, human capital has positive externalities.

2. Spatial agglomeration and spillover effect

Because of the regional development differences, it also makes the return of human capital investment biased. At the same time, human capital has liquidity, so high-quality human capital will move to developed areas to pursue higher returns. With the regional agglomeration of human capital, human capital elements will produce positive externalities and form scale effect on the whole. At the same time, the spatial agglomeration and spillover effect of human capital will provide a strong driving force for the economic development of concentrated regions and promote the development of regional economy. This process can also further strengthen the effect of human capital agglomeration and spillover, and promote high-quality human capital to realize its effect and obtain higher income. In addition, with the accumulation of high-quality human capital, regional competition will further stimulate stronger productivity. It can also promote regional economic development and a new round of industrial structure optimization and upgrading.

3. Resource allocation effect

The allocation effect of human capital means that, in the face of complex and changeable market, people can adjust and reallocate various production factors to cope with changes. Not for production effect, but as an economic subject, human capital is no longer regarded as a production factor. Human capital can improve the ability of workers to reallocate other factors of production, so as to promote the flow of other factors. For example, when the society has a new demand for talents, workers will increase their investment in themselves.

4. Effect of technological progress

Human capital is the decisive factor of technological progress and innovation. This is because technological innovation depends on people's professional knowledge and skills. The way to acquire these knowledge and skills is to invest in human capital. Technological innovation is an accidental human practice, but it cannot do without human initiative. This work must be done by people with high level of knowledge and skills. In addition, human capital is an important source of technological progress and innovation, and a necessary condition and foundation for technology diffusion and application. The regions with low technology level often need to introduce technology, and the human capital quality of the region determines the ability of introducing technology. Regions with higher human capital level tend to absorb and introduce technology more quickly, and on this basis, they are more likely to carry out further innovation. At the same time, workers with higher level of human capital can combine material capital with new technology more effectively, so as to use new technology more efficiently.

In addition to the economic effect of human capital, urban-rural income gap reveals the difference of urban and rural productivity. Human capital is an important factor in determining various factors of production. On the one hand, while the upgrading of industrial structure changes the supply and demand of various factors in the market economy, human capital itself, as an important factor of production, influences the supply and demand structure of various regional factors relying on its own economic effect. With the upgrading of industrial structure, the development of various industries will rely more on new production factors such as human capital. On the other hand, the production effect and technological progress effect of human capital will increase the marginal productivity of each factor, and then affect the income gap between urban and rural areas. The owners of human capital can promote the productivity of other factors as well as the productivity themselves. It can be said that the differences in human capital between urban and rural areas directly determine the difference of factor productivity, and then determine the income gap between urban and rural areas.

Specifically, in the mechanism of industrial structure affecting income gap, human capital has played a moderating role. First of all, human capital reduces the negative effect of urban-rural income gap expansion in the initial stage of industrial structure upgrading through production effect and resource allocation effect. Rural residents will identify the requirements of the market for labor according to the market employment information. Knowing the information, they can form their own human capital through education and training, so as to obtain more employment opportunities and obtain higher income. During this process, labor productivity will be promoted and competitive advantages can be cultivated in the labor market. With the overall improvement of regional human capital level, especially the improvement of rural human capital level, structural unemployment will naturally disappear in the process of upgrading industrial structure. Finally, the transfer of rural surplus labor force from the primary industry to the secondary industry and tertiary industry will be realized, and the income of rural residents will be increased. Meanwhile, along with the upgrading of industrial structure, rural human capital is accumulating continuously. Rural human capital has production effect and technological progress effect, which can narrow the income gap between rural areas and urban areas. The quality of human capital of rural residents often determines their ability to absorb and use advanced technology. Therefore, only higher quality rural human capital can play the role of urban technology diffusion, thus promoting the development of agricultural modernization. In addition, the linkage effect between urban and rural areas will further promote the process of urban-rural integration, and then narrow the urban-rural income gap.

In conclusion, the upgrading of industrial structure based on human capital can play a positive role in narrowing the income gap between urban and rural areas. In the process of upgrading the industrial structure, we must pay attention to improve the quality of rural workers and realize the integration of urban and rural areas.

Next, this chapter will further elaborate how the matching of human capital and industrial structure upgrading affects urban inequality from three dimensions including human capital stock, structure distribution and human capital quality.

1. The regulating function of human capital stock

Human capital stock plays a fundamental role in the income distribution effect of industrial structure upgrading. The upgrading of industrial structure in a region depends on a certain level of human capital. Generally, with the upgrading of industrial structure, a high level of human capital stock is needed to adapt to it. When the industrial structure is upgraded to a certain level, if the overall human capital stock is not enough, it will inevitably cause serious structural unemployment. The improvement of resource utilization efficiency of production factors depends on the level of human capital of labor force. From the perspective of urban and rural areas, with the upgrading of the industrial structure, the proportion of the primary industry has decreased significantly, the proportion of the secondary industry and the tertiary industry has gradually increased. However, the number of low skilled rural labor force is huge, and most of the rural labor force is difficult to smoothly realize the transfer from the primary industry to other industries, and is facing serious structural unemployment problem. Therefore, with the increase of rural human capital stock in a certain extent, it will improve the knowledge level of rural low skilled labor force, increase the employment opportunities of rural low skilled labor force to non-agricultural industry, link structural unemployment problem, and then weaken the problem of urban-rural income gap expansion in the initial stage of industrial structure upgrading. With the increase of rural human capital stock, it can promote the rational allocation of production factors between urban and rural areas, inhibit the expansion of urban-rural income gap in the early stage of industrial structure upgrading, and strengthen the reduction of urban-rural income gap in the later stage of industrial structure upgrading.

2. The adjustment function of human capital distribution structure

Compared with the human capital stock, the distribution structure of human capital has a greater impact on the income distribution effect of industrial structure upgrading. The upgrading of industrial structure is accompanied by the advancement of technology, which puts forward higher requirements for high-quality workers. Once a region lacks high-quality human capital, it is not conducive to the adjustment of regional industrial structure. For a long time, China has shown an obvious dual-economic phenomenon. Most of the high-quality human capital is concentrated in the cities, while the low-quality human capital is detained in the rural areas, which further aggravates the contradiction between the upgrading of industrial structure and the adjustment of employment structure, resulting in the difficulty of rural labor force to benefit from the upgrading of industrial structure. It restricts the upgrading of industrial structure and broadens the income gap between urban and rural areas.

In conclusion, the dual structure of urban and rural human capital is an important reason for the upgrading of industrial structure and it may lead to the difficulty in narrowing the income gap between urban and rural residents. The dual structure of urban and rural human capital plays a negative role in the whole stage of industrial structure upgrading, affecting urban and rural income distribution. This dual structure will significantly enlarge the effect of industrial structure upgrading on urban-rural income gap. Because of the high level of human capital, urban areas have a strong advantage in industrial development. At the same time, the spatial aggregation effect and spillover effect of human capital will strengthen the agglomeration of capital, technology and other elements resources in the process of industrial structure upgrading. The agglomeration effect will further promote a new round of industrial structure upgrading. The new round of industrial structure upgrading will accelerate the factor resources gathering in the city, and then expand the scale effect of urban industrial development. However, due to the low quality of production factors after the upgrading of rural structure, it is difficult for rural labor force to flow to the city, which is not conducive to the increase of rural residents' income.

3. The regulating function of human capital quality

Human capital not only matches the upgrading of industrial structure in quantity, but also matches industrial structure in types. Only by matching the structure and type can the upgrading of industrial structure play a role in narrowing the gap between urban and rural areas as soon as possible. The most important reason is the mismatch between human capital structure and industrial structure. With the upgrading of industrial structure, the demand for high-quality human capital is higher and higher. In reality, China has a large number of low-quality human capitals and the internal structure of human capital cannot be adjusted in a short time, which will inevitably lead to the problems of structural unemployment.

Scholars generally believe that human capital has obvious heterogeneity. Generally speaking, the higher the education level and the higher the technical literacy, the stronger the role of human capital in promoting economic growth, technological progress and innovation. In the income distribution effect caused by the upgrading of industrial structure, the economic effect of higher quality human capital is higher than that of low quality human capital, so it can adapt to the employment fluctuation caused by industrial structure upgrading faster.

In reality, with the optimization of the internal structure of human capital, the quality difference of urban and rural human capital will be greater, which will aggravate the effect of industrial structure upgrading on the expansion of urban-rural income gap in the early time. The optimization of the internal structure of human capital most directly depends on the higher quality human capital investment of urban and rural residents. However, in reality, the willingness of urban and rural residents to make high-quality human capital investment is quite different. Compared with the rural areas, the urban departments have the awareness of cultivating a good environment for human capital to make self-investment to a certain extent. Due to the high quality of human capital, urban residents get more benefits from the upgrading of industrial structure. They can timely grasp the market demand for high-quality human capital, strengthen their own human capital investment, timely adjust and optimize the structure of human capital, so as to adapt to the industrial structure caused by employment structure fluctuations, and always in a dominant position in the employment market. On the contrary, because of their low quality, rural residents can not enjoy the dividend brought by the industrial structure, which will lead to their low willingness to invest in themselves. This difference in human capital investment between urban and rural areas will lead to the further expansion of the quality gap between urban and rural human capital. This will further aggravate the widening income gap between urban and rural areas. The cycle of the two is not conducive to narrowing the income gap between urban and rural areas.

Specifically, with the optimization of the internal structure of human capital, rural areas rely on the stock of human resources to improve the quality of human capital. With the continuous improvement of the quality of rural residents, their employment opportunities in urban non-agricultural sectors will be greater. At the same time, the high income of the city will also drive part of the labor force to migrate to the city permanently. The urban area is the gathering area of high-quality human capital. In a long period of time, it can give full play to the spatial agglomeration and spillover effects brought by high-quality human capital, promote regional technological progress, promote industrial scale expansion, improve production efficiency, and then increase the income of urban residents. Of course, with the passage of time, high-quality human capital will play a positive role in the change of urban-rural income gap through the role of technological progress and technology diffusion.

9.4. Findings and Discussion

From the macroscopic level of China, the increase of human capital stock, the imbalance of human capital spatial distribution and the quality of human capital will affect the income gap between urban and rural areas. With the overall improvement of China's human capital stock, the problem of unbalanced distribution of urban and rural human capital is more serious. And it will restrict the upgrading of the industrial structure between urban and rural areas.

From the regional level, first of all, there is an obvious gap between urban and rural income distribution effect of industrial structure upgrading in different regions. At present, the upgrading of industrial structure in the eastern region is conducive to narrowing the income gap between urban and rural areas, while the central and western regions are still dominated by heavy industry due to the low level of industrial structure upgrading, so the upgrading of industrial structure will expand the income gap between urban and rural areas. This shows that the impact of industrial structure upgrading on the urban-rural income gap is periodic.

When the level of industrial structure is low, the upgrading of industrial structure will expand the income gap between urban and rural areas, but when the upgrading level of industrial structure reaches a certain level, the upgrading of industrial structure can expand the income gap between urban and rural areas. Among them, there are differences in the regulation of the stock, spatial distribution and quality of human capital. The increase of human capital stock in eastern China and the imbalance of urban and rural human capital distribution inhibit the upgrading of industrial structure and narrow the income gap between urban and rural areas, while the optimization of internal structure of human capital plays an inverted U-shaped regulatory role. The improvement of human capital stock and the optimization of internal structure in Central China will always enlarge the income gap between urban and rural areas due to the upgrading of industrial structure. The increase of human capital stock in the western region will inhibit the expansion of industrial structure upgrading on the income gap between urban and rural areas, while the unbalanced distribution of urban and rural human capital and the optimization of internal structure will amplify this effect.

Therefore, on the one hand, the early upgrading of industrial structure is mainly realized as the adjustment and optimization of urban industrial structure, the flow of labor, capital, technology and other resources to the city, and a large number of effective resources gather in the city, resulting in the slow upgrading of rural industrial structure. Therefore, relevant policies and measures can be implemented to reduce the income gap between urban and rural areas by upgrading industrial structure

1. Promoting the rational distribution of resources between urban and rural areas

As for the upgrading for China's industrial structure, the government should pay more attention to the upgrading of industrial structure in rural areas. The government also needs to promote the development of agricultural modernization process. It is better to improve the marginal productivity of rural residents, and solve the long-standing hidden unemployment problem in rural areas. These measures can release the surplus labor force and provide space for the development of the secondary and tertiary industries in rural areas, so as to broaden the source of farmers' income and increase their income. However, in reality, the lack of funds and technology in rural areas leads to the slow upgrading of rural industrial structure. Therefore, the government should give more preferential policies to rural areas and increase financial expenditure on rural areas,

2. In the city, we should pay attention to the development of modern service industry

In the process of promoting the upgrading of urban industrial structure, the government should attach importance to the development of modern service industry and spare all efforts for the absorption capacity of light industry and tertiary industry to rural surplus labor force. Meanwhile, the government needs to continue to push ahead with economic restructuring, gradually reducing registered residence system, wage and housing barriers, and realizing the flow of human capital between urban and rural areas, and increasing farmers' income.

3. The government should devote to the interaction between the upgrading of industrial structure and the process of urban-rural integration

The government should strengthen the layout awareness of the development of industrial structure and realize the complementarity of urban and rural industrial development. At the same time, we should improve the integration of urban and rural social security, so that rural residents who are employed in urban areas can enjoy the same welfare treatment as urban residents, and fully enjoy the reform dividend brought by industrial structure upgrading and technological progress.

On the other hand, human capital plays an important role in the urban and rural income distribution of industrial structure upgrading. The upgrading of industrial structure is inseparable from the matching quantity, structure and quality of human capital. Therefore, first of all, the government should pay attention to the accumulation of rural human capital and increase public investment in rural education and medical care. At the beginning of industrial structure upgrading, a series of structural unemployment problems are mainly due to the low level of human capital of rural residents, which is difficult to meet the needs of urban industrial structure upgrading for higher quality labor. To fundamentally reduce the differences between urban and rural areas and between regions, the government must increase the accumulation of rural human capital, so that rural residents can achieve higher human capital reporting in the process of industrial structure upgrading. Secondly, the government should pay attention to optimizing the rational capital structure, especially the transformation from rural primary human capital to intermediate technical human capital. With the continuous development of industrial structure upgrading, the demand for high-level human capital is growing. Therefore, we should promote the rural labor force to meet the needs of technological progress and agricultural modernization. Finally, the government can try to guide and encourage college students to return home for employment and entrepreneurship, so as to realize the two-way flow of human capital between urban and rural areas. The government can attract high-level talents through preferential policies of rural employment to improve the quality of rural human capital.

Chapter 10

THE ROLE OF HUMAN CAPITAL

10.1. INTRODUCTION

The issue of economic growth and transformation has always been the focus of attention of all sectors of society, because it plays an irreplaceable role in the development of a country and social stability. This book introduces the relationship between human capital and technology diffusion, industrial structure adjustment, development strategy and unbalanced spatial development. We can find that the role of human capital is very obvious in the development and transformation stage of an economy, especially for a developing country like China. Therefore, this chapter will continue to elaborate the mechanism of human capital affecting economic growth and transformation, which is to find the answer to the question whether human capital plays the most important role.

10.2. PRODUCTION OF HUMAN CAPITAL

The special production function of human capital determines its significant correlation with the evolution of economic structure and economic growth. And it also determines the important position of human capital in economic activities. Therefore, we can analyze the role of human capital in economic development by analyzing the production function of human capital. From the perspective of human capital production process, it has two production functions including factor and efficiency.

10.2.1. The Production Function of Human Capital

The factor production function of human capital is an indispensable input factor in the process of human capital production. In the production process, in addition to the need to invest material capital, but also must invest human capital. The knowledge and skills of workers have become the core elements in a country's economic growth. From the course of economic development in various countries in the world, there are great differences in the situation of economic development among countries. The root cause lies in the level of labor productivity. Generally speaking, labor productivity is affected by human capital, material capital, technical knowledge and natural resources. For a long time, natural resources are the most important among the four factors affecting labor productivity. However, with the increasing advancement of science and technology, the importance of natural resources begins to decline in the specific production process, and the production function of human capital is more obvious. At the same time, the application of knowledge, the progress of technology and the innovation of management all depend on human capital in essence. Although both human capital and material capital are essential elements in the process of enterprise production and operation, the rate of return on investment of human capital is higher than that of material capital because of its subjective initiative in the production process. Therefore, human capital is the most active factor in economic activities.

10.2.2. Efficiency Production Function of Human Capital

The efficiency production function of human capital shows that human capital is the core element to improve the efficiency of labor production. This function is mainly realized through the following two ways.

- Firstly, the increase of human capital investment can bring about the improvement of production efficiency

As a result of education investment, the cultural quality of workers has been improved, which can make the workers' learning and adaptation ability stronger, and the time to learn new knowledge and master new skills is shorter. The investment in health will improve the physical quality of labor force, extend the necessary working time and improve the work efficiency per unit time. Investment in skills will lead to the improvement of other technical capabilities, which can make the laborer improve their work proficiency and improve the efficiency of resource utilization. The investment in on-the-job training can improve the management ability of the enterprise, reduce the internal transaction cost and reduce the production cost. From the above analysis, the more labor capital investment workers make, the greater the extent of their related quality and ability progress, and ultimately the higher the quality of labor production. Generally speaking, the stock and quality of human capital directly determine labor productivity. Therefore, if the input of other material resources remains unchanged in the production process, only relying on the improvement of labor quality can bring about the increase of output. In addition, workers' knowledge, skills, health and other qualities are difficult to be deprived or destroyed, as long as the labor force continues to exist. Once human capital can combine with other material resources, economic growth can be achieved.

- Secondly, the increase of human capital investment can improve the production efficiency of other input factors

Increasing the investment of human capital can improve the marginal productivity of other input factors used in production, so as to increase the output level of the whole production process per unit time. This phenomenon is called the external effect of human capital.

10.3. THE KNOWLEDGE EFFECTS OF HUMAN CAPITAL

The knowledge effect of human capital includes the demand effect, income effect and substitution effect of knowledge progress.

Firstly, from the perspective of knowledge progress demand effect of human capital, when the quality of human capital is poor, it is difficult to learn advanced production technology and management concepts. When the quality of human capital is high, the learning ability of labor for production technology and management concept will be improved, which can promote the improvement of labor productivity, and promote the further development, transformation and upgrading of a country's economy. In western countries, the improvement of the quality of human capital can lead to the input of other factors of production, including increasing the types of capital input, expanding the scope of capital input and using the relevant foreign available resources, and so on, which will lead to the improvement of output level.

Secondly, from the perspective of knowledge income effect of human capital, it means that the workers who have received relevant education and training will have higher productivity. Because these labor forces have more distinguishing ability in the market, they can make enterprises grasp more profit opportunities. In the era of knowledge economy, if the labor force has the relevant knowledge and skills of Internet, artificial intelligence and other skills required by emerging industries, it can help enterprises seize market opportunities and obtain new economic growth points.

Thirdly, from the perspective of knowledge substitution effect of human capital, in economic activities, with the development of science and technology, human capital can play a role of substitution for material capital to a certain extent. For the whole world economy, material capital is limited, so it can maintain a country's stable economic growth with the substitution of human capital. At the same time, the substitution effect is also reflected in the fact that human capital can weaken the adverse impact of the law of diminishing marginal utility of material capital on the economy.

The growth of knowledge economy comes from the innovation, dissemination and application of knowledge. The key to the innovation, dissemination and application of knowledge lies in the continuous investment in human capital. In other words, without effective and sustained human capital investment, there will be no knowledge economy. In modern economic society, due to the accumulation of relevant knowledge and experience of workers, the understanding of objective laws is gradually deepened. In this process, workers can better combine with material capital and reduce the contradiction between man and nature. It can also reduce some unnecessary waste and loss. Secondly, the improvement of the quality of workers leads to technological progress, thus increasing the labor growth rate and further promoting economic growth. In addition, due to the popularization of education, the subjective initiative and professionalism of workers are cultivated. In this case, relying on values is more conducive to sustainable economic growth.

10.4. Human Capital and Industrial Structure

The adjustment of industrial structure is a dynamic process, and it is also an important economic development problem faced with the whole world. Whether the industrial structure is reasonable is an important standard to judge whether the economy can develop healthily and sustainably. In essence, the process of economic growth can be seen as a process of continuous adjustment and upgrading with the industrial structure. On the one hand, the emergence of up-to-date industries will change the original industrial structure. On the other hand, the continuous shrinking of some traditional industries will also change the original industrial structure. The premise to ensure the smooth adjustment of industrial structure is the continuous improvement of the quality of human capital.

From the experience of world economic development, if a country's human capital and industrial structure can adapt to each other and develop together, it will play a huge role in promoting the development of the country's economy. Generally speaking, the process of economic development is the process of continuous adjustment and upgrading of industrial structure. The speed of industrial structure adjustment and upgrading also restricts the speed of economic development. In this process, the effective supply of human capital can accelerate the speed of industrial structure adjustment, and then accelerate the speed of economic development and transformation. The core problem of industrial structure adjustment is industrial transformation. Industrial transformation refers to the process of transferring from mature industry or declining industry to emerging industry or growing industry. At this point, we assume that there are only three sectors of society, including agriculture industry, manufacturing industry and services industry. In different period of economic development, the proportions of each sector in economic activities are different. In the early stage, agriculture industry accounted for the largest proportion of economic activities, and the contribution rate of human capital to economic growth was the lowest. At this time, economic growth mainly depends on the input of land and primary labor force. In the mid-term, the proportion of industry in economic activities is increasing, the requirements for labor quality are gradually improving, and the contribution rate of human capital to economic growth is also gradually increasing. In the post-industrial era, the service industry accounts for the largest proportion of economic activities. At the same time, human capital has the greatest contribution to economic growth and the optimization and upgrading of industrial structure.

The human capital situation of a country or region largely determines the efficiency and effect of industrial transformation and upgrading in that country or region. If a country's human capital supply is sufficient, it can provide necessary support for the establishment of the leading industry of knowledge economy. Generally speaking, industries with high human capital stock can respond to different needs of customers quickly, change product structure according to market demand, and finally promote the coordinated development of upstream and downstream industries. In addition, the process of industrial transformation and upgrading has largely changed the economic and technological links between the original industries, causing changes in the market. That is to say, enterprises with large stock of human capital can adapt to the quick market changes, even turbulence, and also adapt to the new market environment more quickly. It is worth noting that the transformation and upgrading of industrial structure must be based on the original industry and make full use of the relevant resources of the original industry. Human capital can significantly improve the elasticity of industrial resource transfer. Compared with ordinary labor force, high-quality labor force can adapt to the new environment more quickly and effectively. Therefore, industries with large human capital stock encounter relatively small resistance in industrial transformation and upgrading.

From the course of national development, countries with large stock of human capital are prone to trigger technological revolution, which is just an important driving force of a country's economic growth, and even a turning point of the times. The industrial revolution will first promote the adjustment and upgrading of the economic structure of developed countries, promote the export of related products of these countries, and further promote the adjustment and upgrading of the industrial structure of the whole world. To sum up, human capital is the motivation and determinant factor of industrial structure adjustment and upgrading. At the same time, the adjustment and upgrading of industrial structure in turn promotes the level of human capital stock again. The interaction between the two promotes the further economic growth of a country.

10.5. Human Capital and Employment

Human capital investment will also have a great impact on the employment of a country, mainly reflected in the two aspects of labor employment demand and labor employment supply.

10.5.1. The Impact of Human Capital Investment on Labor Employment Demand

Human capital investment itself, as an investment activity to improve the quality of labor force, will have a certain impact on the employment demand of a country or region.

Firstly, the promotion of human capital investment on labor employment demand is reflected in the formation process of human capital, that is, human capital investment itself can expand employment capacity and provide new employment opportunities. First of all, in order to improve the stock level of human capital in the region, it is necessary not only to increase the degree education support for labor force, but also to actively promote the development of vocational training education. In this process, with the gender male of vocational training institutions, vocational schools, technical schools and so on, a large number of jobs will be increased and a large number of employees will be absorbed. Secondly, the investment in human capital can also promote the further investment of material capital, and then play a certain role in promoting employment. Material capital investment also plays a positive role in supporting the improvement of human capital level. For example, if we want to vigorously set up academic education, vocational training institutions, vocational schools and technical schools to improve the level of human capital stock, we must invest a certain amount of material capital such as houses, tables and chairs, teaching materials. The health investment of labor force needs a certain amount of physical capital investment, such as health board institutions, fitness venues, equipment and so on. Investment in labor technology and skill progress also requires a certain amount of field capital investment, such as operating machines and sites. Similarly, scientific research and invention also requires a certain amount of investment in instruments, equipment and laboratories. The occurrence of the above shows that human capital investment can promote the further development of related industries and enterprises, so as to create more job opportunities and absorb more labor employment.

Secondly, human capital investment will create more job opportunities in the process of output and income, and further reduce the employment night, thus having an indirect impact on labor employment demand to a certain extent. First of all, human capital investment can improve the level of labor productivity and economic efficiency of enterprises, so as to expand the market share of related products and services. At the same time, the scale of enterprises will also expand. Therefore, enterprises can absorb more labor force to enter the enterprise for employment. The improvement of employees' professional quality, practical operation ability, professional labor skills and the ability to adapt and accept new technology and new equipment all come from continuous human capital investment. This situation enables the same worker to make full and reasonable use of more input factors in other production processes under the same other production conditions, so as to improve the level of labor productivity and promote the growth of enterprises. Generally speaking, the more enterprises attach importance to on-the-job training of employees, the better the quality of their products or services, thus making them more competitive in the market. It is of great strategic significance for enterprises to improve the market share of relevant products and services to solve the employment problem and economic growth problem of a country or region. Secondly, human capital investment can not only promote the economic growth of a country or region, but also increase the number of employed population in a country or region. Many scholars' research on human capital theory and economic growth theory shows that when the economic and social development to a certain extent, the contribution of human capital investment to economic growth is more important than material capital. Half said that there is a significant positive correlation between the economic growth rate and the employment level, that is, if the economic growth rate of a country or region is slow or even retrogressive, then the demand for labor in the country or region will naturally decrease. Related to it, if the economic growth of a country or region tells growth, then the demand for labor in that country or region will naturally increase. In other words, a country's labor employment depends on the economic development, and human capital investment is exactly the main factor of economic growth to the East. Therefore, sustainable and reasonable investment in human capital can not only promote economic growth, but also reduce the unemployment rate.

10.5.2. The Impact of Human Capital Investment on Labor Employment Supply

Firstly, human capital investment can delay the employment of some workers to a certain extent. This situation can appropriately reduce the current employment pressure. For example, in 2020, the world will face a new epidemic, global economic development will almost stagnate, and a large number of enterprises will go bankrupt. As a result, China has expanded the scale of graduate enrollment in order to postpone the employment of some workers, improve the quality of the labor force, and appropriately reduce the employment pressure under the epidemic situation. First of all, for the whole society, human capital investment methods such as diploma education, pre job training and continuing education can not only increase the human capital stock of newly added labor force, the number of workers receiving education and training, and the time for workers to receive education, but also delay the time for them to enter the labor market. In this way, we can absorb a certain number of new labor force that should have flowed into the labor market in the way of "learning" in a certain period of time, thus playing an important role in easing the current employment pressure. Secondly, through the forms of human capital investment, such as laid-off training, job transfer training and continuing education, the laid-off and about to be laid-off personnel can enter vocational training institutions, vocational schools, technical schools or regular colleges and universities to improve and improve their human capital level, rather than let them directly enter the labor market. Finally, it can alleviate the current employment pressure.

Secondly, the continuous investment in human capital can provide more labor supply with higher human capital stock level, and reduce the labor supply quantity with lower human capital stock level. The above methods can alleviate the structural unemployment and adjust the structural imbalance of labor supply and demand to a certain extent. The structural imbalance of labor supply and demand will lead to the coexistence of long-term vacancies of highly technical and professional jobs, rising unemployment rate and long-term crowding of general posts. With the continuous transformation and upgrading of the industrial structure of a country and region, emerging industries will continue to develop. If the supply of high-quality labor is insufficient, and the labor demand and supply do not match, the employment pressure of related industries will be more and more serious. By increasing the investment in knowledge, skills and health of workers, the stock of human capital is gradually increased, which further improves the ability of labor force to choose jobs and adapt to the position. Only by solving the problem of low human capital stock in some industries can a country or region fundamentally solve the problem of employment structural imbalance.

Based on the above analysis, human capital plays a decisive role in promoting economic growth. For a country or region, human capital investment can affect economic growth through the factor production capacity of human capital, the efficiency production function of human capital, and the knowledge effect of human capital. It can also take human capital investment as a starting point to promote the adjustment and upgrading of industrial structure, promote the balance of labor market and affect economic growth. In view of the important role of human capital in modern economic development, if a country or region vigorously improves the stock and quality of human capital, and maintains the investment in human capital, it will achieve stable economic growth and virtuous circle.

Chapter 11

A THEORETICAL MODEL

11.1. INTRODUCTION

The theoretical analysis in this chapter aims to wrap up all those analyses in earlier chapters. In this chapter we will build a theoretical model in which we deliberately avoid explicit mentioning of technological progress and capital accumulation as factors that foster economic growth and transformation. Our aim in building the model in this chapter is simply to reveal the fact that besides factors such as technological progress and capital accumulation, other important factors may also contribute to China's rapid growth and development over the past decades. Therefore, this chapter is an integral part of the present study in the sense that it aims to complement and wrap up all the analyses of the earlier chapters. An abridged version of the model analysis below was contained in one of the authors' earlier work Jiang (2016).

11.2. An Infra-Marginal Analysis

In this section, we present a brief description of Cheng, Sachs, and Yang (2000)'s infra-marginal analysis of the Ricardian Model, which will form the basis of the theoretical model in the next section.

There are two countries in the world, Country Home (H) and Country Foreign (F). Each country has only one factor of production, human capital, and each country is able to produce two goods, x and y. Each individual in both countries is endowed with one unit of human capital, and the total number of individuals is L in Home and L^* in Foreign. Individuals within a country are assumed to be identical. The utility function for the representative consumer-producer in Home is assumed to take the Cobb-Douglas form:

$$U = (x + k\hat{x})^{\alpha} (y + k\hat{y})^{1-\alpha}$$

where x and y are quantities of good x and good y that are produced *and* consumed by the representative Home consumer-producer, while $\hat{x}$ and $\hat{y}$ are quantities of good x and good y that are produced in Foreign but consumed by the representative Home consumer (i.e., imported goods the Home consumer consumes). k is the transaction efficiency coefficient, $0 < k < 1$. The transaction cost is assumed to take the iceberg form: for each unit of a good bought, the buyer only receives k units of the good (i.e., when the buyer pays one dollar, he gets only k dollars' worth of the good, $0 < k < 1$); the rest is lost in transit. The transaction cost may result from different sources: costs of storage, costs of transportation, and costs of finding a transaction partner, to name only a few.

Analogously, the utility function of the representative consumer in Foreign is:

$$U^* = (x^* + k\hat{x}^*)^{\alpha} (y^* + k\hat{y}^*)^{1-\alpha}$$

where x^* and y^* are quantities of good x and good y that are produced and consumed by the representative Foreign consumer-producer, while $\widehat{x}^*$ and $\widehat{y}^*$ are quantities of good x and good y that are produced in Home but consumed by the Foreign consumer (i.e., imports the Foreign consumer consumes). The unit human capital requirements for good x and good y are a_x and a_y respectively in Home and are a_x^* and a_y^* respectively in Foreign. Therefore the production function for each consumer-producer in Home is:

$$x + \breve{x} = l_x / a_x \text{ and } y + \breve{y} = l_y / a_y \text{, with } l_x + l_y = 1$$

where $\breve{x}$ and $\breve{y}$ are quantities of good x and good y produced by the representative Home consumer-producer but exported to Foreign. l_x and l_y are the fraction of human capital of the consumer-producer engaged in the production of good x and good y respectively. Analogously, the production function for the representative Foreign consumer-producer is:

$$x^* + \breve{x}^* = l_x^* / a_x^* \text{ and } y^* + \breve{y}^* = l_y^* / a_y^* \text{, with } l_x^* + l_y^* = 1$$

For simplicity of analysis, we arbitrarily assume that Home has a comparative advantage in producing good x, that is:

$$a_x / a_y < a_x^* / a_y^*$$

Intuitively, with a sufficiently high k (close to 1), trade is possible and desirable between the two countries. On the other hand, if k is sufficiently low, the two countries may find themselves better off remaining in autarky. Generally, there are three possible modes of division of human capital between the two countries: (1) Each country is completely specialized in the production of the good where it has a comparative advantage, i.e., Home only produces good x and Foreign only produces good y; (2) One country is completely specialized in the production of the good where it has a comparative advantage, while the other country produces both goods; (3) Each country remains in autarky, producing both goods.

The general equilibrium is found in two steps. First, we find the (corner) equilibrium for each mode, then we identify the range of the transaction efficiency, k, within which each corner equilibrium is the general equilibrium.

11.2.1. Equilibrium in Mode (1)

In this mode of division of human capital, Home will exclusively produce and export good x, and Foreign will exclusively produce and export good y. Therefore, for Home $x, \breve{x}, \hat{y} > 0$, and $\hat{x}, y, \breve{y} = 0$; for Foreign $y^*, \breve{y}^*, \hat{x}^* > 0$, and $\hat{y}^*, x^*, \breve{x}^* = 0$. The decision-making of the representative consumer in Home is described by:

$$MaxU = x^{\alpha} (k\hat{y})^{1-\alpha}$$

subject to: $x + \breve{x} = 1/a_x$, $\hat{y} = p\breve{x}$, where $p \equiv p_x / p_y$.

Inserting the constraints into the utility function, we get:

$$U = (1/a_x - \breve{x})^{\alpha} (kp\breve{x})^{1-\alpha}$$

Letting $u \equiv \ln U = \alpha \ln(1/a_x - \breve{x}) + (1-\alpha)\ln(kp\breve{x})$, the maximization of u (hence of U) requires:

$$\frac{-\alpha}{1/a_x - \breve{x}} + \frac{(1-\alpha)kp}{kp\breve{x}} = 0,$$

which implies:

$$\breve{x} = \frac{1-\alpha}{a_x},$$

Inserting this result back into the constraints gives us:

$$x = \frac{\alpha}{a_x}, \quad \widehat{y} = p \cdot \frac{1-\alpha}{a_x}$$

Analogously, the decision-making of the representative foreign consumer is described by:

$$MaxU^* = (k\widehat{x}^*)^\alpha y^{*1-\alpha}$$

subject to: $y^* + \breve{y}^* = 1/a_y^*$, $\breve{y}^* = p\widehat{x}^*$.

By the same trick we can obtain the following results:

$$\breve{y}^* = \frac{\alpha}{a_y^*}, \quad y^* = \frac{1-\alpha}{a_y^*} \text{ and } \widehat{x}^* = \frac{1}{p} \cdot \frac{\alpha}{a_y^*}$$

In equilibrium, $\breve{x}L = \widehat{x}^* L^*$ (and also $\widehat{y}L = \breve{y}^* L^*$), from which we can solve for the equilibrium relative price p :

$$p = \frac{\alpha}{1-\alpha} \cdot \frac{L^*/a_y^*}{L/a_x}$$

In equilibrium, the individual utility levels in Home and Foreign are respectively:

$$U = \alpha \cdot \left(\frac{1}{a_x}\right)^{\alpha} \cdot \left(\frac{kL^*}{a_y^* L}\right)^{1-\alpha}, \text{ and } U^* = (1-\alpha) \cdot \left(\frac{kL}{a_x L^*}\right)^{\alpha} \cdot \left(\frac{1}{a_y^*}\right)^{1-\alpha}$$

11.2.2. Equilibrium in Mode (2)

In this mode of division of human capital, one country will specialize in producing the one good where it has a comparative advantage while the other country will produce both goods. This is further divided into two sub-modes: Mode (2a) and Mode (2b).

In Mode (2a), we assume Home produces both good x and good y while Foreign completely specializes in the production of good y (where it has been assumed to have a comparative advantage). In Mode (2a), it can be seen for Home, $x, \breve{x}, y, \widehat{y} > 0$, $\widehat{x}, \breve{y} = 0$, while for Foreign, $y^*, \breve{y}^*, \widehat{x}^* > 0$, $\widehat{y}^*, x^*, \breve{x}^* = 0$. The maximization problem for the Home consumer is now:

$$Max U = x^{\alpha}(y + k\widehat{y})^{1-\alpha}$$

subject to: $x + \breve{x} = l_x / a_x$, $y = l_y / a_y$, $l_x + l_y = 1$, and $\widehat{y} = p\breve{x}$.

Inserting the constraints into the utility function gives:

$$U = (l_x / a_x - \breve{x})^{\alpha}[(1 - l_x)/a_y + kp\breve{x}]^{1-\alpha}$$

where in order for Home to produce both goods, p must be such that:

$$k \cdot (p_x / a_x)/p_y = 1/a_y \Leftrightarrow p = a_x / (ka_y)$$

Letting $u \equiv \ln U = \alpha \ln(l_x / a_x - \breve{x}) + (1-\alpha)\ln[(1-l_x)/a_y + kp\breve{x}]$, then the maximization of u (hence of U) requires (taking $\breve{x}$ as a function of l_x),

$$\frac{-\alpha}{l_x / a_x - \breve{x}} + \frac{(1-\alpha)kp}{(1-l_x)/a_y + kp\breve{x}} = 0$$

Solving for $\breve{x}$ and inserting the result back into the constraints, we get:

$p = a_x /(ka_y)$, $\breve{x} = (l_x - \alpha)/a_x$, $x = \alpha / a_x$, $y = (1-l_x)/a_y$,
and $\widehat{y} = (l_x - \alpha)/(ka_y)$.

The utility maximization problem for the representative Foreign consumer is as follows:

$$MaxU^* = (k\widehat{x}^*)^{\alpha} {y^*}^{1-\alpha}$$

subject to: $y^* + \breve{y}^* = 1/a_y^*$, and $\breve{y}^* = p\widehat{x}^*$

The first-order condition requires:

$$\frac{\alpha k}{k\widehat{x}^*} = \frac{(1-\alpha)p}{1/a_y^* - p\widehat{x}^*}$$

which in turn implies that:

$$\widehat{x}^* = \frac{\alpha k a_y}{a_x a_y^*}, \quad \breve{y}^* = \frac{\alpha}{a_y^*} \text{ and } y^* = \frac{1-\alpha}{a_y^*}.$$

In equilibrium, $\breve{x}L = \widehat{x}^* L^*$, therefore:

$$\breve{x}L = \hat{x}^* L^* \Leftrightarrow \frac{l_x - \alpha}{a_x} \cdot L = \frac{\alpha k a_y}{a_x a_y^*} \cdot L^* \Rightarrow l_x = \frac{\alpha k a_y L^*}{a_y^* L} + \alpha$$

$l_x = \dfrac{\alpha k a_y L^*}{a_y^* L} + \alpha < 1$ if and only if $k < \dfrac{1-\alpha}{\alpha} \cdot \dfrac{L / a_y}{L^* / a_y^*}$, thus we have to require that $k < \dfrac{1-\alpha}{\alpha} \cdot \dfrac{L / a_y}{L^* / a_y^*}$ in order for l_x to be less than 1.

In equilibrium, it is straightforward to see that the individual utility levels in Home and Foreign are respectively:

$$U = \left(\frac{\alpha}{a_x}\right)^{\alpha} \cdot \left(\frac{1-\alpha}{a_y}\right)^{1-\alpha}, \text{ and } U^* = \left(\frac{\alpha k^2 a_y}{a_x a_y^*}\right)^{\alpha} \left(\frac{1-\alpha}{a_y^*}\right)^{1-\alpha}.$$

In Mode (2b) of division of human capital, however, Home only produces and exports good x, where it has a comparative advantage, while Foreign produces both good x and good y. In Mode (2b), for Home, $x, \breve{x}, \hat{y} > 0,\ \hat{x}, y, \breve{y} = 0$, while for Foreign, $x^*, \hat{x}^*, y^*, \breve{y}^* > 0,\ \breve{x}^*, \hat{y}^* = 0$.

The utility maximization problem for the representative Home consumer is:

$$MaxU = x^{\alpha} (k\hat{y})^{1-\alpha}$$

subject to: $x + \breve{x} = 1 / a_x$ and $\hat{y} = p\breve{x}$

The utility maximization problem for the representative Foreign consumer is:

$$MaxU^* = (x^* + k\hat{x}^*)^{\alpha} y^{*1-\alpha}$$

subject to: $x^* = l_x^* / a_x^*$, $y^* + \breve{y}^* = l_y^* / a_y^*$, $l_x^* + l_y^* = 1$ and $\breve{y}^* = p\hat{x}^*$.

Following the same procedure as in Mode (2a), we can obtain the following results:

$$p = ka_x^* / a_y^*,\ \breve{y}^* = \frac{\alpha - l_x^*}{a_y^*},\ y^* = \frac{1-\alpha}{a_y^*},\ \widehat{x}^* = \frac{\alpha - l_x^*}{ka_x^*},$$

$$\breve{x} = \frac{1-\alpha}{a_x},\ x = \frac{\alpha}{a_x},\ \widehat{y} = \frac{k(1-\alpha)a_x^*}{a_x a_y^*},\ \text{and } l_x^* = \alpha - \frac{k(1-\alpha)a_x^* L}{a_x L^*}.$$

In order for $0 < l_x^* < 1$ to hold, we have to require that:

$$k < \frac{\alpha}{1-\alpha} \cdot \frac{L^* / a_x^*}{L / a_x}$$

In equilibrium, the individual utility levels in Home and Foreign are respectively:

$$U = \left(\frac{\alpha}{a_x}\right)^{\alpha} \left(\frac{k^2(1-\alpha)a_x^*}{a_x a_y^*}\right)^{1-\alpha},\ \text{and } U^* = \left(\frac{\alpha}{a_x^*}\right)^{\alpha} \left(\frac{1-\alpha}{a_y^*}\right)^{1-\alpha}$$

11.2.3. Equilibrium in Mode (3)

It is possible that both countries choose to remain in autarky. In this case, both countries obviously produce both goods. The utility maximization problem for the Home consumer is then:

$$MaxU = x^{\alpha} y^{1-\alpha}$$

subject to: $x = l_x / a_x$, $y = l_y / a_y$, $l_x + l_y = 1$

It is easy to see that in equilibrium:

$x = \alpha / a_x$ and $y = (1-\alpha) / a_y$

Therefore in equilibrium, the individual utility level in Home is:

$$U = (\alpha / a_x)^{\alpha}[(1-\alpha)/a_y]^{1-\alpha}$$

Analogously, in equilibrium, for Foreign, we have:

$$x^* = \alpha / a_x^*, \; y^* = (1-\alpha)/a_y^*$$
$$U^* = (\alpha / a_x^*)^{\alpha}[(1-\alpha)/a_y^*]^{1-\alpha}$$

11.2.4. The General Equilibrium

Now we come to the important analysis on how individuals in the two countries choose among the different modes of division of human capital and what the general equilibrium mode will be with different values of the transaction efficiency, k.

First, consider Mode (2a). In order for Mode (2a) to be the general equilibrium structure, then at the (corner) equilibrium relative price $p = a_x/(ka_y)$, individuals in Foreign must prefer complete specialization in good y to autarky. Thus, the following condition must hold:

$$\left(\frac{\alpha k^2 a_y}{a_x a_y^*}\right)^{\alpha}\left(\frac{1-\alpha}{a_y^*}\right)^{1-\alpha} \geq \left(\frac{\alpha}{a_x^*}\right)^{\alpha}\left(\frac{1-\alpha}{a_y^*}\right)^{1-\alpha} \Leftrightarrow k \geq \left(\frac{a_x / a_y}{a_x^* / a_y^*}\right)^{1/2}$$

Also, individuals in Home must prefer Mode (2a) to complete specialization in good x *and* to autarky, that is:

$$\left(\frac{\alpha}{a_x}\right)^{\alpha}\left(\frac{1-\alpha}{a_y}\right)^{1-\alpha} \geq \left(\frac{\alpha}{a_x}\right)^{\alpha}\left(\frac{kp(1-\alpha)}{a_x}\right)^{1-\alpha} \Leftrightarrow \frac{a_x}{a_y} \geq kp = \frac{a_x}{a_y},$$

which holds automatically; and

$$\left(\frac{\alpha}{a_x}\right)^{\alpha}\left(\frac{1-\alpha}{a_y}\right)^{1-\alpha} \geq \left(\frac{\alpha}{a_x}\right)^{\alpha}\left(\frac{1-\alpha}{a_y}\right)^{1-\alpha},$$

which also holds automatically.

Further, as noted earlier, in order for l_x to be less than 1 (i.e., the representative individual in Home produces both goods) we have to require that $k < \frac{1-\alpha}{\alpha} \cdot \frac{L/a_y}{L^*/a_y^*}$.

Therefore, in order for the (corner) equilibrium in Mode (2a) to be the general equilibrium, we have to require that:

$$\left(\frac{a_x/a_y}{a_x^*/a_y^*}\right)^{1/2} \leq k < \frac{1-\alpha}{\alpha} \cdot \frac{L/a_y}{L^*/a_y^*}$$

Further, in order for $\left(\frac{a_x/a_y}{a_x^*/a_y^*}\right)^{1/2} < \frac{1-\alpha}{\alpha} \cdot \frac{L/a_y}{L^*/a_y^*}$ to hold, we must have:

$$\left(\frac{a_x a_y}{a_x^* a_y^*}\right)^{1/2} < \frac{1-\alpha}{\alpha} \cdot \frac{L}{L^*}.$$

Let $k_0 \equiv \left(\frac{a_x/a_y}{a_x^*/a_y^*}\right)^{1/2}$ and $k_1 \equiv \frac{1-\alpha}{\alpha} \cdot \frac{L/a_y}{L^*/a_y^*}$, then based on the analysis above, if $\left(\frac{a_x a_y}{a_x^* a_y^*}\right)^{1/2} < \frac{1-\alpha}{\alpha} \cdot \frac{L}{L^*}$ *and if* $k_0 \equiv \left(\frac{a_x/a_y}{a_x^*/a_y^*}\right)^{1/2} \leq k < k_1 \equiv \frac{1-\alpha}{\alpha} \cdot \frac{L/a_y}{L^*/a_y^*}$, the (corner) equilibrium in Mode (2a) will be the general equilibrium.

Now consider Mode (2b). In order for Mode (2b) to be the general equilibrium structure, then at the (corner) equilibrium relative price $p = ka_x^* / a_y^*$, Home individuals must prefer complete specialization in good x to autarky. Therefore, the following condition must hold:

$$\left(\frac{\alpha}{a_x}\right)^{\alpha}\left(\frac{k^2(1-\alpha)a_x^*}{a_x a_y^*}\right)^{1-\alpha} \geq \left(\frac{\alpha}{a_x}\right)^{\alpha}\left(\frac{1-\alpha}{a_y}\right)^{1-\alpha},$$

which exactly implies that:

$$k \geq k_0 \equiv \left(\frac{a_x / a_y}{a_x^* / a_y^*}\right)^{1/2}$$

Also, individuals in Foreign must prefer Mode (2b) to complete specialization in good y *and* to autarky. Thus the following conditions must hold:

$$\left(\frac{\alpha}{a_x^*}\right)^{\alpha}\left(\frac{1-\alpha}{a_y^*}\right)^{1-\alpha} \geq \left(\frac{k\alpha}{pa_y^*}\right)^{\alpha}\left(\frac{1-\alpha}{a_y^*}\right)^{1-\alpha} \Leftrightarrow \frac{ka_x^*}{a_y^*} \leq p = \frac{ka_x^*}{a_y^*},$$

which holds automatically; and

$$\left(\frac{\alpha}{a_x^*}\right)^{\alpha}\left(\frac{1-\alpha}{a_y^*}\right)^{1-\alpha} \geq \left(\frac{\alpha}{a_x^*}\right)^{\alpha}\left(\frac{1-\alpha}{a_y^*}\right)^{1-\alpha}$$

which also holds automatically.

Further, as noted earlier, in order for $0 < l_x^* < 1$ to hold, we have to require that:

$$k < \frac{\alpha}{1-\alpha} \cdot \frac{L^* / a_x^*}{L / a_x}$$

Let $k_2 \equiv \frac{\alpha}{1-\alpha} \cdot \frac{L^* / a_x^*}{L / a_x}$, then if $\left(\frac{a_x a_y}{a_x^* a_y^*} \right)^{1/2} > \frac{1-\alpha}{\alpha} \cdot \frac{L}{L^*}$, *and* if $k_0 \le k < k_2$, then the (corner) equilibrium in Mode (2b) is the general equilibrium.

Now let's consider Mode (1), in which both countries are in complete specialization. In order for the (corner) equilibrium in Mode (1) to be the general equilibrium structure, then at the equilibrium relative price $p = \frac{\alpha}{1-\alpha} \cdot \frac{L^* / a_y^*}{L / a_x}$, individuals in both countries must prefer complete specialization to autarky. Therefore, for Home, the following condition must hold:

$$\alpha \cdot \left(\frac{1}{a_x} \right)^{\alpha} \left(\frac{kL^*}{a_y^* L} \right)^{1-\alpha} \ge \left(\frac{\alpha}{a_x} \right)^{\alpha} \left(\frac{1-\alpha}{a_y} \right)^{1-\alpha} \Leftrightarrow k \ge k_1 \equiv \frac{1-\alpha}{\alpha} \cdot \frac{L / a_y}{L^* / a_y^*}$$

For Foreign, instead, the following condition has to be met:

$$(1-\alpha) \cdot \left(\frac{kL}{a_x L^*} \right)^{\alpha} \left(\frac{1}{a_y^*} \right)^{1-\alpha} \ge \left(\frac{\alpha}{a_x^*} \right)^{\alpha} \left(\frac{1-\alpha}{a_y^*} \right)^{1-\alpha} \Leftrightarrow k \ge k_2 \equiv \frac{\alpha}{1-\alpha} \cdot \frac{L^* / a_x^*}{L / a_x}$$

When $\left(\frac{a_x a_y}{a_x^* a_y^*} \right)^{1/2} < \frac{1-\alpha}{\alpha} \cdot \frac{L}{L^*}$, it is easy to see that $k_2 < k_0 < k_1$, while when $\left(\frac{a_x a_y}{a_x^* a_y^*} \right)^{1/2} > \frac{1-\alpha}{\alpha} \cdot \frac{L}{L^*}$, we have $k_1 < k_0 < k_2$. Therefore, The equilibrium in Mode (1) is the general equilibrium structure if:

$$k \in [k_1,\ 1) \text{, when } \left(\frac{a_x a_y}{a_x^* a_y^*} \right)^{1/2} < \frac{1-\alpha}{\alpha} \cdot \frac{L}{L^*}$$

$$k \in [k_2,\ 1),\ \text{when} \left(\frac{a_x a_y}{a_x^* a_y^*}\right)^{1/2} > \frac{1-\alpha}{\alpha} \cdot \frac{L}{L^*}$$

Finally we are left with Mode (3), in which both countries are in autarky. Following essentially the same reasoning as above, it is not difficult to show that the (corner) equilibrium in Mode (3) becomes the general equilibrium whenever $0 < k \leq k_0$.

To sum up, we have so far obtained the following results:

If $0 < k \leq k_0$, then the general equilibrium structure is Mode (3), with both countries remaining in autarky;

If $\left(\frac{a_x a_y}{a_x^* a_y^*}\right)^{1/2} < \frac{1-\alpha}{\alpha} \cdot \frac{L}{L^*}$, and if $k_0 \leq k < k_1$, then the general equilibrium structure is Mode (2a), with Home producing both good x and good y while Foreign completely specializing in the production of good y;

If $\left(\frac{a_x a_y}{a_x^* a_y^*}\right)^{1/2} < \frac{1-\alpha}{\alpha} \cdot \frac{L}{L^*}$, and if $k_1 \leq k < 1$, then the general equilibrium structure is Mode (1), with the two countries engaging in complete specialization according to their respective comparative advantage;

If, instead, $\left(\frac{a_x a_y}{a_x^* a_y^*}\right)^{1/2} > \frac{1-\alpha}{\alpha} \cdot \frac{L}{L^*}$, and if $k_0 \leq k < k_2$, then the general equilibrium structure is Mode (2b), where Foreign produces both good x and good y while Home completely specializes in the production of good x;

If $\left(\frac{a_x a_y}{a_x^* a_y^*}\right)^{1/2} > \frac{1-\alpha}{\alpha} \cdot \frac{L}{L^*}$, and if $k_2 \leq k < 1$, then the general equilibrium structure is Mode (1), with the two countries engaging in complete specialization according to their respective comparative advantage.

The parameters are $k_0 \equiv \left(\frac{a_x / a_y}{a_x^* / a_y^*}\right)^{1/2}$, $k_1 \equiv \frac{1-\alpha}{\alpha} \cdot \frac{L / a_y}{L^* / a_y^*}$, and $k_2 \equiv \frac{\alpha}{1-\alpha} \cdot \frac{L^* / a_x^*}{L / a_x}$.

If $\left(\frac{a_x a_y}{a_x^* a_y^*}\right)^{1/2} = \frac{1-\alpha}{\alpha} \cdot \frac{L}{L^*}$ happens to hold, then we will have $k_0 = k_1 = k_2$. This simply implies that under the condition $\left(\frac{a_x a_y}{a_x^* a_y^*}\right)^{1/2} = \frac{1-\alpha}{\alpha} \cdot \frac{L}{L^*}$, the two countries will either be in complete autarky or in complete specialization, depending on the value of the actual k: if $0 < k \le k_0$, the two countries will remain in autarky; if $k_0 \le k < 1$, the two countries will engage in complete specialization according to their respective comparative advantage. Mode (2) (i.e., Mode (2a) and Mode (2b)) simply cannot be the general equilibrium structure under the condition $\left(\frac{a_x a_y}{a_x^* a_y^*}\right)^{1/2} = \frac{1-\alpha}{\alpha} \cdot \frac{L}{L^*}$.

The results above have revealed that when the transaction efficiency coefficient k increases from a low value to k_0, and further to k_1 or k_2, the general equilibrium will then jump from complete autarky (Mode (3)) to incomplete division of human capital (Mode (2a) or (2b)) and finally to complete specialization (Mode (1)). Whether the transformational structure is Mode (2a) or Mode (2b) depends on the relative size (as indicated by L / L^*), the relative productivity (as indicated by a_x^* / a_x, a_y^* / a_y) of the two countries, and individuals' relative preference for the two goods (as indicated by $\alpha /(1-\alpha)$). The major point of all this analysis is that the level of transaction efficiency k really *does* matter in determining the pattern of division of human capital and hence the pattern of trade between two countries. As a general result, the economy develops as the transaction efficiency k increases from a sufficiently low level to a sufficiently high level. In this simple model, the (exogenous) transaction efficiency is the final determinant for the level of development of the economy. Unlike in the neoclassical growth models, here in this model, we do not need "technological progress" or capital accumulation to explain changes in the economy.

11.3. CROSS-REGIONAL INEQUALITY

In this section, we develop a theoretical model to show the impact of transaction efficiency on intra-regional inequality in the welfare (utility) level.

Again, there are two countries, Home (H) and Foreign (F). The general specification of this model is the same as that of the model in the preceding section. The difference is that now in the present model, Home is divided into two regions (e.g., a developed region versus a backward region, or the urban region versus the rural region, etc.), denoted H_1 and H_2 respectively. Individuals in the two regions are otherwise the same, except for their transaction efficiency with country Foreign (F). Individuals in H_1 are assumed to have a sufficiently high transaction efficiency coefficient k such that the general equilibrium structure of division of human capital between H_1 and F is Mode (1) – complete specialization with H_1 exclusively producing good x and F exclusively producing good y). Based on our analysis, in order for Mode (1) between H_1 and F to be the general equilibrium structure, we have to assume here that $1 > k > k_1 \equiv \frac{1-\alpha}{\alpha} \cdot \frac{L_1 / a_y}{L^* / a_y^*}$ if $\left(\frac{a_x a_y}{a_x^* a_y^*}\right)^{1/2} < \frac{1-\alpha}{\alpha} \cdot \frac{L_1}{L^*}$ and $1 > k > k_2 \equiv \frac{\alpha}{1-\alpha} \cdot \frac{L^* / a_x^*}{L_1 / a_x}$ if $\left(\frac{a_x a_y}{a_x^* a_y^*}\right)^{1/2} > \frac{1-\alpha}{\alpha} \cdot \frac{L_1}{L^*}$.

In contrast, individuals in H_2 are assumed to have such a low transaction efficiency coefficient k' that no *direct* trade is possible between H_2 and F. However, (domestic) trade is possible between H_1 and H_2, and the transaction efficiency coefficient between H_1 and H_2 is assumed to be τ, where $0 < \tau < 1$. Therefore, *indirect* trade between H_2 and F is possible via H_1 if τ is not too low. It is easy to see that there are three possible modes of trade between H_1 and H_2: Mode (1^d), in which H_2 exclusively produces good x and sells good x to H_1 in exchange for good y (originally produced in F) from H_1; Mode ($2a^d$), in which H_2 produces both goods and sells good x to H_1 in exchange for good y (originally produced in F) from H_1; Mode (3^d), in which H_2 is completely self-sufficient, producing both goods for itself and has no trade with H_1 at all.

Next we are going to find out the (corner) equilibrium for each trade mode between H_1 and H_2, given that the general equilibrium trade mode between H_1 and F has been assumed to be Mode (1).

11.3.1. Equilibrium in Mode (1d)

In Mode (1^d), H_2 exclusively produces good x and sells good x to H_1 in exchange for good y (originally produced in F) from H_1.

The utility maximization problems for the representative individual in H_1, H_2 and F are respectively:

$$MaxU_1 = (1/a_x + t\widehat{x}_{1d} - \breve{x}_1)^\alpha (k\widehat{y}_1 - \breve{y}_{1d})^{1-\alpha}$$

subject to: $\widehat{y}_1 = p\breve{x}_1$, $\breve{y}_{1d} = p_d\widehat{x}_{1d}$

$$MaxU_2 = (1/a_x - \breve{x}_{2d})^\alpha (t\widehat{y}_{2d})^{1-\alpha}$$

subject to: $\widehat{y}_{2d} = p_d\breve{x}_{2d}$

$$MaxU^* = (k\widehat{x}^*)^\alpha (1/a_y^* - \breve{y}^*)^{1-\alpha}$$

subject to: $\breve{y}^* = p\widehat{x}^*$

For the representative individual in H_1, inserting the constraints into the utility function gives:

$$U_1 = (1/a_x + t\widehat{x}_{1d} - \breve{x}_1)^\alpha (kp\breve{x}_1 - p_d\widehat{x}_{1d})^{1-\alpha}$$

The first-order condition requires:

$$\frac{-\alpha}{1/a_x+\tau\widehat{x}_{1d}-\breve{x}_1}+\frac{(1-\alpha)kp}{kp\breve{x}_1-p_d\widehat{x}_{1d}}=0$$

which implies:

$$\breve{x}_1=\frac{1-\alpha}{a_x}+\left((1-\alpha)\tau+\frac{\alpha p_d}{kp}\right)\widehat{x}_{1d},\ \widehat{y}_1=\left[\frac{1-\alpha}{a_x}+\left((1-\alpha)\tau+\frac{\alpha p_d}{kp}\right)\widehat{x}_{1d}\right]p$$

For the representative individual in H_2, inserting the constraint gives:

$$U_2=(1/a_x-\breve{x}_{2d})^{\alpha}(\tau p_d\breve{x}_{2d})^{1-\alpha}$$

The first-order condition requires:

$$\frac{-\alpha}{1/a_x-\breve{x}_{2d}}+\frac{1-\alpha}{\breve{x}_{2d}}=0$$

which implies:

$$\breve{x}_{2d}=\frac{1-\alpha}{a_x},\ \widehat{y}_{2d}=\frac{(1-\alpha)p_d}{a_x}$$

For the representative individual in F, inserting the constraint gives:

$$MaxU^*=(k\widehat{x}^*)^{\alpha}(1/a_y^*-p\widehat{x}^*)^{1-\alpha}$$

The first-order condition requires:

$$\frac{\alpha}{\widehat{x}^*}+\frac{-(1-\alpha)p}{1/a_y^*-p\widehat{x}^*}=0$$

which implies:

$$\widehat{x}^* = \frac{1}{p} \cdot \frac{\alpha}{a_y^*}, \; \breve{y}^* = \frac{\alpha}{a_y^*}$$

In equilibrium, we must have $\breve{x}_1 L_1 = \widehat{x}^* L^*$ and $\breve{x}_{2d} L_2 = \widehat{x}_{1d} L_1$. These two equations combined imply that:

$$\widehat{x}_{1d} = \frac{(1-\alpha)L_2}{a_x L_1}$$

$$\breve{x}_1 = \frac{1}{p} \cdot \frac{\alpha L^*}{a_y^* L_1} = \frac{1-\alpha}{a_x} + \left((1-\alpha)\tau + \frac{\alpha p_d}{kp}\right)\widehat{x}_{1d} = \frac{1-\alpha}{a_x} + \left((1-\alpha)\tau + \frac{\alpha p_d}{kp}\right)\frac{(1-\alpha)L_2}{a_x L_1}$$

In equilibrium, it is easy to show that if an H_1 individual is willing to buy good y from F at the (relative) price p and resell it to H_2 at the (relative) price p_d, the domestic relative price p_d must be such that $p_d = \tau k p$. Inserting this back into the equation above and rearranging, we get:

$$p = \frac{\alpha a_x L^*}{(1-\alpha)a_y^*(L_1 + \tau L_2)}, \; p_d = \frac{\tau k \alpha a_x L^*}{(1-\alpha)a_y^*(L_1 + \tau L_2)}$$

and,

$$\breve{x}_1 = \frac{(1-\alpha)(L_1 + \tau L_2)}{a_x L_1}, \; \widehat{y}_1 = \frac{\alpha L^*}{a_y^* L_1}$$

We can now calculate the utility levels of individuals in H_1, H_2 and F:

$$U_1 = (1/a_x + \tau\widehat{x}_{1d} - \breve{x}_1)^{\alpha} (kp\breve{x}_1 - p_d \widehat{x}_{1d})^{1-\alpha}$$

$$= \left(\frac{1}{a_x} + \frac{\tau(1-\alpha)L_2}{a_x L_1} - \frac{(1-\alpha)(L_1 + \tau L_2)}{a_x L_1}\right)^{\alpha} \left(\frac{k\alpha L^*}{a_y^* L_1} - \frac{\tau k \alpha a_x L^*}{(1-\alpha)a_y^*(L_1 + \tau L_2)} \cdot \frac{(1-\alpha)L_2}{a_x L_1}\right)^{1-\alpha}$$

$$=\alpha\left(\frac{1}{a_x}\right)^{\alpha}\left(\frac{kL^*}{a_y^*(L_1+\tau L_2)}\right)^{1-\alpha}$$

$$U_2=(1/a_x-\breve{x}_{2d})^{\alpha}(\tau\widehat{y}_{2d})^{1-\alpha}$$

$$=\left(\frac{1}{a_x}-\frac{1-\alpha}{a_x}\right)^{\alpha}\left(\tau\cdot\frac{(1-\alpha)}{a_x}\cdot\frac{\tau k\alpha a_x L^*}{(1-\alpha)a_y^*(L_1+\tau L_2)}\right)^{1-\alpha}$$

$$=\alpha\left(\frac{1}{a_x}\right)^{\alpha}\left(\frac{k\tau^2L^*}{a_y^*(L_1+\tau L_2)}\right)^{1-\alpha}$$

$$U^*=(k\widehat{x}^*)^{\alpha}(1/a_y^*-\breve{y}^*)^{1-\alpha}$$

$$=\left(k\cdot\frac{(1-\alpha)a_y^*(L_1+\tau L_2)}{\alpha a_x L^*}\cdot\frac{\alpha}{a_y^*}\right)^{\alpha}\left(\frac{1}{a_y^*}-\frac{\alpha}{a_y^*}\right)^{1-\alpha}$$

$$=(1-\alpha)\left(\frac{k(L_1+\tau L_2)}{a_x L^*}\right)^{\alpha}\left(\frac{1}{a_y^*}\right)^{1-\alpha}$$

11.3.2. Equilibrium in Mode (2ad)

In Mode ($2a^d$), H_2 produces both goods and sells good x to H_1 in exchange for good y (originally produced in F) from H_1.

The utility maximization problems for the representative individual in H_1, H_2 and F are respectively:

$$MaxU_1=(1/a_x+\tau\widehat{x}_{1d}-\breve{x}_1)^{\alpha}(k\widehat{y}_1-\breve{y}_{1d})^{1-\alpha}$$

subject to: $\widehat{y}_1=p\breve{x}_1$, $\breve{y}_{1d}=p_d\widehat{x}_{1d}$

$$MaxU_2 = \left(\frac{l_{2x}}{a_x} - \breve{x}_{2d}\right)^{\alpha}\left(\frac{1-l_{2x}}{a_y} + \tau\overset{\frown}{y}_{2d}\right)^{1-\alpha}$$

subject to: $\overset{\frown}{y}_{2d} = p_d \breve{x}_{2d}$

$$MaxU^* = (k\overset{\frown}{x}^*)^{\alpha}(1/a_y^* - \breve{y}^*)^{1-\alpha}$$

subject to: $\breve{y}^* = p\overset{\frown}{x}^*$

Since H_2 produces both goods, in equilibrium we must have:

$$p_d = \frac{a_x}{\tau a_y}$$

Following the same procedure as above, we get:

$$\breve{x}_1 = \frac{1-\alpha}{a_x} + \left((1-\alpha)\tau + \frac{\alpha p_d}{kp}\right)\overset{\frown}{x}_{1d},$$

$$\overset{\frown}{y}_1 = \left[\frac{1-\alpha}{a_x} + \left((1-\alpha)\tau + \frac{\alpha p_d}{kp}\right)\overset{\frown}{x}_{1d}\right]p,$$

$$\breve{x}_{2d} = \frac{l_{2x}-\alpha}{a_x},\ \overset{\frown}{y}_{2d} = \frac{l_{2x}-\alpha}{\tau a_y},$$

$$\overset{\frown}{x}^* = \frac{1}{p}\cdot\frac{\alpha}{a_y^*},\ \breve{y}^* = \frac{\alpha}{a_y^*}$$

In equilibrium, we must have $\breve{x}_1 L_1 = \overset{\frown}{x}^* L^*$ and $\breve{x}_{2d} L_2 = \overset{\frown}{x}_{1d} L_1$. These two equations combined imply that:

$$\widehat{x}_{1d} = \frac{(l_{2x} - \alpha)L_2}{a_x L_1}$$

$$\breve{x}_1 = \frac{1}{p} \cdot \frac{\alpha L^*}{a_y^* L_1} = \frac{1-\alpha}{a_x} + \left((1-\alpha)\tau + \frac{\alpha p_d}{kp}\right)\widehat{x}_{1d} = \frac{1-\alpha}{a_x} + \left((1-\alpha)\tau + \frac{\alpha p_d}{kp}\right)\frac{(l_{2x} - \alpha)L_2}{a_x L_1}$$

Again, in equilibrium, we must have $p_d = \tau kp$, using this and inserting $p_d = \dfrac{a_x}{\tau a_y}$ back into the equation above, we get:

$$p = \frac{a_x}{k\tau^2 a_y}, \; l_{2x} = \frac{\alpha k \tau a_y L^*}{a_y^* L_2} - \frac{(1-\alpha)L_1}{\tau L_2} + \alpha$$

Since H_2 produces both goods, we must have $l_{2x} < 1$, therefore:

$$l_{2x} = \frac{\alpha k \tau a_y L^*}{a_y^* L_2} - \frac{(1-\alpha)L_1}{\tau L_2} + \alpha < 1 \Rightarrow \tau < \frac{L_2 + \sqrt{L_2^{\,2} + 4\alpha k a_y L^* L_1 / [(1-\alpha)a_y^*]}}{2\alpha k a_y L^* / [(1-\alpha)a_y^*]}$$

Further, $l_{2x} \geq \alpha$ must hold (since α is the equilibrium human capital input in the production of good x under autarky), which implies that $\tau \geq \left(\dfrac{(1-\alpha)a_y^* L_1}{k\alpha a_y L^*}\right)^{1/2}$ (With our earlier assumptions concerning k, it is easy to see that $\left(\dfrac{(1-\alpha)a_y^* L_1}{k\alpha a_y L^*}\right)^{1/2} < 1$)

It is now easy to obtain the utility levels of individuals in H_1, H_2 and F:

$$U_1 = (1/a_x + \tau\widehat{x}_{1d} - \breve{x}_1)^\alpha (kp\breve{x}_1 - p_d \widehat{x}_{1d})^{1-\alpha} = \left(\frac{\alpha}{a_x}\right)^\alpha \left(\frac{1-\alpha}{\tau^2 a_y}\right)^{1-\alpha}$$

$$U_2 = \left(\frac{l_{2x}}{a_x} - \breve{x}_{2d}\right)^{\alpha}\left(\frac{1-l_{2x}}{a_y} + \tau\widehat{y}_{2d}\right)^{1-\alpha}$$

$$= \left(\frac{l_{2x}}{a_x} - \frac{l_{2x}-\alpha}{a_x}\right)^{\alpha}\left(\frac{1-l_{2x}}{a_y} + \frac{l_{2x}-\alpha}{a_y}\right)^{1-\alpha} = \left(\frac{\alpha}{a_x}\right)^{\alpha}\left(\frac{1-\alpha}{a_y}\right)^{1-\alpha}$$

$$U^* = (k\widehat{x}^*)^{\alpha}(1/a_y^* - \breve{y}^*)^{1-\alpha}$$

$$= \left(k \cdot \frac{k\tau^2 a_y}{a_x} \cdot \frac{\alpha}{a_y^*}\right)^{\alpha}\left(\frac{1}{a_y^*} - \frac{\alpha}{a_y^*}\right)^{1-\alpha} = \left(\frac{k^2\tau^2\alpha a_y}{a_x a_y^*}\right)^{\alpha}\left(\frac{1-\alpha}{a_y^*}\right)^{1-\alpha}$$

11.3.3. Equilibrium in Mode (3 d)

In Mode (3^d), H_2 is completely self-sufficient, producing both goods for itself and has no trade with H_1 at all. Based on the relevant analysis in Section 7.2, it is now easy to find that in this case:

$$\breve{x}_1 = \frac{1-\alpha}{a_x}, \ \widehat{y}_1 = p \cdot \frac{1-\alpha}{a_x}, \widehat{x}^* = \frac{1}{p} \cdot \frac{\alpha}{a_y^*}, \ \breve{y}^* = \frac{\alpha}{a_y^*},$$

and $p = \dfrac{\alpha}{1-\alpha} \cdot \dfrac{L^*/a_y^*}{L_1/a_x}$

In equilibrium, the individual utility levels in H_1, H_2 and F are respectively:

$$U_1 = \alpha \cdot \left(\frac{1}{a_x}\right)^{\alpha}\left(\frac{kL^*}{a_y^* L_1}\right)^{1-\alpha},$$

$$U_2 = \left(\frac{\alpha}{a_x}\right)^{\alpha}\left(\frac{1-\alpha}{a_y}\right)^{1-\alpha}$$

$$U^* = (1-\alpha)\left(\frac{kL_1}{a_x L^*}\right)^{\alpha}\left(\frac{1}{a_y^*}\right)^{1-\alpha}$$

11.3.4. The General Equilibrium

Now we can turn to a discussion of the resulted general equilibrium structures based on the interactions of individuals in H_1, H_2 and F.

First, consider the equilibrium in Mode ($2a^d$). In order for the equilibrium in Mode ($2a^d$) to be the general equilibrium structure, then at the equilibrium relative price $p = \frac{a_x}{k\tau^2 a_y}$, individuals in F must prefer complete specialization in good y to autarky. Thus, the following condition must hold:

$$\left(\frac{k^2\tau^2\alpha a_y}{a_x a_y^*}\right)^{\alpha}\left(\frac{1-\alpha}{a_y^*}\right)^{1-\alpha} \geq \left(\frac{\alpha}{a_x^*}\right)^{\alpha}\left(\frac{1-\alpha}{a_y^*}\right)^{1-\alpha} \Leftrightarrow \tau \geq \left(\frac{a_x a_y^*}{k^2 a_x^* a_y}\right)^{1/2}$$

Comparing this result with our earlier requirement that $\tau \geq \left(\frac{(1-\alpha)a_y^* L_1}{k\alpha a_y L^*}\right)^{1/2}$, under the assumptions we have made concerning the value of k, it is easy to see that:

$$\left(\frac{(1-\alpha)a_y^* L_1}{k\alpha a_y L^*}\right)^{1/2} > \left(\frac{a_x a_y^*}{k^2 a_x^* a_y}\right)^{1/2}$$

Also, at $p_d = \frac{a_x}{\tau a_y}$, individuals in H_2 must prefer Mode ($2a^d$) to complete specialization in good x *and* to autarky. That is:

$$\left(\frac{\alpha}{a_x}\right)^{\alpha}\left(\frac{1-\alpha}{a_y}\right)^{1-\alpha} \geq \left(\frac{\alpha}{a_x}\right)^{\alpha}\left(\frac{\tau(1-\alpha)p_d}{a_x}\right)^{1-\alpha} \Leftrightarrow \frac{a_x}{a_y} \geq \tau p_d = \frac{a_x}{a_y}$$

Which holds automatically, and

$$\left(\frac{\alpha}{a_x}\right)^{\alpha}\left(\frac{1-\alpha}{a_y}\right)^{1-\alpha} \geq \left(\frac{\alpha}{a_x}\right)^{\alpha}\left(\frac{1-\alpha}{a_y}\right)^{1-\alpha},$$

which also holds automatically.

Still, at $p = \frac{a_x}{k\tau^2 a_y}$ and $p_d = \frac{a_x}{\tau a_y}$ individuals in H_1 must prefer Mode ($2a^d$) to Mode (3^d) concerning trade with H_2. Therefore, we should have:

$$\left(\frac{\alpha}{a_x}\right)^{\alpha}\left(\frac{1-\alpha}{\tau^2 a_y}\right)^{1-\alpha} \geq \left(\frac{\alpha}{a_x}\right)^{\alpha}\left(k \cdot \frac{a_x}{k\tau^2 a_y} \cdot \frac{1-\alpha}{a_x}\right)^{1-\alpha},$$

which holds automatically.

Therefore, in order for the (corner) equilibrium in Mode ($2a^d$) to be the general equilibrium structure, we have to require that:

$$\tau_0 \equiv \left(\frac{(1-\alpha)a_y^* L_1}{k\alpha a_y L^*}\right)^{1/2} \leq \tau < \frac{L_2 + \sqrt{{L_2}^2 + 4\alpha k a_y L^* L_1 /[(1-\alpha)a_y^*]}}{2\alpha k a_y L^* /[(1-\alpha)a_y^*]} \equiv \tau_1$$

A prerequisite for the inequality above to hold is obviously:

$$\left(\frac{(1-\alpha)a_y^* L_1}{k\alpha a_y L^*}\right)^{1/2} < \frac{L_2 + \sqrt{{L_2}^2 + 4\alpha k a_y L^* L_1 /[(1-\alpha)a_y^*]}}{2\alpha k a_y L^* /[(1-\alpha)a_y^*]}$$

which can be shown to hold automatically.

Further, for $\tau_1 \equiv \frac{L_2 + \sqrt{L_2^2 + 4\alpha k a_y L^* L_1 / [(1-\alpha)a_y^*]}}{2\alpha k a_y L^* / [(1-\alpha)a_y^*]} < 1$ to hold, it is easy to show that we have to further assume that $k > \frac{1-\alpha}{\alpha} \cdot \frac{L / a_y}{L^* / a_y^*}$, where $L \equiv L_1 + L_2$.

Now, in order for the (corner) equilibrium in Mode (1^d) to be the general equilibrium structure, then at the corner equilibrium relative price $p = \frac{\alpha a_x L^*}{(1-\alpha)a_y^*(L_1 + \tau L_2)}$, individuals in F must prefer complete specialization in good y to autarky. Thus, the following condition must hold:

$$(1-\alpha)\left(\frac{k(L_1 + \tau L_2)}{a_x L^*}\right)^{\alpha}\left(\frac{1}{a_y^*}\right)^{1-\alpha} \geq \left(\frac{\alpha}{a_x^*}\right)^{\alpha}\left(\frac{1-\alpha}{a_y^*}\right)^{1-\alpha} \Leftrightarrow \tau \geq \frac{\alpha a_x L^*}{k(1-\alpha)a_x^* L_2} - \frac{L_1}{L_2}$$

With our earlier assumptions concerning k, it is easy to see that $\frac{\alpha a_x L^*}{k(1-\alpha)a_x^* L_2} - \frac{L_1}{L_2} < 0$. Therefore the condition $\tau \geq \frac{\alpha a_x L^*}{k(1-\alpha)a_x^* L_2} - \frac{L_1}{L_2}$ holds automatically.

Also, for the equilibrium in Mode (1^d) to be the general equilibrium structure, at $p_d = \frac{\tau k \alpha a_x L^*}{(1-\alpha)a_y^*(L_1 + \tau L_2)}$, individuals in H_2 must prefer Mode (1^d) to autarky, thus the following must hold:

$$\alpha\left(\frac{1}{a_x}\right)^{\alpha}\left(\frac{k\tau^2 L^*}{a_y^*(L_1 + \tau L_2)}\right)^{1-\alpha} \geq \left(\frac{\alpha}{a_x}\right)^{\alpha}\left(\frac{1-\alpha}{a_y}\right)^{1-\alpha}$$

$$\Rightarrow \tau \geq \frac{L_2 + \sqrt{L_2^2 + 4\alpha k a_y L^* L_1 / [(1-\alpha)a_y^*]}}{2\alpha k a_y L^* / [(1-\alpha)a_y^*]}$$

Still, at $p = \frac{\alpha a_x L^*}{(1-\alpha)a_y^*(L_1 + \tau L_2)}$ and $p_d = \frac{\tau k \alpha a_x L^*}{(1-\alpha)a_y^*(L_1 + \tau L_2)}$ individuals in H_1 must prefer Mode (1^d) to Mode (3^d) concerning trade with H_2. Therefore, we should have:

$$\alpha\left(\frac{1}{a_x}\right)^{\alpha}\left(\frac{kL^*}{a_y^*(L_1 + \tau L_2)}\right)^{1-\alpha} \geq$$

$$\left(\frac{\alpha}{a_x}\right)^{\alpha}\left(k \cdot \frac{\alpha a_x L^*}{(1-\alpha)a_y^*(L_1 + \tau L_2)} \cdot \frac{1-\alpha}{a_x}\right)^{1-\alpha},$$

which holds automatically.

Therefore, in order for the equilibrium in Mode (1^d) to be the general equilibrium structure, we have to require that:

$$\tau \geq \frac{L_2 + \sqrt{L_2{}^2 + 4\alpha k a_y L^* L_1 / [(1-\alpha)a_y^*]}}{2\alpha k a_y L^* / [(1-\alpha)a_y^*]} \equiv \tau_1$$

Now, consider the (corner) equilibrium in Mode (3^d). In order for this to be the general equilibrium structure, we have to make a series of comparisons.

First, at the corner equilibrium relative prices $p = \frac{\alpha a_x L^*}{(1-\alpha)a_y^* L_1}$ and $p_d = \frac{\tau k \alpha a_x L^*}{(1-\alpha)a_y^* L_1}$, compare the utility levels of H_1, H_2 and F in Mode (3^d) against the corresponding utility levels of H_1, H_2 and F in Mode (1^d). In order for Mode (3^d) to be the general equilibrium structure, the following must be required:

$$\alpha \cdot \left(\frac{1}{a_x}\right)^{\alpha}\left(\frac{kL^*}{a_y^*L_1}\right)^{1-\alpha} \geq \left(\frac{\alpha}{a_x}\right)^{\alpha}\left(\frac{k\alpha L^*}{a_y^*L_1} - \frac{\tau k\alpha a_x L^*}{(1-\alpha)a_y^*L_1} \cdot \frac{(1-\alpha)L_2}{a_x L_1}\right)^{1-\alpha}$$

which holds automatically, and

$$\left(\frac{\alpha}{a_x}\right)^{\alpha}\left(\frac{1-\alpha}{a_y}\right)^{1-\alpha} \geq \left(\frac{1}{a_x} - \frac{1-\alpha}{a_x}\right)^{\alpha}\left(\tau \cdot \frac{(1-\alpha)}{a_x} \cdot \frac{\tau k\alpha a_x L^*}{(1-\alpha)a_y^*L_1}\right)^{1-\alpha}$$

$$\Leftrightarrow \tau \leq \left(\frac{(1-\alpha)a_y^*L_1}{k\alpha a_y L^*}\right)^{1/2}$$

and

$$(1-\alpha)\left(\frac{kL_1}{a_x L^*}\right)^{\alpha}\left(\frac{1}{a_y^*}\right)^{1-\alpha} \geq \left(k \cdot \frac{(1-\alpha)a_y^*L_1}{\alpha a_x L^*} \cdot \frac{\alpha}{a_y^*}\right)^{\alpha}\left(\frac{1}{a_y^*} - \frac{\alpha}{a_y^*}\right)^{1-\alpha}$$

which holds automatically.

Therefore, in order for Mode (3^d) to be the general equilibrium structure, we have to require that:

$$\tau \leq \left(\frac{(1-\alpha)a_y^*L_1}{k\alpha a_y L^*}\right)^{1/2} \equiv \tau_0$$

To sum up, we have so far reached the following results:

If $0 < \tau \leq \left(\frac{(1-\alpha)a_y^*L_1}{k\alpha a_y L^*}\right)^{1/2} \equiv \tau_0$, the general equilibrium trade structure between H_1 and H_2 is Mode (3^d), in which H_2 is completely self-sufficient, producing both goods for itself and has no trade with H_1 at all.

If $\tau_0 \equiv \left(\frac{(1-\alpha)a_y^* L_1}{k\alpha a_y L^*}\right)^{1/2} \leq \tau < \frac{L_2 + \sqrt{L_2^{\,2} + 4\alpha k a_y L^* L_1 / [(1-\alpha)a_y^*]}}{2\alpha k a_y L^* / [(1-\alpha)a_y^*]} \equiv \tau_1$, the general equilibrium trade structure between H_1 and H_2 is Mode ($2a^d$), in which H_2 produces both goods and sells good x to H_1 in exchange for good y (originally produced in F) from H_1.

If $\tau_1 \equiv \frac{L_2 + \sqrt{L_2^{\,2} + 4\alpha k a_y L^* L_1 / [(1-\alpha)a_y^*]}}{2\alpha k a_y L^* / [(1-\alpha)a_y^*]} \leq \tau < 1$, the general equilibrium trade structure between H_1 and H_2 is Mode (1^d), in which H_2 exclusively produces good x and sells good x to H_1 in exchange for good y (originally produced in F) from H_1.

11.3.5. Comparative Statics

Under all of our earlier assumptions concerning the value of k, we can now carry out a comparative static analysis of the individual utility levels in H_1, H_2 and F with respect to the value of τ.

When $0 < \tau \leq \left(\frac{(1-\alpha)a_y^* L_1}{k\alpha a_y L^*}\right)^{1/2} \equiv \tau_0$, the general equilibrium trade structure between H_1 and H_2 is Mode (3^d). The individual utility levels in H_1, H_2 and F are respectively:

$$U_1 = \alpha \cdot \left(\frac{1}{a_x}\right)^{\alpha} \left(\frac{kL^*}{a_y^* L_1}\right)^{1-\alpha}, \quad U_2 = \left(\frac{\alpha}{a_x}\right)^{\alpha} \left(\frac{1-\alpha}{a_y}\right)^{1-\alpha}, \text{ and}$$

$$U^* = (1-\alpha)\left(\frac{kL_1}{a_x L^*}\right)^{\alpha} \left(\frac{1}{a_y^*}\right)^{1-\alpha}$$

Obviously, when τ increases within the interval $(0, \tau_0]$, U_1, U_2 and U^* all remain unchanged.

Next, when $\tau_0 \equiv \left(\frac{(1-\alpha)a_y^* L_1}{k\alpha a_y L^*}\right)^{1/2} \leq \tau < \frac{L_2 + \sqrt{L_2^2 + 4\alpha k a_y L^* L_1 / [(1-\alpha)a_y^*]}}{2\alpha k a_y L^* / [(1-\alpha)a_y^*]}$ $\equiv \tau_1$, the general equilibrium trade structure between H_1 and H_2 is Mode ($2a^d$). The individual utility levels in H_1, H_2 and F are respectively:

$$U_1 = \left(\frac{\alpha}{a_x}\right)^{\alpha}\left(\frac{1-\alpha}{\tau^2 a_y}\right)^{1-\alpha}, \; U_2 = \left(\frac{\alpha}{a_x}\right)^{\alpha}\left(\frac{1-\alpha}{a_y}\right)^{1-\alpha}, \; U^* = \left(\frac{k^2\tau^2\alpha a_y}{a_x a_y^*}\right)^{\alpha}\left(\frac{1-\alpha}{a_y^*}\right)^{1-\alpha}$$

First, at $\tau = \tau_0$, it is easily seen that there is no discontinuous jump for U_1, U_2 and U^*. Then when τ increases continuously within the interval $[\tau_0, \tau_1)$, we can see that U_1 decreases continuously, U_2 remains unchanged, and U^* increases continuously.

Finally, when $\tau_1 \equiv \frac{L_2 + \sqrt{L_2^2 + 4\alpha k a_y L^* L_1 / [(1-\alpha)a_y^*]}}{2\alpha k a_y L^* / [(1-\alpha)a_y^*]} \leq \tau < 1$, the general equilibrium trade structure between H_1 and H_2 is Mode (1^d). The individual utility levels in H_1, H_2 and F are respectively:

$$U_1 = \alpha\left(\frac{1}{a_x}\right)^{\alpha}\left(\frac{kL^*}{a_y^*(L_1+\tau L_2)}\right)^{1-\alpha},$$

$$U_2 = \alpha\left(\frac{1}{a_x}\right)^{\alpha}\left(\frac{k\tau^2 L^*}{a_y^*(L_1+\tau L_2)}\right)^{1-\alpha}$$

$$U^* = (1-\alpha)\left(\frac{k(L_1+\tau L_2)}{a_x L^*}\right)^{\alpha}\left(\frac{1}{a_y^*}\right)^{1-\alpha}$$

First, it is easy to see that at $\tau = \tau_1$, there is no discontinuous jump for U_1, U_2 and U^*. Then, when τ increases continuously within the interval

$[\tau_1,1)$, we can see that U_1 decreases continuously, U_2 increases continuously, and U^* increases continuously.

We can also carry out a comparative static analysis of the individual utility levels in H_1, H_2 and F with respect to the trade pattern between H_1 and F. Suppose initially the transaction efficiency coefficient k between H_1 and F is so low that in equilibrium no trade is possible between H_1 and F (that is Mode (3) between H_1 and F). We can study how the individual utility levels in H_1, H_2 and F will change if k jumps from such a low value $\underline{k}$ to a sufficiently high value $\bar{k}$ (which meets all of our earlier assumptions and with which the general equilibrium mode of trade between H_1 and F is Mode (1)).

With the initial low value $\underline{k}$, there is no trade between the two countries, and obviously there is no domestic trade between H_1 and H_2. Therefore, with any $\tau \in (0,1)$, we always have:

$$U_1 = U_2 = \left(\frac{\alpha}{a_x}\right)^{\alpha}\left(\frac{1-\alpha}{a_y}\right)^{1-\alpha}, \quad U^* = \left(\frac{\alpha}{a_x^*}\right)^{\alpha}\left(\frac{1-\alpha}{a_y^*}\right)^{1-\alpha}$$

Now, suppose the transaction efficiency coefficient k between H_1 and F jumps to a sufficiently high value $\bar{k}$ (one that meets all of our earlier assumptions).

Now at $\bar{k}$, if τ happens to be such that $0 < \tau \le \left(\frac{(1-\alpha)a_y^* L_1}{\bar{k}\alpha a_y L^*}\right)^{1/2} \equiv \bar{\tau}_0$, then we have:

$$U_1 = \alpha \cdot \left(\frac{1}{a_x}\right)^{\alpha}\left(\frac{kL^*}{a_y^* L_1}\right)^{1-\alpha}, \quad U_2 = \left(\frac{\alpha}{a_x}\right)^{\alpha}\left(\frac{1-\alpha}{a_y}\right)^{1-\alpha}, \quad U^* = (1-\alpha)\left(\frac{kL_1}{a_x L^*}\right)^{\alpha}\left(\frac{1}{a_y^*}\right)^{1-\alpha}$$

It is easy to show that with this upward jump in k from $\underline{k}$ to $\bar{k}$, if $0<\tau\leq\overline{\tau_0}$, then U_1 unambiguously jumps upward, U_2 remains unchanged, and U^* unambiguously jumps upward.

Instead, at the new level of the transaction efficiency coefficient $\bar{k}$, if τ happens to be such that $\overline{\tau_0}\equiv\left(\frac{(1-\alpha)a_y^*L_1}{\bar{k}\alpha a_y L^*}\right)^{1/2}\leq\tau<\frac{L_2+\sqrt{L_2{}^2+4\alpha\bar{k}a_yL^*L_1/[(1-\alpha)a_y^*]}}{2\alpha\bar{k}a_yL^*/[(1-\alpha)a_y^*]}$ $\equiv\overline{\tau_1}$, then we have: $U_1=\left(\frac{\alpha}{a_x}\right)^{\alpha}\left(\frac{1-\alpha}{\tau^2 a_y}\right)^{1-\alpha}$, $U_2=\left(\frac{\alpha}{a_x}\right)^{\alpha}\left(\frac{1-\alpha}{a_y}\right)^{1-\alpha}$, $U^*=\left(\frac{k^2\tau^2\alpha a_y}{a_x a_y^*}\right)^{\alpha}\left(\frac{1-\alpha}{a_y^*}\right)^{1-\alpha}$

It is also easy to show that with the upward jump in k from $\underline{k}$ to $\bar{k}$, if $\overline{\tau_0}\leq\tau<\overline{\tau_1}$, then U_1 unambiguously jumps upward, U_2 remains unchanged, and U^* unambiguously jumps upward.

Finally, at the new level of the transaction efficiency coefficient $\bar{k}$, if τ happens to be such that $\overline{\tau_1}\equiv\frac{L_2+\sqrt{L_2{}^2+4\alpha\bar{k}a_yL^*L_1/[(1-\alpha)a_y^*]}}{2\alpha\bar{k}a_yL^*/[(1-\alpha)a_y^*]}\leq\tau<1$ we then have:

$$U_1=\alpha\left(\frac{1}{a_x}\right)^{\alpha}\left(\frac{kL^*}{a_y^*(L_1+\tau L_2)}\right)^{1-\alpha},$$

$$U_2=\alpha\left(\frac{1}{a_x}\right)^{\alpha}\left(\frac{k\tau^2L^*}{a_y^*(L_1+\tau L_2)}\right)^{1-\alpha}$$

$$U^*=(1-\alpha)\left(\frac{k(L_1+\tau L_2)}{a_xL^*}\right)^{\alpha}\left(\frac{1}{a_y^*}\right)^{1-\alpha}$$

It is easy to show that with the upward jump in k from $\underline{k}$ to $\bar{k}$, if $\overline{\tau_1} \leq \tau < 1$, then U_1 unambiguously jumps upward, U^* unambiguously jumps upward, and U_2 remains unchanged (if exactly $\tau = \overline{\tau_1}$) or jumps upward (if $\overline{\tau_1} < \tau < 1$).

Also, it is easy to see another related fact: if k is now sufficiently high so that the general equilibrium trade mode between H and F is Mode (1), then a marginal increase in k (one such that it does not cause the general equilibrium between H_1 and H_2 to shift from one mode to another) will leave individuals in F strictly better off, and individuals in H_1 and H_2 at least no worse off than before the increase in k.

Next, let's study the model from another perspective. Now, suppose as before, k meets all our earlier assumptions so that with this value of k, the general equilibrium trade structure between H and F is Mode (1). The domestic transaction efficiency coefficient may fall into any one of the three intervals, $(0, \tau_0]$, $[\tau_0, \tau_1)$, and $[\tau_1, 1)$. Now suppose both k and τ are fixed, but the border between H_1 and H_2 shifts so that H_1 is now larger and H_2 smaller (i.e., L_1 increases and L_2 decreases, with the total population of H fixed at $L = L_1 + L_2$). Let's now study the effects of an increase in L_1 on the individual utility levels of H_1, H_2 and F, holding both k and τ fixed. First, we have to note that a change in L_1 shifts the dividing points τ_0 and τ_1. It is not difficult to show that:

$$\frac{\partial \tau_0}{\partial L_1} = \frac{1}{2}\left(\frac{(1-\alpha)a_y^*}{k\alpha a_y L^*}\right)^{1/2} L_1^{-1/2} > 0$$

$$\frac{\partial \tau_1}{\partial L_1} = \frac{1}{M}\{-1 + [(L - L_1)^2 + 2ML_1]^{-1/2}(-L + L_1 + M)\} > 0$$

where $M \equiv 2\alpha k a_y L^* /[(1-\alpha)a_y^*]$. With our earlier assumption that $k > \frac{1-\alpha}{\alpha} \cdot \frac{L/a_y}{L^*/a_y^*}$, it is not difficult to show that $M > 2L$, which in turn can be easily shown to imply that $[(L-L_1)^2 + 2ML_1]^{-1/2}(-L+L_1+M)>1$, hence $\frac{\partial \tau_1}{\partial L_1} > 0$.

If a marginal increase in L_1 is such an increase that it does not shift the general equilibrium trade structure between H_1 and H_2, then it is straightforward to see that this marginal increase in L_1 will make individuals in F strictly better off (if Mode (1^d) or Mode (3^d) is the general equilibrium structure between H_1 and H_2) or at least no worse off (if Mode ($2a^d$) is the general equilibrium structure between H_1 and H_2), make individuals in H_1 strictly worse off (if Mode (1^d) or Mode (3^d) is the general equilibrium structure between H_1 and H_2) or no better off (if Mode ($2a^d$) is the general equilibrium structure between H_1 and H_2), and make individuals in H_2 strictly worse off (if Mode (1^d) is the general equilibrium structure between H_1 and H_2) or no better off (if Mode ($2a^d$) or Mode (3^d) is the general equilibrium structure between H_1 and H_2).

At a sufficiently high level of k and a given level of τ, suppose now there is such a discontinuous upward jump in L_1 that causes the equilibrium structure between H_1 and H_2 to shift from Mode (1^d) to Mode ($2a^d$). It is easy to see that U_1 unambiguously decreases, U_2 unambiguously decreases, and U^* unambiguously increases as a result. If instead this upward jump in L_1 has caused the equilibrium structure between H_1 and H_2 to shift from Mode ($2a^d$) to Mode (3^d), then as a result, U_1 unambiguously increases, U_2 does not change, and U^* unambiguously decreases.

In sum we see, for example, if the transaction cost between the "developed" part of Country Home, H_1 and the "underdeveloped" part of it, H_2, is already low enough (We can roughly interpret this as the fact that there are not much transaction "barrier" between the two parts of the country), then ceteris paribus, further lifting the transaction barrier between the two parts will make the residents in the "underdeveloped" area better off at the sacrifice of the welfare of the residents in the "developed" area. This is one way through which changing transaction efficiency may affect the welfare distribution of the residents residing in different areas of the same country. What is more relevant here with our study of human capital is that we have concluded in our model that if a marginal increase in human capital in the developed part is such an increase that it does not shift the general equilibrium trade structure between the two parts, then it is the case that this marginal increase in the developed part will make individuals in the rest of the world strictly better off or at least no worse off, make individuals in the developed part of the country strictly worse off or no better off, and make individuals in the underdeveloped part of the country strictly worse off or no better off.

REFERENCES

Akhvlediani, T., A. Cieślik. (2020), "Human Capital, Technological Progress and Technology Diffusion across Europe: Education Matters," *Journal of European Economics,* 47(3), 475-493.

Amsden, A. H. (1989), "The Political Economy of the New Asian Industrialism. Frederic C. Deyo," *Economic Development and Culture Change,* 94(5), 854-869.

Anderson, G. L. (2015), "Why Nations Fail: the Origins of Power, Prosperity, and Poverty," *International Journal on World Peace,* 32(2), 153-158.

Ang, J. B. and Madsen, J. B., Islam, M. R. (2011), "The Effects of Human Capital Composition on Technological Convergence," *Journal of Macroeconomics,* 33(3), 465-476.

Arrow, K. J. (1962), "The Economic Implications of Learning by Doing," *The Review of Economic Studies,* 29(3), 155-173.

Apergis, N., C. Economidou, I. Filippidis (2008), "Innovation, Technology Transfer and Labor Productivity Linkages: Evidence from a Panel of Manufacturing Industries," *Review of World Economics,* 144(3), 491-508.

Azarnert, L. V. (2010), "Free Education, Fertility and Human Capital Accumulation," *Journal of Population Economics,* 23(2), 449-468.

Bai, Jing, and Feng Xiaoyang (2020), "Empirical Test of Human Capital on the Development of Advanced Industrial Structure," *Statistics and Decision Making,* 36 (4), 67-71.

Baldacci, E., B. Clements, S. Gupta, Q. Cui (2007), "Social Spending, Human Capital, and Growth in Developing Countries," *World Development,* 36(8), 1317-1341.

Barro, R. J. (2001), "Human Capital and Growth," *American Economic Review,* 91(2), 12-17.

Batabyal, A. A., and H. Beladi (2013), "Human Capital, Knowledge Spillovers, and One Kind of Semi-endogenous Regional Economic Growth," *Letters in Spatial and Resource Sciences,* 6(3), 121-135.

Becker, G. S. (1962), "Investment in Human Capital: A Theoretical Analysis," *Journal of Political Economy,* 70(5), 9-49.

Becker, G. S. and B. R. Chiswick (1966), "Education and the Distribution of Earnings," *The American Economic Review,* 56(1/2), 358-369.

Bi, Yuhui (2008), "Government Transformation: Target Mode and Path Selection," *Journal of Guangdong University of administration,* 2008 (04), 14-16 + 19.

Bryant C. E., and R. G. Javalgi (2016), "Global Economic Integration in Developing Countries: The Role of Corruption and Human Capital Investment," *Journal of Business Ethics,* 136(3).

Carlsson, B. and E. Taymaz (1993), "Technological Capabilities and International Competitiveness in the Engineering Industries," *Review of Industrial Organization,* 8(3), 437-450.

Castelló-Climent, A., and R. Doménech (2008), "Human Capital Inequality, Life Expectancy and Economic Growth," *The Economic Journal,* 118(528), 654-667.

Chari V. V., and Hugo Hopenhayn (1991), "Vintage Human Capital, Growth, and the Diffusion of New Technology," *Journal of Political Economy,* 99(6), 1142-1165.

Chen, Jiaxu and Ren Yao (2020), "The Upgrading of Human Capital Structure, Industrial Structure and Economic Growth -- Based on the Perspective of New Structural Economics," *Exploration of Economic Problems,* 2020 (07), 180-190.

Chen, Rui, Lili Ma, Xuan Chen (2019), "Human Capital Structure Evolution and China's Economic Growth: Empirical Evidence from Provincial Level," *Business Research,* 2019 (01), 60-70.

Chen, Xuting (1991), "Realizing the Transformation from Scale and Speed Type to Quality and Efficiency Type -- Also on the Operation and Development Strategy of Agricultural Bank of China," *Jiangsu Rural Finance,* 1991 (07), 20-22.

Chung C. C., H. Y. Park, J. Y. Lee, K. Kim (2015), "Human capital in multinational enterprises: Does strategic alignment matter?," *Journal of International Business Studies*,46(7), 806-829.

Ciccone, A., and E. Papaioannou (2009), "Human Capital, the Structure of Production, and Growth," *The Review of Economics and Statistics,* 91(1), 66-82.

Coe, D. T. and, E. Helpman (1995), "International R&D spillovers," *European Economic Review*, 39(5), 859-887.

Dai, Kuizao, Li, Xiaoli, Luo, Junhan (2020), "Advanced Human Capital Structure, Development of Factor Market and Upgrading of Service Industry Structure," *Finance and Trade Economy,* 41 (10), 129-146.

Day, C. and S. Dowrick (2013), "Endogenous Growth with R&D and Human Capital: The Role of Returns to Scale," *Oxford Economic Papers,* 65(2), 312-322.

Duan, Xin and Mingrui Li (2020), "The Impact of Inter-regional Physical Capital and Heterogeneous Human Capital on Economic Growth -- From the Perspective of Industrial Structure Optimization," *Western Finance,* 2020 (08), 15-21.

Duan, Xin and Xiaoyang Ren (2020), "The Impact of Physical Capital, Human Capital and R & D Investment on Economic Growth -- Based on the Perspective of Industrial Structure Optimization," *Journal of Hubei University of Arts and Sciences,* 41 (05), 40-48.

Enke, S. (1962), "Economic Development with Unlimited and Limited Supplies of Labour," *Oxford Economic Papers,* New Series, 14(2), 158-172.

Fan, Tian, Liu Liu (2019), "The Impact of Intellectual Capital Spillover on Total Factor Productivity: An Empirical Study in Coastal Regions of China," *Journal of Coastal Research*, 94(sp1).

Feng, Xi, Huang Yanshan (2018), "Discussion on Economic Development and Transformation of Economic Development Mode in 40 Years of China's Reform and Opening up," *Qingjiang forum,* 2018 (04) : 25-33.

Fleisher, B., Haizheng Li, Min Qiang Zhao (2010), "Human Capital, Economic Growth, and Regional Inequality in China," *Journal of Development Economics,* 92(2), 215-231.

Frank, A. G. (2015), "Human Capital and Economic Growth: The Role of Governance," *The Pakistan Development Review,* 54(4), 529-548.

Frantzen D. (2000), "R&D, Human Capital and International Technology Spillovers: A Cross-country Analysis," *Scandinavian Journal of Economics,* 102(1), 57-75.

Griliches, Z. (1997), "Education, Human Capital, and Growth: A Personal Perspective," *Journal of Labor Economics,* 15(1), 330-344.

Gundlach, E. (1995), "The Role of Human Capital in Economic Growth: New Results and Alternative Interpretations," *Weltwirtschaftliches Archive,* 131(2), 383-402.

Hobday, M. (1995), "Innovation in East Asia: Diversity and Development," *Technovation,* 15(2), 55-63.

Li, Zhen, Yongchun Yang (2019), "The Evolution of China's Human Capital Structure and its Spatial Differentiation Mechanism," *Economic Geography,* 39 (10), 104-111

Liu, Zhiyong, Haizheng Li, Yongyuan Hu, Chenhua Li (2018), "The Upgrading of Human Capital Structure and Economic Growth -- Also on the Formation and Narrowing of the Gap between Eastern, Central and Western Regions," *Economic Research,* 53 (3) : 50-63.

Lodde, S. (2008), "Human Capital and Productivity Growth in Italian Regional Economies: A Sectoral Analysis, *Rivista Internazionale di Scienze Sociali,* 116(2), 211-233.

Jadoon, K., H. A. Rashid, A. Azeem (2015), "Trade Liberalization, Human Capital and Economic Growth: Empirical Evidence from Selected

Asian Countries," *Pakistan Economic and Social Review,* 53(1), 113-132.

Jess, B., and S. Mark M. (1994), "The role of human capital in economic development evidence from aggregate cross-country data," *Journal of Monetary Economics,* 34(2), 143-173.

Jiang, Y. (2016), "Trade Integration and Regional Inequality: A Theoretical Framework with Empirical Implications for China," *Journal of Chinese Economic and Business Studies,* 14(4), 365–384.

Jing, Weimin, Yao Wang, Longjiong Mo (2019), "Educational Human Capital Structure, Technological Transformation and Upgrading and High Quality Development of Regional Economy," *Macro quality Research,* 7 (4): 18-32.

Kalaitzidakis, P. T. P. Mamuneas, A. Savvides, T. Stengos (2001), "Measures of Human Capital and Nonlinearities in Economic Growth," *Journal of Economic Growth,* 6(3), 229-254.

Krolzig, H., and Asoka W. (1999), "Learning-by-Doing, Human Capital, and Growth: An Integrated Perspective," *Jahrbücher für Nationalökonomie und Statistik,* 218(1/2), 241-248.

Krugman, P. (1979), "A Model of Innovation, Technology Transfer, and the World Distribution of Income," *Journal of Political Economy,* 87(2), 253-266.

Kuznets, S. (1955), "Economic Growth and Income Inequality," *The American Economic Review,* 45(1), 1-28.

Madsen, J. B. (2014), "Human Capital and the World Technology Frontier," *Review of Economics and Statistics,* 96(4), 676-692.

Malinen, T. (2012), "Estimating the Long-run Relationship between Income Inequality and Economic Development," *Empirical Economics,* 42(1), 209-233.

Mamuneas, T. P., A. Savvides, T. Stengos (2006), "Economic Development and the Return to Human Capital: A Smooth Coefficient Semiparametric Approach," *Journal of Applied Econometrics,* 21(1), 111-132.

Mansfield, E. (1961), "Technical Change and the Rate of Imitation," *Econometrica,* 29(4), 741-766.

Mincer, J. (1958), “Investment in Human Capital and Personal Income Distribution,” *Research in Economics,* 66(4), 281-302.

Moretti, E. (2003), “Estimating the Social Return to Higher Education: Evidence from Longitudinal and Repeated Cross-sectional Data,” *Journal of Econometrics,* 121(1), 175-212.

Nelson, R. R. and E. S. Phelps. (1966), “Investment in Humans, Technological Diffusion, and Economic Growth,” *The American Economic Review,* 56(1/2), 69-75.

Padhi. S. P. (2014), “Human Capital Formation, Good Employment Opportunities & the Firm,” Indian Journal of Industrial Relations, 50(2), 213-223.

Papageorgiou, C. (2002), “Technology Adoption, Human Capital, and Growth Theory,” *Review of Development Economics,* 6(3), 351-368.

Pei, Mengdi, Dachun Fang. (2019), “Industrial Structure Upgrading, Regional Innovation and Economic Growth -- GMM Analysis Based on Provincial Panel Data,” *Journal of Jilin University of technology and industry,* 35 (05), 21-25.

Peng, Siqing, Lan Li, Jiancheng Pan, Dahai Hao, Youlan Han, Jian Han, Yunfeng Wang, Bo Dong. (2013), “Economic Transformation and Innovation: Understanding, Problems and Countermeasures -- a Special Investigation Report on the Growth and Development of Chinese Entrepreneurs in 2013,” *Management world,* 2013 (09).

Rehme, G. (2007), “Education, Economic Growth and Measured Income Inequality,” *Economica,* 74(295), 493-514.

Romer, P. M. (1990), “Endogenous Technological Change,” *Journal of Political Economy,* 98(5), S71-S102.

Salop, S. J. Stiglitz. B. and Ripoffs (1977), “A Model of Monopolistically Competitive Price Dispersion,” *The Review of Economic Studies,* 44(3), 493-510.

Schultz, T. W. (1960), “Capital Formation by Education,” *Journal of Political Economy,* 68(6), 571-583.

Schultz, T. W. (1961), “Investment in Human Capital: Reply,” *The American Economic Review,* 51(5), 1035-1039.

Shaffer, H. G. (1961), "Investment in Human Capital: Comment," *The American Economic Review,* 51(5), 1026-1035.

Solow, R. M. (1956), "A Contribution to the Theory of Economic Growth," *The Quarterly Journal of Economics,* 70(1), 65-94.

Stokey, N. L. (2015), "Catching Up and Falling Behind," *Journal of Economic Growth,* 20(1), 1-36.

Tai, Hang, Xiaoyun Cui (2019), "Human Capital Structure and Technological Progress: Heterogeneity Impact Analysis and Transnational Empirical Evidence," *Nankai Economic Research,* 2019 (04), 143-166

Teles, V. K. (2005), "The Role of Human Capital in Economic Growth," *Applied Economics Letters,* 12(9), 583-587.

Turnovsky, S. J. (2011), "The Accumulation of Human Capital and Income Inequality in a Two-Sector Economy," *Journal of Human Capital,* 5(4), 418-452.

Turnovsky, S. J. and A. Mitra. (2013), "The Interaction between Human and Physical Capital Accumulation and the Growth-Inequality Trade-off," *Journal of Human Capital,* 7(1), 26-75.

Van, C. L., T. Nguyen, M. Nguyen, T. B. Luong (2010), "New Technology, Human Capital, and Growth in a Developing Country," *Mathematical Population Studies,* 17(4), 215-241.

Veltri, S. and A. Silvestri (2017), "Investing in Human Capital: an Analysis of the Mismatch between Theoretical Claim and Managerial Behaviour," *Int. J. of Knowledge-Based Development,* 8(1), 5-23.

Vernon, R. (1966), "International Investment and International Trade in the Product Cycle," *Thunderbird International Business Review,* 8(4), 16.

Walder, A.G. (2002), "Income Determination and Market Opportunity in Rural China, 1978–1996," *Journal of Comparative Economics,* 30(2), 354-375.

Wang, Haichen and Dachun Fang (2016), "Industrial Structure Upgrading, Human Capital and Economic Growth -- Based on GMM Analysis of Provincial Dynamic Panel Data," *Journal of Guangxi University of Finance and economics*, 29 (03), 11-16.

Wang, Jiaxin (1996), "On the Transformation Mechanism from Speed Economy to Benefit Economy," *Nanjing Social Sciences,* 1996 (07), 54-59.

Wang, Jinjin and Baoping Ren (2017), "The Rise and Fall of China's Economic Transformation from the Perspective of Science," *Jiangsu Social Science,* 2017(1).

Wang, Ting and Dachun Fang (2019), "Human Capital Dividend, Industrial Structure Upgrading and Economic Growth -- Based on GMM Analysis of Provincial Panel Data," *Journal of Jilin University of technology and industry,* 35 (01), 54-60.

Xie, Bojie, and Rong Zhang, Shuai Sun (2019), "Impacts of Marine Industrial Structure Changes on Marine Economic Growth in China," *Journal of Coastal Research,* 98(sp1).

Yakita, A. (2010), "Human Capital Accumulation, Fertility and Economic Development," *Journal of Economics,* 99(2).

Yang, Chao (2016), "The Classification and Measurement of Human Capital," *Management Window,* 2(3).

Yang, D. T. (2003), "Education and Allocative Efficiency: Household Income Growth during Rural Reforms in China," *Journal of Development Economics,* 74(1).

Yang, Jie (2019), "70 Years of New China's Economic System Transformation and Development," *Modern Economic Information,* 2019 (23).

Zhang, Guang-jin and Chao-shuang Long (2003), "On the Importance of Human Capital for Continuous Growth of Chinese Economy," *Journal of Beijing University* (Social Science Edition), 3(2).

Zhang, Nan and Hongmin Fan, Huaizhong Mu (2020), "Economic Growth Effect of Human Capital Gradient Upgrading," *Population and Economy,* 2020 (02).

Zhu, Mei and Ying Song (2018), "Empirical Analysis of Human Capital, Industrial Structure Change and Regional Economic Growth," *Journal of Jining University*, 39 (02).

About the Authors

Yanqing Jiang, PhD

Professor, School of Economics and Finance,
Shanghai International Studies University, P.R. China
Email: yjiang@shisu.edu.cn

Yanqing Jiang, Professor of Economics at the School of Economics and Finance, Shanghai International Studies University, received his PhD in economics from the Hanken School of Economics in Finland. Professor Jiang's recent research works include over fifty journal articles and more than ten research monographs published by well-known academic publishers.

Yingjie Li

Postgraduate Student, School of Economics and Finance,
Shanghai International Studies University, P.R. China
Email: 0193100031@shisu.edu.cn

Yingjie Li is a postgraduate student in economics at the School of Economics and Finance, Shanghai International Studies University, whose main research field is international economics. She has published several academic papers in various journals such as "Bilingual teaching, exchange visits and college students' international ability: an empirical analysis based on the survey data of Yangzhou University" in *Jiangsu Science and technology information*.

INDEX

A

adjustment of industrial structure, 38, 117, 121, 177
agricultural modernization, 23, 160, 165, 170, 172
artificial intelligence, 134, 139, 148, 176

B

backward association, 115, 116

C

capital intensive industry, 38, 158
competitive advantage, 134, 139, 142, 143, 144, 145, 147, 164
Consumer Price Index (CPI), 83

D

double-track influence mechanism, 141
dual economic structure, 9
dual-economic phenomenon, 166

E

economic transformation, v, vii, 1, 2, 3, 4, 6, 9, 11, 12, 14, 15, 25, 27, 77, 96, 97, 104, 124, 140, 147, 157, 226, 228
educational attainment levels, 127, 129
elasticity, 117, 118, 179
employment migration, 32
employment pressure, 182, 183
entrepreneurship, 146, 147, 172

F

factor aggregation effect, 121, 122, 160
factor endowment, 27, 36, 114
factor replacement effect, 121, 122
factor substitution, 162
financial crisis, 135
forward association, 115
frictional unemployment, 43

G

Gini coefficient, 156, 157

Gross Domestic Productivity (GDP), 6, 9, 20, 22, 43, 44, 83, 84, 85, 94, 116, 124, 126, 136

H

human capital stock, 30, 74, 77, 111, 113, 117, 119, 120, 121, 124, 127, 130, 143, 165, 166, 169, 179, 180, 182, 183

I

imperfect information, 4
income distribution gap, 39
income gap, 155, 156, 157, 160, 161, 164, 165, 166, 168, 169, 170
industrial relevance theory, 115
Industry 4.0, 135
Industry Life Cycle Theory, 5
Institution Change Theory, 5
integration of urban and rural areas, 165
inter-industry transformation, 23
intermediate demand, 116
intra-regional inequality, 200

K

knowledge intensive industry, 38

L

labor employment demand, 180, 181
labor employment supply, 180, 182
labor force human capital, 83, 84, 85, 86, 87, 88, 89, 90, 91, 92, 93, 94, 96
labor intensive industry, 38
labor productivity, 13, 23, 35, 120, 136, 137, 138, 152, 162, 164, 174, 175, 176, 181, 221
labor-capital intensive industry, 38
learning by doing, 31, 144, 152

M

marginal productivity, 23, 138, 139, 144, 158, 164, 170, 176
market demand mechanism, 113, 114, 115, 118, 121, 130
market economy, 3, 14, 15, 33, 77, 102, 114, 124, 150, 164

N

nominal and real labor force human capital, 83, 84, 85, 86, 87, 88, 91, 92

P

Per Capita Disposable Income (DPI), 8, 20
planned economy, 12, 13, 14, 15, 17
primary industry, 7, 9, 94, 95, 96, 124, 127, 129, 130, 159, 164, 165
psychological contract, 153

R

reindustrialization, 136, 137
resource allocation mechanism, 121

S

school and enterprise cooperation, 151
secondary industry, 7, 95, 96, 124, 127, 129, 130, 164, 165
service-oriented manufacturing industry, 136
shock therapy, 3
socialist market economy, 12, 15, 17
spatial agglomeration, 162, 169

spillover effect, 109, 140, 141, 144, 152, 160, 161, 162, 167, 169
structure transformation, 2, 3, 4
supply-side reform, 21
surplus labor force, 160, 161, 164, 170, 171
sustainable economic growth, 177

T

technological imitation activity, 102
technological innovation activity, 102
technological learning activity, 102
technological progress, 17, 31, 37, 97, 102, 103, 106, 109, 110, 111, 114, 120, 130, 133, 134, 138, 148, 151, 162, 163, 164, 165, 167, 169, 171, 172, 177, 185, 199, 221, 227
technology diffusion, v, 37, 96, 97, 98, 102, 108, 109, 163, 165, 169, 173, 221
technology intensive industry, 38, 158
technology transfer, 107, 108, 109, 221, 225
tertiary industry, 7, 23, 95, 96, 124, 127, 129, 130, 159, 161, 164, 165, 171
the law of diminishing marginal productivity, 139
the law of diminishing marginal utility of material capital, 177
the post-industrial era, 178
the supply side, 17, 113, 141
theoretical model, v, 185, 186, 200

U

upstream and downstream industries, 142, 179
urban inequality, 165

V

vocational education, 58, 110, 148